PHYSICAL FITNESS GAMES & ACTIVITIES KIT

Mary Kotnour

illustrated by Leslie Landwehr

PARKER PUBLISHING COMPANY
West Nyack, New York 10995

PARKER PUBLISHING COMPANY, INC.

West Nyack, NY

10   9   8   7   6   5   4   3   2   1

I thank and praise my Lord and Savior, Jesus Christ,
who has blessed me with the gifts that I am honored
to share with you now. I pray that these ideas will
enhance your teaching as well as inspire you to create
new ideas.—M.K.

I dedicate this book to all my precious students who
bring me joy and satisfaction through their interest,
enthusiasm, and understanding. Also to those
administrators and staff members in the Coeur d'Alene
School District who have supported and encouraged me
in my professional and personal growth.—M.K.

Library of Congress Cataloging-in-Publication Data

Kotnour, Mary, 1956–
    Physical fitness games & activities kit / Mary Kotnour ;
illustrated by Leslie Landwehr.
        p. cm.
    Includes bibliographical references.
    ISBN 0-13-665613-7
    1. Physical education for children. 2. Games. 3. Physical
fitness for children. I. Title. II. Title: Physical fitness games
and activities kit.
GV443.K67 1990
372.86—dc20   89-49664
                                                              CIP

ISBN 0-13-665613-7

PARKER PUBLISHING COMPANY
BUSINESS & PROFESSIONAL DIVISION
A division of Simon & Schuster
West Nyack, New York 10995

Printed in the United States of America

About the Author

Mary Kotnour has been an elementary physical education instructor in the schools of Coeur d'Alene since 1979. During the 1985–1986 school year when physical education was eliminated, she served as the district Elementary Physical Education Coordinator for eight schools, showing classroom teachers how to teach Physical Education through modeling, observing, and providing instructional materials. She earned her B.S. in Physical Education from Winona (Minnesota) State University and her M.E. in Guidance and Counseling from the University of Idaho in 1983. In addition to teaching elementary physical education, she serves as an affiliate staff member of the University of Idaho and has compiled curriculum materials (e.g., bicycle safety and recess resources) and supervised student teachers (since her second year of teaching). She has also been a District Representative on the State Board of the Idaho Alliance of Health, Physical Education, Recreation, and Dance.

Among her other activities, Miss Kotnour has worked with Special Olympics, co-coached the Hayden Hopper Jump Rope Team, served on the Big Brothers/Big Sisters Board of Directors, and has traveled abroad with the People-to-People High School Student Ambassador Program. She is a presenter at state and regional physical education conferences on "Mastery Teaching in Physical Education" (based on Dr. Madeline Hunter's Principles of Learning) and state reading conferences on "Learning Academics through Physical Activity."

Mary was chosen an Outstanding Young Woman of America in 1984 for her contributions to her profession and community; was nominated for Idaho's Outstanding Physical Education Teacher of the Year in 1986; and was the youngest ever to receive the Winona State University Distinguished Young Alumni Award in 1987 for her contributions to the teaching profession. Besides her individual honors she has led her students in 1983, 1984, and 1985 to the Presidential Physical Fitness State Champions Award. She has been the coordinator for the All-City Jump Rope for Heart (American Heart Association) and has had the winning team in 1985, 1986, and 1987. In 1989 she implemented the Physical Best Program (AAHPERD) for the 550 kindergarten through fifth grade students.

About this Teacher's Resource

The purpose of the *Physical Fitness Games & Activities Kit* is to move from the focus on competition to a focus on cooperation, skill development, and fitness in the elementary physical education program. Physical education class should be a time to learn and practice skills, and to develop such social skills as cooperation and good sportsmanship. It should be a class where students can learn to enjoy physical activities and their benefits even if they are not "gifted athletes." If the focus is on involvement and having fun, then we encourage and foster fitness for all.

The activities featured in this kit are designed to give your students in grades K–6 maximum involvement as well as to develop their physical, social, and mental skills.

Learning Games involve active participation in academic skills. The twenty-seven games in "Get Totally Fit with Learning Games" add a new and exciting dimension to learning and keep students' interest level high. Classroom teachers can use these games to practice and reinforce academic skills. Physical educators can use them to promote transfer between physical education and academics.

Outdoor Games provide an opportunity for students to expend their energy in a positive, active manner. Many of the thirty-two activities in "Outdoor Fun for Everyone" are done in relay formation so you can incorporate them together for a lesson. This provides diversity in skills and activity.

Cooperative Games are an ideal way to get students to work together toward a common goal. The twenty games in "Everyone's a Winner in Cooperative Games" include everyone, and everyone is indeed a winner. These activities foster a sense of belonging, a positive self-image, and an understanding of how to work with others. Students are much happier, and the task goes more smoothly when all are included and all are succeeding. A sense of accomplishment is experienced by all as they complete the task. This cooperative aspect applied to team sports is a perfect way to get the apprehensive child involved and to focus on the value of teamwork. Learning to cooperate is a lifetime skill, and is one of the most important things we can teach our students.

Finding unique ways to increase fitness level is always a challenge for physical educators. The more than forty activities in *Fun With Innovative Fitness Activities* will develop the students' fitness level without their even realizing it, because they will be having so much fun. The activities include many unique ideas that don't involve a lot of costly equipment. Most of the equipment needed can be made or obtained through donation. The uniqueness grabs students' attention and keeps them motivated and interested.

Giving students a chance to use their creativity, work at their own level, and problem solve are just a few of the benefits of the over fifty activities in *Individualized Activities for Fitness and Fun.* Each student has his or her own piece of equipment and own space, which allows for total participation. There is no right or wrong way to respond to the stated task. Rather, each allows the student to take in what he or she hears, add that to his or her peception, analysis, and creativity to demonstrate his or her personal response.

Lead-up Games for Super Sports presents over fifty games that give students opportunities to master learned skills through applying them in a game situation. After skills are broken down and taught with various drills, they are then applied in a game that focuses on that particular skill. The benefits of this approach are increased motivation since it makes skills practice fun, practice that leads to mastery in a skill, and an opportunity for all students to be active all the time.

Mary Kotnour

Contents

Section 2
RUNNING AND RELAY FUN FOR EVERYONE • 18

Section 3
EVERYONE'S A WINNER WITH COOPERATIVE GAMES • 33

Section 4
FUN WITH INNOVATIVE FITNESS ACTIVITIES • 44

Section 5
INDIVIDUALIZED ACTIVITIES FOR FITNESS AND FUN • 106

Section 6
LEAD-UP GAMES FOR SUPER SPORTS • 155

xviii *Contents*

Section **1**

Get Totally Fit
With Learning Games

```
┌─────────────────────────────────────────────────────────────────┐
│                         TEACHING HINTS                            │
│                                                                   │
│   1. These games reinforce or add a new twist to learning and     │
│      reinforcing academic skills.                                 │
│   2. These games involve active learning.                         │
│   3. Some of the Learning Games are in the Classroom Games        │
│      Chapter because they work best in a classroom setting. The   │
│      Learning Games are best suited for a larger area, but can    │
│      be adapted to the classroom if necessary.                    │
│   4. When learning games from other countries, point out to       │
│      students the country's location on a map or globe, and show  │
│      where it is in relation to where they live.                  │
│   5. These games are assigned a suggested grade level, but may    │
│      be adjusted for your specific class situation.               │
│   6. The suggested group size for the activities may need to be   │
│      adjusted according to the space available.                   │
│                                                                   │
└─────────────────────────────────────────────────────────────────┘
```

GAMES USING LETTERS AND WORDS

■ Alphabet Sequence (1–2)

Skills: Knowledge of the alphabet, rolling/throwing, and catching

Supplies: A playground ball for each group

Formation: Divide the class into groups of 6-8 students each. Have each group form a circle. Give each group a ball.

Description: The student with the ball says "A" and a word that begins with the letter *a*, then rolls the ball to another player who says "B" and a word that begins with the letter *b*. This continues all through the alphabet.
VARIATION: Have the students throw the ball instead of roll it.

■ Body-Built Letters and Numbers (1–3)

Skills: Forming letters and numbers, alphabetical order, math computation

Supplies: None

Formation: Each student in a personal space. Students can form letters and numbers while standing, sitting, or lying down.

Description: This is a great activity for students to creatively use their bodies. There are a few ways you can use this activity:

1. Name a letter, and have the students form that letter with their bodies.
2. For third graders you can play the "Decoding Game", where a number is assigned to each letter of the alphabet ($a = 1$, $b = 2$ . . . $z = 26$). When you say the number, the students have to figure out which letter it is and make that letter with their bodies. Have them say the letter out loud in unison.
3. Say a number, and have the students form that number with their bodies.
4. Give the students a math problem, and have them make the answer with their bodies.

VARIATION: Have students get in groups of six, and form the letters/numbers using everyone in the group. This is a great cooperative activity and it is interesting to watch the students interact.

■ Jump Rope Letters and Words (1–3)

Skills: Practice in forming letters, spelling

Supplies: A jump rope for each student

Formation: Scattered about with ample space between students

Description: Help each student find a personal space, then give each of them a jump rope. Have the students form small letters of the alphabet with their jump ropes, making the letter go the correct way as they sit looking at it. Then have the students figure out a way to jump around, over, and in and out of their rope letter. Repeat with capital letters.

VARIATIONS:

1. Decoding: each letter of the alphabet is given a number ($a=1$, $b=2$, $c=3$ . . . $z=26$). State the number, students decode that into the correct letter, and without saying it, they form the letter with their jump ropes. When everyone is done, have the students say the letter out loud together, then have them jump rope the number of times indicated by the number you stated.

2. Spelling: Using spelling words, have the students group according to the number of letters in the words. When the word is given, the students in each group form the letters in the word with their jump ropes. Have one student in each group lead the group through a pattern of jumping around, in, out of, and over, their word, or have each student in each group use his/her own ideas to jump the word.

■ Scramble Spell (1–6)

Skills: Spelling, locomotor skills, teamwork

Supplies: Three sets of alphabet cards

Formation: Divide the class into three groups. Have each group form a circle. Each member of each group holds an alphabet card, and the remaining cards are put face up in a pile in the center of their circle.

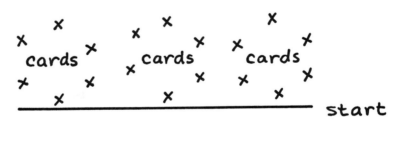

Description: This spelling activity is great for focusing on teamwork as well as spelling. The teacher calls out a word to be spelled. Members of each group see if they have the letters in their hands needed to spell the word. If they do not, they may exchange their letters, one at a time, for a letter in their pile. When a team is able to spell the word, the students run to their designated spelling line and hold their letters above their heads in the correct order. Scoring can be on a 5-3-1 basis so that each team scores in every game. Cards are shuffled and new cards are selected for each game. For younger students (1–2) you may want to have them do a specific locomotor movement to the spelling line to add variety and practice basic motor skills.

■ Spelling Race (1–6)

Skills: Spelling

Supplies: Cards with the letters of the alphabet on them for each group with two of each vowel, and two each of *t, r,* and *l.* A list of spelling words for the teacher.

Formation: Divide the class into as many teams as you have space available. Each team stands in a designated place and each has a team captain who changes with every new word to be spelled. Each team member holds several letters of the alphabet. There is a designated spelling area for each group.

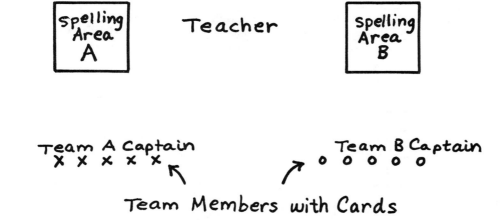

Description: This is a fantastic, active way to practice spelling. The captain of each team goes to the teacher who whispers a word to them. At the signal, the captains run to their teams. The captain pulls those team members holding the appropriate letters to the designated spelling area to spell the word, and places them in order to correctly spell the word given. One point is given to the first team that spells the word correctly. A new captain from each team is picked and the old captain takes his/her place. This continues until all players have had an opportunity to be captain. A variation would be to have the captain take the correct cards from his team members, one at a time, and spell the word by laying the letters on the floor.

■ Body Spelling (2–4)

Skills: Spelling, movement, cooperation

Supplies: None

Formation: Divide the class into groups of five to eight players each. Have each group get in its own space.

Description: The teacher gives a word and each group spells out the word with their bodies. All members of the group must be used in spelling out the word.
VARIATION: One group demonstrates the word with their bodies and other groups guess the word.

■ Putting Movement Words Into Action (4–6)

Skills: Defining words, translating words into actions, creativity

Supplies: Lists of movement words for each group, paper and pencil for each group to write down their action, any equipment students may choose to use in their created actions

Formation: Divide the class into groups of four to six students each. Have the groups choose a word from each of the categories, find a space, and work together to come up with an action involving those words.

Description: This is a great activity for using creativity in combining words and actions. Either give each group a list of the words, or put the different categories of words in separate bags and have each group pull a word from each of the bags. You may choose to use all of the categories or just a few of them. After the groups have had time to create an action, have each group teach their action while all the other students perform the action.

TRAVELING WORDS

run	dash
skip	stamp
creep	whirl
rush	waddle
flee	skate
slither	jump
hop	bounce
gallop	slide
dart	kick
spin	totter
sneak	crawl
step	stride
shuffle	

STOPPING ACTIONS

freeze	hold
perch	grip
anchor	pause
settle	stop
collapse	slide
flop	crumple

JUMPING ACTIONS

leap	hurl
toss	bound
prance	bounce
soar	fly

VIBRATING WORDS

shiver	shake
quiver	tremble
wobble	vibrate
patter	shudder
rattle	gyrate
tumble	wriggle
squirm	snake

PERCUSSIVE ACTIONS

stamp	punch
explode	pound
patter	

NONTRAVELING WORDS

flick	jerk
twitch	squeeze
writhe	compress
explode	spread
contract	fold
splatter	punch
jab	slash
chop	saw
stab	grip
release	tense
relax	push
pull	press
lower	drag
dangle	drip

SINKING ACTIONS

collapse	sink
lower	fall
drip	melt
flop	spin
turn	drop
squash	shrink
pounce	

FUNNY-SOUNDING WORDS

snickersnack	brip
gallumph	bruttle-battle
cavort	achoo
flip-flop	crinkle
grunch	swoosh
hiccup	squizzog
zigzag	crickcrock
kerumph	
blump	
snap-crackle	
wheezey	

SEQUENCES OF ACTION WORDS

run—freeze—skip
dart—collapse—pop
grow—spin—deflate
writhe—jerk—pop
slither—inflate—explode
squeeze—jump—release
creep—pounce—explode
slip—pause—flop
rise(turn)—twitch—skip
gallop—stamp—screw
jump—freeze—jab
chop—whirl—slash

RISING AND EXPANDING

grow	reach
release	open
spread	evaporate
float	pop
rise	lift
turn	blossom
spin	swell
inflate	

DESCRIPTIVE WORDS

droopy	tired
happy	greedy
prickly	bubbling
excited	heavy
strong	loving
spongy	nervous
light	tense
floppy	gentle
big	unsure
springy	fierce
carefree	small
confident	sharp
spikey	rounded
soft	hard
enormous	square
bold	angular
curvey	tiny
afraid	

■ Invent a Game (4–6)

Skills: Defining words, creativity

Supplies: Any equipment listed under "Things" and "Places" that the students choose to use in their games

Formation: Divide the class into groups of four to six students each. Have each group choose a word from each category below, find a space to work in, and create a game together as a group that they can teach to the rest of the class.

Description: This is a great activity for encouraging creativity. It empowers the students, because they have created a new game that will be taught to the rest of the class. There is also a focus on cooperation. An exciting addition to this activity is to make a booklet of the games students created and place a copy in the school library.

THINGS

bats	rope
rackets	batons
balls	boxes
hoops	cones
beanbags	nets
pins	plastic shapes
pucks	plastic containers
sticks	carpets
wands	streamers

PEOPLE

solo
trio
partner
small group
large group

MAKING IT HARDER

goal keeping	smashing
switching hands or feet	serving
screening	saving
passing ahead	attacking
rebounding	double teaming
cooperating	scoring
switching players	feinting
defending	tackling
dodging	fast breaking
retrieving	checking a player
blocking	

PLACES

hills	square	corner
pits	wall	trees
corridor	trestle	steps
pillar	basket	rocks
circle	lines	air
bars	nets	court
bins	backstop	floor
bleachers	hall	field
triangle	stumps	goals

ACTIONS

counting	heading	passing	alternating
slowing	spiking	taking	keeping together
speeding	using rhythm	giving	tagging
spinning	freezing	putting down	dribbling
going backwards	striking	picking up	shooting

reversing	hitting	jumping	aiming
stopping	sending away	juggling	running
hurdling	catching	balancing	keeping away
kicking	throwing	changing	tugging
			exchanging

■ Activity: Busy Bee (K–2)

Skills: Movement, identification of body parts, cooperation.

Supplies: None.

Formation: Scattered.

Description: This is a great active way of practicing identification of body parts. When the direction "Busy Bee" is given, the students move around the area without touching anyone. When the teacher calls out a specific direction (e.g., back to back; head to nose, etc.) students get with the person closest to them and touch those body parts. Allow the students to use their creativity in ways to accomplish the task. You will see a variety of "right" ways. In between each body direction say "Busy Bee."

■ Bones (4–6)

Skills: Recall, transfer, movement

Supplies: A skeletal diagram with the bones labeled, drawings of individual bones

Formation: Each student in a personal space.

Description: The study of bones can be practiced in a variety of ways. At first, using a labeled skeletal diagram, play "Simon Says" (Simon says, "Touch your tibia." Simon says, "Put your right hand on your patella; wave your phalanges," and so on). If the leader prefaces the direction with "Simon says," students must follow the direction. If the leader does not preface the direction with "Simon says," the students do not follow the direction given.

VARIATIONS: (Take the skeletal chart down.):

1. Show a labeled drawing of an individual bone and have students point to that bone. Later see if they can identify the bone by its shape without the label.

2. Set up various stations with bone drawings. Students rotate to the stations and do an exercise that affects the muscles around that bone.

3. Put music on and have students rotate to the various stations and move the appropriate part of the body, or do an exercise involving that part of the body to the music.

GAMES USING NUMBERS AND CONCEPTS

■ Locomotor Math (1–2)

Skills: Math computation, locomotor movements

Supplies: Numbered cards

Formation: The class in a circle

Description: Give each player a numbered card. Have the students ⌐ ̣ a locomotor movement in a circle (walk, skip, gallop, etc.). The teacher calls out a math problem, the student with the correct answer card runs to the center of the circle. Rotate the cards periodically.

■ Nine-Square Math and Spelling (1–3)

Skills: Hopping, math skills, alphabetical order, spelling

Supplies: Chalk for drawing hopscotch designs

Formation: Draw as many hopscotch designs as possible and divide the class into groups, assigning each group a hopscotch design.

1.

2.

S	E	B
D	A	C
I	O	T

3.

1	4	7
9	3	2
5	6	8

Description: This activity is great for practicing letters, spelling, and math along with the skill of hopping. There are several ways to use this activity:

1. Hop from blank square to blank square, counting. See how many hops you can do without missing.
2. Hop from blank square to blank square, and call out a set of multiples.
3. Hop out the answer to a math problem.
4. Hop and recite the alphabet. See how far you can get without missing.
5. Hop and spell words.

In a pattern with lettered squares:

1. Spell certain words called from a prepared list.
2. Spell as many words as possible that you can find in the lettered squares.
3. One student spells a word while another student hops it.
4. Each student thinks of a word and hops it while the other students try to guess the word.

In a pattern with numbered squares:

1. Add numbers together as you hop.
2. Subtract numbers as you hop.

■ Magic Carpet (1–3)

Skills: Math facts

Supplies: Pieces of paper with numbers on them placed around the area on the floor. The numbers need to correspond with the answers for the given math problems.

Formation: Students are in scattered formation and move around the area until a math problem is given.

Description: This activity is great for practicing math facts and can be done in the classroom as well as the gymnasium. As the students move around the area, state a math problem. Students move to the number that is the answer to the math problem and touch it with their feet. NOTE: You can either have several papers with the same numbers or a few papers with the same numbers (with a few, the students would have to come up with a way to cooperatively touch the number).
VARIATIONS:

1. Use names of states or countries or both to practice geography and social studies facts.
2. Use colored construction paper to practice:
   a. Color identification
   b. Mood questions (examples: What color do you feel is a sad color; a happy color; a quiet color; a fast color; a rainy day color?)
   c. Art questions (example: When you mix blue and yellow, what color do you get?)

■ Jump Rope Math (1–3)

Skills: Math

Supplies: A segmented plastic jump rope for each student

Formation: Each student in a personal space

Description: Students can practice a variety of math skills with the use of a segmented jump rope. The activities that can be done include:

1. Put geometric shapes on the floor and have the students place their ropes over the shapes or duplicate them with their ropes.
2. Have the students count the number of plastic sections in their ropes.
3. Have the students measure a partner to see how many "pieces" tall they are. Have older students multiply the number of sections by the length of each section to come up with inches/feet.
4. The ropes can be stretched on the floor and the students can see how many pieces long they can jump with a one foot take-off, a two foot take-off, and a running start.
5. State a math problem and have the students form the answer with their rope.

■ Five Dollars (2–3)

Skills: Adding, subtracting, throwing, catching

Supplies: A ball for every three or four students.

Formation: Divide the class into groups of three or four students. Have each group find a space, and give each group a ball. Have one player in each group be the leader. The other players stand in a side-by-side line with space between them.

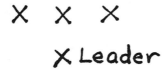

Description: This activity involves adding and subtracting money as well as developing throwing and catching skills. The leader of each group has the ball and faces the line of players. The leader throws the ball to each player in turn. The players catch the ball and return the throw. The object is for each player to try to earn five dollars and become the leader.

The scoring is: Add $1.00 for a caught fly ball; $.50 for a ball caught on a bounce. Subtract $1.00 for a dropped fly ball; $.50 for a dropped ball on a bounce. The first player to get $5.00 is the new leader, and all players start over with no money. Make sure each player has a chance to be leader.

■ Group Math (2–6)

Skills: Cooperation, movement

Supplies: None

Formation: Each student in a personal space

Description: This is an active way to practice arithmetic facts. Have the students move around the area either in a designated locomotor movement or one they choose. The teacher calls out a math problem (for example 2 × 2), the students come up with the answer (4) and form groups with that many students. If there are students left over, they get in a group and use body parts to signify the balance needed to reach the answer (two students, each with one hand raised, equals four). Then you can give another math problem or have the students do an exercise in their groups (four jumping jacks, for example) counting the answer out loud.

VARIATION: Give a math problem and have the students say the answer out loud in unison. Then the class responds by performing a certain movement (for example, marching in place, running in place, or toe touches).

■ Hoop Math (2–6)

Skills: Math skills, shooting with accuracy

Supplies: Two playground balls, question cards with math problems, markers for placement of baskets, shooting line markers, and team line markers

Formation: Divide the class into two teams. Two players from each team go out to the designated spot and join hands to form a basket. The remaining team members line up side by side behind a line, at a distance from the baskets. The teacher lines up between the two baskets with the question cards and playground balls.

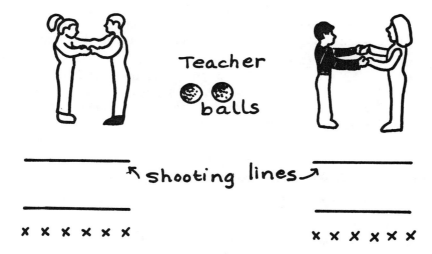

Description: The teacher selects a card and reads the math problem. Players in each line take turns running to the teacher and whispering the answer. The first player from each team with the correct answer picks up the ball, runs to his shooting line, and attempts to make a basket. The first player to score is awarded two team points. A player giving an incorrect answer must return to his line and the next player runs up to answer the problem, if the other team has not scored.

After each basket, the two basket players go to the end of their respective lines, and the first two players in line form the next basket. Continue this rotation until all players have had an opportunity to form the basket.

GAMES FROM OTHER CULTURES

■ Cat-and-Mouse Weave, China (K–2)

Skills: Chasing, dodging, tagging

Supplies: None

Formation: The class forms a circle with one player in the center as the mouse and another player on the outside of the circle as the cat.

Description: The object of this game is for the cat to catch the mouse. The mouse starts running and weaving between the students in the circle. The cat must follow the exact same path as the mouse. If the cat catches the mouse, they change roles, then a new cat and mouse are chosen.

■ Wolf, Are You Ready? Peru (K–2)

Skills: Running, chasing, tagging

Supplies: None

Formation: Have the class form a circle, and choose one player to be the wolf, who hides in a place near the students. Select a designated area for the students to run to.

Description: The game begins with the class saying in unison, "Wolf are you ready?" The wolf responds, "No, I'm not ready. I'm putting on my shoes." Each time the class calls to the wolf, the wolf responds that s/he is not ready because s/he is putting on another piece of clothing. When the wolf chooses, s/he responds with "I am ready." S/he then runs from his/her hiding place and chases the class members, trying to tag them before they get to their designated safe area. Choose a new wolf.

■ Walk Around and Around, New Guinea (1-3)

Skills: Running, chasing, dodging

Supplies: Two cones

Formation: Have the class form a circle around the cone designated for the standing circle, with one student as the chaser. The other cone marks the center of the sitting circle.

Description: The game begins with the players in the standing circle. The chaser walks around the outside of the circle, and when s/he wants the other players to run, s/he says, "Walk around and around." Players, at their own discretion, try to run to and sit in the sitting circle before the chaser tags them. Those tagged go to the halfway point between the two designated circle areas while the chaser walks around the sitting circle. When the players begin to run to the standing circle (after chaser says "Walk around and around"), the players tagged get to help the chaser tag players. This continues back and forth until there is one player left. That person can choose to be the chaser or choose someone else to be the chaser.

■ Jump the Ditch, Holland (1-3)

Skills: Jumping

Supplies: Two ropes for each group

Formation: Divide the class into groups of four to six players each. Have each group line up single file behind one rope, and place the second rope a short distance from the first rope.

Description: The first student in line stands behind the closest rope, and at the signal jumps over both ropes. After each student in line has jumped, move the ropes farther apart and repeat. *NOTE:* This is safest done outside on the grass.

■ Find the Stone, Greece (1–3)

Skills: Running, chasing, tagging, strategy

Supplies: A pebble

Formation: Have the students stand in a line side by side with their hands cupped to receive the stone. One student is selected to be in possession of the stone.

Description: The object of the game is to have the players and the person who is "It" trick the others into believing they do or do not have the stone. The player who is "It" walks down the line pretending to put the stone in each player's hands. Each player closes his hands together like he received the stone. The player who is "It" continues down the whole line whether he has given the stone to someone or not.

The players, whether they have the stone or not, at some point, run to the designated area. The players chase and try to tag the player who they think has the stone. Each player tagged must stop and open his/her hands to prove whether they have the stone or not.

If a player tags the player with the stone, s/he gets to be "It." If the player with the stone makes it to the designated area without being tagged, s/he is "It."

■ Where Do I Go? Australia (1–6)

Skills: Giving and following directions

Supplies: A blindfold and a flat rock or large piece of paper for each group

Formation: Divide the class into groups of four to six students each. Have each group form a circle, with one student standing in the center of the circle with a blindfold on.

Description: This activity is fun and provides an opportunity to practice responding to oral directions without using your visual sense. After the student is blindfolded, place a piece of paper on the floor inside the circle away from the blindfolded player. The rest of the group sits in a circle and tries to direct the blindfolded player to the rock/paper with verbal cues (for example, move to your right; move forward). Change the center player. Continue this until all players have had a chance to be blindfolded.

■ Group Line Hop, China (3–6)

Skills: Balance, coordination, hopping, cooperation

Supplies: None

Formation: Divide the class into groups of about five people. Have each group line up single file.

Description: All but the first person in each line lifts and extends his/her left leg forward. The person in front of them grabs the left ankle of the person behind them. Then each person places his/her right hand on the right shoulder of the person in front of them. The first person lifts his/her left foot off the ground. You are now ready for the group hop. At the signal, the groups begin hopping on their right feet.

■ Keep It Up, Arctic (3–6)

Skills: Hitting with accuracy

Supplies: A beachball or volleyball for each group

Formation: Divide the class into groups of six players each. Have each group form a circle, kneeling. Give each circle a ball.

Description: The object of the game is for each circle to keep the ball in the air by tapping it with one hand. There are two ways you can play the game:

1. If a player misses a ball or uses two hands, s/he is eliminated from the circle. The game continues until one player is left. Begin again with all players.
2. For a designated period of time, count how many taps you get in a row, as a team, without missing. Begin again. See if your team can improve its score.

■ Taking Balls, New Guinea (3–6)

Skills: Movement, strategy

Supplies: Five balls, four hoops, one long rope to form the center circle

Formation: A large center circle is made with four smaller circles located outside of it. The five balls are placed in the large center circle. One player stands in each of the four outside circles. Set a time limit (for example, one minute). If you have the space and the equipment, set up more than one game.

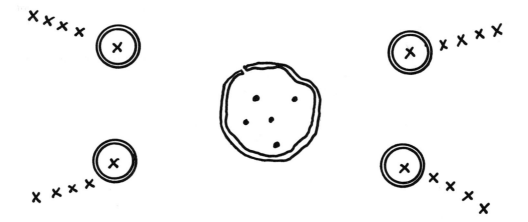

Description: The object of this game is for each of the four players to try to get three balls into his/her circle before the time is up. At the signal, the players begin. They can take the balls from the center circle or from another player's circle, but they can only take one ball at a time. Players cannot guard their balls. Balls must be placed (not rolled or thrown) in their circle. At the end of the time limit, rotate players. Continue until all students have had a turn.

■ Human Obstacle Course, China (3–6)

Skills: Cooperation, creativity

Supplies: Equipment to set up an obstacle course, or playground equipment

Formation: Have the class get into groups of three to five students each, and hold hands.

Description: There are two different ways to do this activity. One involves the use of equipment; one does not.

1. Set up an obstacle course using equipment (for example, chairs, tables, cones, ropes, and beams). The object is to get everyone in the group through the course without letting go of hands.
2. Make an obstacle course with groups of students making the obstacles with their bodies. Have each group go through the course individually.

■ Foot-Net-Ball, Malaysia (3–6)

Skills: Kicking with accuracy, teamwork

Supplies: A net, standards, ball (beachball would be best)

Formation: Set up the net at badminton height (low enough so players can kick the ball over the net). Have at least three players on each side.

Description: The object of the game is to keep the ball in the air and have it go back and forth over the net. All contact is made with the feet and body, no hands can be used. Use as many hits as needed on a side to get the ball over the net.

Section 2

Running and Relay
Fun For Everyone

```
┌─────────────────────────────────────────────────────────────┐
│                      TEACHING HINTS                           │
│                                                               │
│  1. Running games are great for expending energy. They also   │
│     give students ideas for playing at recess.                │
│  2. For the running games, have designated lines marked for   │
│     students to line up at when necessary. Mark the lines     │
│     with cones, jump ropes, or gym lines.                     │
│  3. Teach running without touching others or things.          │
│  4. Individual relays can be used as a warm-up activity;       │
│     several relays can be put together for an activity time.  │
│  5. Relays apply to any age group. Just hearing the word      │
│     "relays" excites kids. Choose the ones you feel           │
│     comfortable with in regard to safety and the ones your    │
│     particular class can handle and will enjoy.               │
│  6. You do not have to focus on winning. Tell the class that  │
│     the idea is to do the relay correctly, to have fun doing  │
│     it, and that you will not be keeping track of which team  │
│     comes in first.                                           │
└─────────────────────────────────────────────────────────────┘
```

RUNNING GAMES

■ Around the World (K–2)

Skills: Running, color recognition

Supplies: Paper for each class member in at least four colors

Formation: Have the class form a circle, and give each student a piece of colored paper.

Description: The game begins with the teacher calling out a color. The students with that color run to the right around the outside of the circle. The student who returns to his/her place first is the winner. Then another color is called. After calling all the colors have the students exchange colors with another student.
VARIATIONS:
1. Divide the class into smaller groups, having each group form a circle. This provides a safer and more individualized activity.
2. Have the students use different locomotor movements to move around the outside of their circle.

■ Brownies and Elves (1–2)

Skills: Running, chasing, tagging, dodging

Supplies: Line markers

Formation: Divide the class into two teams of equal size. Set up two goal lines a distance apart. Have one team (brownies) line up side-by-side at one goal line, and the other team (elves) line up side-by-side at the other goal line.

Description: The elves stand with their backs to the brownies. Silently, the brownies creep up on the elves and stand behind them. The leader of the brownies calls out, "Run brownies run." The brownies run back to their goal line while the elves turn around and chase the brownies, trying to tag them. Any brownies tagged must go back with the elves to their goal line. Then it is the elves' turn to creep up on the brownies. The team having the most players at the end of the time period is the winner.
VARIATION: Continue to have the brownies creep up on the elves until all the brownies have been tagged, then start a new game with the brownies and elves changing roles.

■ Squirrels in the Tree (1–2)

Skills: Running, chasing, tagging, dodging

Supplies: None

Formation: Divide the class into groups of three. Two of three players in each group grab hands to form an open area (tree) for the squirrel (third player) to stand in. There is one player chosen to be "It." If there are extra players, they can also be squirrels, which will make the game more challenging.

Description: At the teacher's signal, the squirrels leave their tree and try to run to another tree before "It" can tag them. If a squirrel is tagged, s/he then becomes "It," and "It" becomes a squirrel. If "It" does not tag anyone in a reasonable amount of time, designate a new "It." Change players around so that everyone gets to be both squirrels and trees.

■ One Leg Tag (1–2)

Skills: Running, chasing, balancing

Supplies: None

Formation: Players scattered with one player chosen to be "It."

Description: At the signal, "It" begins to chase the other players. For a player to be safe, all s/he has to do is stand on one foot. If "It" tags a player while the player has both feet on the ground, that player becomes "It." If a player is "It" more than once, have him/her choose another player.

■ Run, Rabbit, Run (1–6)

Skills: Running, chasing, dodging, tagging, movement

Supplies: Line markers

Formation: All except two students line up side by side at one goal line. The two students, who are the hunters, stand in the center of the playing area.

Description: The game begins with the hunters calling out a way to move (for example, "Run, rabbit, run," "Hop, rabbit, hop.") The students must perform that movement across the playing area to the other goal line. The hunters must use the same movement. If one of the hunters tags a rabbit, the rabbit must sit down in that spot. The rabbits that are sitting down may try to tag the other rabbits as they go by, but must stay sitting. When all but two rabbits are caught, a new game is started. The last two rabbits are the new hunters or they can choose someone else to be the hunter.

■ Cars (3–4)

Skills: Running, dodging, tagging

Supplies: Line markers

Formation: Students line up side by side along one goal line. Choose one player to be "It," and have him/her stand in the center.

Description: The player who is "It" decides on four kinds of cars (for example, Porsche, BMW, Firebird, and Jaguar). S/he tells the class the four kinds of cars, and each student silently chooses the type of car s/he is going to be. When "It" calls out one of the car names, all of the students who chose that car attempt to run to the other side without being tagged. Then "It" calls out another car name. This continues until s/he has called all four types of cars. You can either have those tagged sit down in the spot where they were tagged, or they can help "It" tag others. When only one player is left, begin a new game. That player can be "It" or choose someone else to be "It."

■ Partner Hook-Up Tag (3–6)

Skills: Running, chasing, dodging

Supplies: None

Formation: Divide the class into pairs. The partners form a circle with space between each set of partners. Designate one player as the chaser and another as the chasee.

Description: This activity adds a new dimension to the game of tag. The object of the game is for the chasee to run in and out of the circle, and before being tagged by the chaser, to hook up with a set of partners. When the chasee hooks up with a set of partners, the outside person must run and is now the chasee. If the chaser tags the chasee before s/he hooks up, s/he becomes the chaser and the chaser becomes the chasee. NOTE: If the chaser is "It" for a long period of time and gets tired, choose someone to take his/her place.

RELAY GAMES

■ Tunnel Relay

Skills: Crawling

Supplies: None

Formation: Divide the class into groups of six students each. Have each group get in a single file line with some distance between each player. Each player needs to stand in a straddle position.

Description: This relay is fun and does not involve a lot of skill. At a signal, the last player in line gets on his/her knees and crawls between the legs of his/her teammates until s/he gets to the front of the line. When s/he gets to the front, s/he stands in a straddle position. Then the next person goes. This continues until the team is back in its original order.

■ Zigzag Relay

Skills: Running, weaving between obstacles

Supplies: None

Formation: Divide the class into groups of about six players each. Have each group get in a single file line with space in between each player.

Description: At the signal, the first player on each team turns, and runs back through the line of players in a zigzag fashion, alternating going to the right of one teammate and to the left of the next teammate. After completing the run, s/he stands a distance away from the last person in line. As soon as s/he gets to the end, s/he says "Go," for the second player to run and weave. This continues until all players are back in their original order.

■ Straddle Relay

Skills: Running through obstacles

Supplies: None

Formation: Divide the class into groups of six students each. Have each group get in a single file line. Have two lines face each other, and sit down in a straddle position with knees straight. Each player puts the soles of his shoes against the soles of the shoes of the player across from him/her.

Description: At the signal, the last couple stands and runs, jumping over legs to the front of the lines, and sit down in a straddle position. As soon as that couple is sitting in position, the next couple goes and does the same thing. This continues until the lines are back in their original order.

■ Two-Legged Relay

Skills: Hopping, balance, cooperation

Supplies: None

Formation: Divide the class into groups of six students each. Have each group get in a single file line. Have the students get a partner in their group.

Description: This is a great cooperative relay. The first partners in each line stand side by side and grasp each other around the waist or shoulders with the inside arm, and lift the inside foot off the ground. At the signal, the first pair in each line, hop to a designated line and back, then the next pair goes. This continues until each pair has gone.

■ Back-To-Back Relay

Skills: Cooperation, moving strategy

Supplies: None

Formation: Divide the class into groups of six students each. Have each group get in a single file line. Have each player get a partner in their line. Have the first pair in each line sit down back-to-back and hook elbows.

Description: This relay brings a lot of laughs. For the relay to work well, the students need to use strategy for moving as well as cooperation. At a signal, the first pair in each line attempts to stand up and move to the designated line and back without unlocking their arms. (One is moving forward and the other is moving backward.) HINT: The player moving forward has his/her feet close together, and the player moving backward moves with his/her feet in a straddle position. This will keep them from hitting feet. Let the students try to figure this out on their own.) When they get back to their line, the second pair sits down, locks arms, attempts to get up and move to the line and back as the first pair did. This continues until all pairs have gone.

■ Skin the Snake

Skills: Cooperation, agility, flexibility

Supplies: None

Formation: Divide the class into groups of six students each. Have each group get in a single file line. Each player extends his left hand back between his/her legs and grasps the right hand of the person behind him/her.

Description: This is a fun relay to do and gives the students a sense of accomplishment if they are able to do it. The last player in line lies down on his/her back still holding on to the player in front of him/her. At the signal, every member (except the last one) starts moving backwards. The second rear player, after passing over the last player, lies down, still maintaining his/her grasp with both hands. This pattern continues until all players are lying down. Then the rear player stands and moves forward, pulling the second player to her feet. This continues until all the players are standing up.

■ Rescue Relay

Skills: Starting, running, stopping, turning, cooperation

Supplies: None

Formation: Divide the class into groups of six students each. Have each group get in a single file line with one player moving to a designated line a distance away.

Description: This is a fun relay which also involves cooperation. At the signal, the single player from each line, runs to the first player in his/her single file line, grabs his/her hand, and runs him/her back to the designated line (rescue). The rescued player becomes the rescuer for the next player in line. S/he runs to the line, grabs the hand of the next player, and runs him/her back to the designated line. This continues until all the players have been rescued.

NOTE: Remember that the player rescued gets to rescue the next player in line. At the end of the relay all team members will be at the designated line, not the starting line.

■ Orbit Relay

Skills: Running, cooperation

Supplies: None

Formation: Divide the class into groups of six students each. Have each group get in a single file line. Divide each group in half and line each group up in shuttle formation, facing each other, some distance apart.

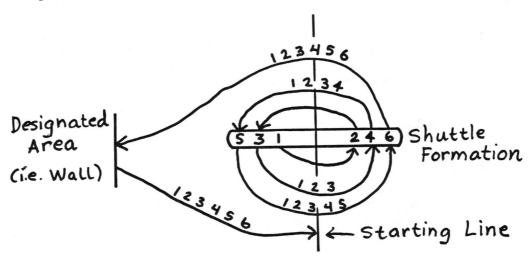

Description: This is a great cooperative relay where the object is for all players to stay connected throughout the race. At the signal, the first player in each line runs to the second player and hooks arms at the elbow. Then players 1 and 2 run to player 3 and hook arms with him/her. This continues until all six players on a team are hooked together. When all players are hooked together they run to a designated area (a wall, for example) and one end player must touch the designated area. Then, still hooked together, they run to the starting line and sit down. The team that finishes first without coming unhooked wins.

■ Car Wreck Relay

Skills: Locomotor movements

Supplies: Line markers

Formation: Divide the class into groups of six students each. Have each group get in a single file line.

Description: Players move to and from a designated turning line using the following actions:
Player 1: Flat tire (gallop).
Player 2: Tires out of line (move on hands and feet).
Player 3: Spark plugs missing (4 steps forward, 1 step backward).
Player 4: Car is idling (fast run).
Player 5: Steering is out of order (full turns).
Player 6: Car being towed (run backwards).
You can either have all students perform the same action, or have each student perform a different action as listed above.

■ Over-and-Under Relay

Skills: Patterning, passing

Supplies: A playground ball for each group

Formation: Divide the class into groups of six students each. Have each group get in a single file line, with the first player in each line holding a playground ball.

Description: At the signal, the first player in each line hands the ball over his/her head to the second player. The second player hands the ball between his/her legs to the third player. This pattern continues (over and under) until the ball gets to the last player in line. The last player runs up to the front of the line with the ball and begins the pattern again (over and under). This continues until the line is back in its original order.

■ Kangaroo Relay

Skills: Running or jumping, coordination

Supplies: A playground ball for each group

Formation: Divide the class into groups of six students each. Have each group get in a single file line. Give a ball to the first player in each line.

Description: The first player in each line holds the ball between his/her knees. At the signal, the first player goes to a designated line and back with the ball between his/her knees. If the ball drops, s/he stops there, puts it between his/her knees, and continues to move. When the first player gets back to his/her line, s/he gives the ball to the second player, and goes to the end of the line. The second player does the same thing. This continues until all the players have had a turn. Students can choose whether to jump or run with the ball between their knees.

■ Ice Cream Cone Relay

Skills: Balance, flipping a ball, catching

Supplies: Three cones per group, one ball per group

Formation: Divide the class into groups of six students each. Have each group get in a single file line. The first player in each line has a cone held upside down with a ball on top of it. The second player in each line has a cone held upside down. There is a foul line a distance from the starting line, and a cone is placed a distance from the foul line.

Description: At the signal, the first player in line runs with the cone and ball to and around the cone. When s/he gets back to the foul line s/he stops and flips the ball to the second player in line, who attempts to catch it with his cone. If the ball falls or is missed, it is picked up, and the player starts from behind the starting line.
Player 1, after flipping the ball to player 2, runs back to his/her line and hands the cone to the third player, and then goes to the end of his line. Player 2 does the same as player 1, flipping the ball to player 3. This continues until all players have had a chance to run with the ball and cone and flip it.

■ Circle-the-Wagon Relay

Skills: Passing, catching, running, teamwork

Supplies: A ball for every two teams

Formation: Divide the class into groups of six students each. Put two teams together. One team forms a circle, and the other team forms a single file line facing the circle, about 10 feet away. The "circle team" has the ball.

Description: The object of this relay is to see how many times the ball can make complete circuits around the circle by passing to each player, while the other team completes a running relay.
At the signal, the ball begins to be passed around the circle. At the same time, each player in turn on the "line team" takes turns running around the outside of the circle and then tags the next runner, until all have run. After the running relay is completed, then the number of times the ball was passed around the circle is stated. This can then be compared with two other teams, if you choose. The teams then change roles and the relay is repeated.

■ One-Step Relay

Skills: Concentration, coordination

Supplies: Two pieces of cardboard for each group

Formation: Divide the class into groups of six students each. Have each group get in a single file line. Give the first player in each line two pieces of cardboard.

Description: At the signal, the first player in each line places one piece of cardboard on the floor and steps on it with one foot, then places the second piece of cardboard on the floor and steps on it with the other foot. Then the player picks up the first piece of cardboard, places it ahead of the other one, and puts his foot on it. This procedure of putting a piece of cardboard on the floor, putting one foot on it, and then placing the other foot on the second piece of cardboard continues to a designated line and back. The players may not put a foot on the floor or put two feet on one piece of cardboard. When the first player returns, the second player goes. This continues until all players have had a turn.

■ Hoop Roll

Skills: Rolling a hoop, running, hand-eye coordination

Supplies: A hoop per group, and two cones per group

Formation: Divide the class into groups of six students each. Have each group get in a single file line. Set the first cone some distance away from the front of the line, and place the hoop over it. Set the second cone a distance away from the first cone.

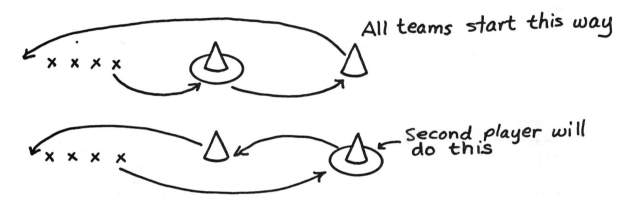

Description: At a signal, the first player in each line runs to the first cone, takes the hoop, rolls it to the second cone, and places the hoop over the cone. Then s/he runs back to the line and tags the next player. The second player runs to the second cone, takes the hoop, rolls it to the first cone, places it over the cone, and runs back to the line and tags the third player. This pattern continues until all players have had a turn.

■ Through-the-Hoop Relay

Skills: Rolling a hoop, running through an obstacle

Supplies: A hoop for each group

Formation: Divide the class into groups of six students each. Have each group get in a single file line. Give the first player in each line a hoop.

Description: At the signal, the first player rolls the hoop to a designated line. The remaining players on each team run to and through their hoop and back to their place behind the starting line. The first player then rolls the hoop back to the starting line, gives it to the second player, and goes to the end of his line. The second player does the same, and the team follows to and through the hoop. This continues until each member has had an opportunity to roll and hold the hoop.

■ Hit-the-Pin Relay

Skills: Rolling a ball with accuracy

Supplies: A ball and a bowling pin for every two groups

Formation: Divide the class into groups of six students each. Have two groups face each other in single file lines with a pin in the center between them. Give a ball to one of the teams.

Description: The object of this relay is to knock down the pin with the ball. The teams facing each other alternate in rolling the ball at the pin. The players in turn try to bowl down the pin. If a player misses the pin, s/he goes to the end of the line to wait for another turn. See which team can be the first to have all its members knock down the pin.

■ Bowl It Down

Skills: Rolling with accuracy

Supplies: A playground ball and a bowling pin for each group

Formation: Divide the class into groups of six students each. Have each group get in a single file line. Place a pin a distance away from each line. Give the first player in each line a ball.

Description: At the signal, the first player in each line rolls the ball toward the pin, attempting to knock it down. If the player is successful, s/he runs and sets up the pin, and rolls the ball back to the next player in line. After doing this, the player would go to a designated area and sit down. If a player misses the pin, s/he runs down and rolls the ball back to the next player, and then goes to the end of the line to wait for a second turn. The relay is over when every player in line knocks down the pin. The last player in line after knocking down the pin, runs down, sets it up, grabs the ball, and kneels behind the pin to show that the team is done.

■ Foot-and-Hand Dribble

Skills: Hand dribbling, foot dribbling

Supplies: Two hoops per group, one soccer ball per group, one basketball per group

Formation: Divide the class into groups of six students each. Have each group get in a single file line. Set up one hoop a distance away from each line, and place a basketball in the center of it. Set up the second hoop a distance away from the first hoop, and place a soccer ball in the center of it.

Description: This relay is fun and works on dribbling skills. At the signal, the first player in each line runs to the first hoop, takes the basketball and dribbles to the second hoop. At the second hoop, the player places the basketball in the center of it, takes the soccer ball, dribbles it back to the first hoop, places the ball in the center of it, runs back, and gets at the end of his line. Then the second player goes. S/he will run to the first hoop, dribble the soccer ball to the second hoop, then dribble the basketball back to the first hoop, and go to the end of his line. This pattern continues until all players have had a turn.

■ Skill Relay

Skills: Jumping rope, tossing, catching, bouncing

Supplies: A jump rope, softball, and playground ball for each group

Formation: Divide the class into groups of six students each. Have each group get in a single file line. In front of each line, place a jump rope, a softball, and a playground ball with about five yards between each.

Description: This relay is good for practicing various skills. At a signal, the first player in each line runs to the jump rope and jumps ten times. Then s/he drops the rope and runs to the softball, tosses it in the air and catches it ten times. Then s/he runs to the playground ball, bounces and catches it ten times, then runs back to the end of the line. The next player does the same thing. This continues until all players have had a turn. VARIATION: Change the three tasks or the number of repetitions.

■ Object Shuffle Relay

Skills: Starting, running, stopping

Supplies: Two hoops for each group, and various small objects (for example, erasers, beanbags, chalk) for each group

Formation: Divide the class into groups of six students each. Have each group get in a single file line. Place one hoop by each line and the other hoop a distance away from the first hoop. Put the objects in the hoop that is a distance away from the lines.

Description: At the signal, the first player in each line runs to the hoop that has the objects in it, picks up one object, runs it back to the other hoop, and places it in the center of the hoop. The player then runs back for a second object. This continues until each object has been moved. The second player starts at the closest hoop then, and does the same thing as the first player except in reverse direction. This continues until all players have had a turn.

■ Spoon It Out

Skills: The sense of touch

Supplies: One each of the following items for each group: a table and chair (desk or floor), one large spoon, two bowls, a blindfold, a stopwatch, cottonballs

Formation: Divide the class into groups of six students each. Have each group get in a single file line. A bowl of cottonballs is set on each table, and an empty bowl is set next to it. A spoon is also placed on the table. The first player is seated and blindfolded.

Description: After the first player in each line is blindfolded, s/he feels where the bowls are in front of them once. They may not touch the bowls or cottonballs at any time after that. Set a time limit for each player to move the cottonballs to the empty bowl. At the signal, the first players begin to move the cottonballs to the empty bowl. At the end of the time limit, the players stop and count how many cottonballs they moved from one bowl to the next (ones outside the bowl do not count).

NOTE: You can either have individual winners OR add up the total number of cottonballs moved by the team to see which team has the most. For a math problem you could have the students average the number of cottonballs moved by the team, the class, or both.

■ Grocery Shopping Relay

Skills: Running, speed, coordination

Supplies: For each group: one grocery bag, one box, five empty food containers (for example, egg cartons, pop cans, or cereal boxes), one hat, one coat or shirt, one cone.

Formation: Divide the class into groups of six students each. Have each group get in a single file line. Place the hat, coat, and grocery bag in front of the lines. Place a box of empty food cartons a distance away from the lines, and a cone a distance away from the box.

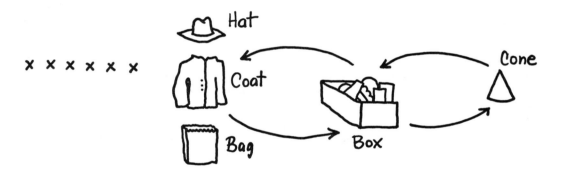

Description: This is a fun relay that is sure to liven up a dreary day. At the signal, the first player in each line puts on the hat and coat, takes the grocery bag, runs to the box, and puts the food containers in the bag one at a time. Then s/he runs to and around the cone and back to the box. S/he empties the bag into the box, runs back to the line, takes off the hat and coat and gives the grocery bag to the next player in line. This continues until each player has had a turn.

■ Sponge Relay

Skills: Hand strength

Supplies: Two buckets and one sponge for each group

Formation: Divide the class into even teams and get them in relay formation.

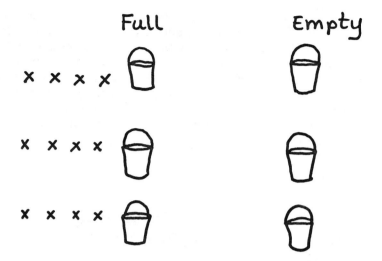

Description: This is a great relay for a hot day or end-of-the-year field day. The buckets at the head of each line are filled with water and contain a sponge. Empty buckets are placed a distance away. At the signal, the first person in each line gets his/her sponge full of water, runs to the empty bucket, squeezes out the water, runs back, hands the sponge to the next person in line, and goes to the end of the line. The relay continues until their empty bucket is filled with water.

■ Cup-and-Bottle Relay

Skills: Hand-eye coordination

Supplies: A cup, a bucket of water, and an empty plastic liter pop bottle for each group.

Formation: This is best done in a grassy area. Divide the class into groups of six students each. Have each group get in a single file line. A bucket of water is set at the head of each line. A cup is given to the second player in each line. The first player in each line takes a pop bottle, lays down on the grass a distance away, and holds the pop bottle above his/her face.

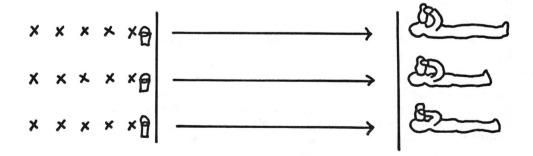

Description: This is a great relay for a hot day or a field day at the end of the school year. All students seem to enjoy this one, but be prepared to get wet. At a signal, the second player in each line fills the cup with water, runs to the first player who is laying down holding the bottle, and attempts to pour the water into the bottle. The second player takes the first player's place on the grass, while the first player takes the cup, runs back to the line, gives the cup to the next person in line, and goes to the end of the line. This pattern continues until the bottle is full of water.
NOTE: The player with the cup becomes the player with the bottle. The player with the bottle goes to the end of his line.

■ Fan The Balloon Relay

Skills: Hand-eye coordination

Supplies: One balloon and a piece of cardboard per group.

Formation: Divide the class into teams and have them get in single file lines. Designate a starting line and turning line.

Description: At the signal, the first player fans the balloon to the turning line and back. Then the second player goes. This continues until all players have had a turn.

■ Throw And Sit Relay

Skills: Throwing and catching.

Supplies: A ball for each group.

Formation: The students stand in a single file line. The first player in each line is the leader. This player has the ball and faces his line.

Description: At the signal, the leader throws the ball to the second player who catches it, throws it back to the leader, and sits down. Then the leader throws the ball to the next player who catches it, throws it back, and sits down. This continues until the leader gets to the last player in line. The last person does not throw the ball back but runs to the front and faces his line. All players stand up. The new leader does the same thing as leader #1 did. This continues until all players have had a turn to be the leader.

■ Eraser Pass And Balance

Skills: Coordination, speed.

Supplies: An eraser for each team.

Formation: Divide the class into equal groups and have each group get in a single file line. Number the players in each line consecutively.

Description: This is a fun activity that involves both speed and the ability to balance. The teacher calls out a number. The student in each line with that number runs to a designated line, picks up the eraser and passes it around his waist three times, stands the eraser on end and runs back to his place. The first player back to his place scores a point for his team. If the eraser falls over, the player must set it back up. Then another number is called. This continues until all players have had a turn.

Section 3

Everyone's A Winner With Cooperative Games

```
TEACHING HINTS

1. These games are great for the beginning of the year to instill the
   attitude of cooperation and to break down barriers. They also take
   a focus off competition.
2. These activities focus on accomplishing a task as a group. Point out
   groups that are cooperating well, not a group that finishes first.
3. Discuss what cooperation means.
4. Though there are suggested grade levels attached to each game,
   the games are not limited to those grade levels. You need to decide
   what you think your particular group of students will enjoy and be
   able to accomplish.
5. To have more students active at a time divide the class into smaller
   groups, with each group playing the same game.
6. You can develop a lesson around several activities that use music,
   for example, Cooperative Musical Hoops, Matching Shapes and
   Colors, and Beachball Carry and Pass.
7. You may want to use the cooperative sports activities with their
   related sports units.
```

COOPERATIVE GAMES

■ Matching Shapes and Colors (K–1)

Skills: Identification of shapes and colors, matching, cooperation

Supplies: Cout-outs of shapes (circles, squares, rectangles, triangles), two of each shape in four different colors (red, yellow, blue, green), music

Formation: Each student in a personal space. Place the shapes on the floor.

Description: As the music starts, the students move around the area. When the music stops, each student picks up a shape and tries to get together with:

1. A student with the same shape.
2. A student with the same color.
3. Everyone with the same shape.
4. Everyone with the same color.
5. A student with the same shape and color.

■ Cooperative Musical Hoops (K–2)

Skills: Problem solving, cooperation

Supplies: Hula hoops

Formation: Place the hoops in a circle with space between them. Have the students stand around the circle outside the hoops.

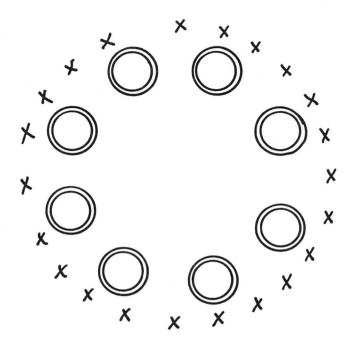

Description: This is another cooperative activity which is patterned after musical chairs with the difference that no student is ever out. Students move around the hoops when the music is playing. When the music stops, they get inside a hoop. Remove a hoop and start the music again. Students need to work together as there are fewer hoops, to ensure that all students can get into a hoop.

■ Body-Built Numbers, Shapes, and Letters (K–2)

Skills: Knowledge of letters, shapes, and numbers, cooperation

Supplies: None

Formation: Divide the class into groups of six students each. Have each group find its own space.

Description: This is a great cooperative activity that involves creating letters, numbers, and shapes. There are a variety of ways you can do this activity:

  1. Ask students to use their whole group to form a shape (circle, triangle, square, etc.), letter, or number.

2. Have groups join together to form a word.

3. Have the class join together to form a sentence.

■ Trust Me (3–6)

Skills: Cooperation, movement, listening, giving directions, trust

Supplies: Equipment for setting up an obstacle course, one blindfold for each set of partners.

Formation: Divide the class into pairs. Each set of partners lines up at the start of the obstacle course, with one partner blindfolded.

Description: This activity involves trust as well as cooperation. Tell the students to pretend that they are in the middle of a blizzard, and one of them is snow-blind, while the other one can see. The object is for the partner who can see to lead the snow-blind partner through the blizzard to safety by guiding him/her (hold hands) and giving oral directions. Have the partners change roles.

■ Elephant, Palm Tree, Camel (3–6)

Skills: Cooperation, reaction time

Supplies: None

Formation: Divide the class into groups of three students each. Have the groups form a circle, with space between each group. One player is "It" and stands in the center of the circle.

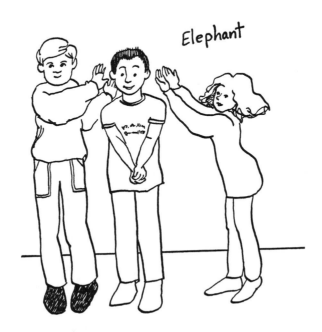
Elephant

Description: This activity is a fun one that involves quick reactions as well as cooperation. It takes three players to make each combination. All three players must make the form together at the same time.

1. Elephant: The center person stands with arms pointed in front, hands clasped together for a trunk. The players on either side cup their hands behind the center person's ears to make the elephant's ears.

2. Palm tree: All three players stand together with arms raised up to form the leaves.

3. Camel: The center person bends over, and the players on either side make humps on his back with their fists.

The player who is "It" spins around, points to a group, and says either "Camel," "Elephant," or "Palm tree." That group must make the formation by the count of three. If one of the three waits too long, s/he becomes "It." After a player has been "It" for three formations, a new "It" is chosen.

■ Cooperative Balloon Tap (3–6)

Skills: Cooperation, striking

Supplies: Balloons

Formation: Divide the class into pairs and give each set of partners a balloon. Mark a starting line, then a finish line about 30 to 40 feet away.

Description: Tapping a balloon is a common activity, but Cooperative Balloon Tap involves working with a partner to tap the balloon. Partners stand side by side at the starting line with inside arms linked together. They hold the balloon in their free hands. At the signal, the partners work together hitting their balloon to the finish line. If the balloon lands on the ground, partners stop and pick it up, but they may not unlink arms. This continues until each set of partners has had a turn. (This can also be incorporated into a relay.)

■ Beach Ball Carry and Pass (3–6)

Skills: Cooperation, balance, teamwork, coordination

Supplies: A beach ball for every two players, music

Formation: Divide the class into pairs. Half of the sets of partners have a beach ball and are connected with the ball between two body parts.

Description: When the music starts, students move around the area with their partners. When the music stops, the partners with the beach balls must pass the balls to a set of partners without a ball, without using their hands.

■ Strike A Pose (3–6)

Skills: Cooperation, sense of touch

Supplies: Blindfolds

Formation: Divide the class into groups of three students each. Have each group find its own space. Each group designates one student as a statue, one as the sculptor, and another as the statue's twin. The sculptor puts on a blindfold. The statue strikes a pose.

Description: This is a fun activity which involves having one sense taken away so that you need to depend on another sense. The sculptor feels the statue, then attempts to shape the twin into the same pose. The sculptor may go back and forth between the two statues. The blindfold is taken off so the sculptor can see how closely the statues resemble each other. Students change roles and repeat. This continues until all students have had a turn as sculptor, statue, and twin.

■ Snake Dodgeball (3–6)

Skills: Cooperation, running, dodging, throwing with accuracy

Supplies: One or several balls

Formation: Class in a large circle

Description: This is a fun variation of dodgeball where the emphasis is on cooperation, not competition. After having the class form a circle, choose three students to go in the middle of the circle and connect by holding onto the waist of the person in front of them. The object is to hit the tail of the snake. When hit, the tail goes to the head. This continues until all three players have been the tail and have been hit. Three more students are chosen to make the snake.

VARIATION: Have several groups of two or three people form snakes, and have several balls. When the tail is hit, s/he goes to the head, the head goes to the circle, and the player who threw the ball becomes the tail.

■ All-End-Up-On-One-Side Dodgeball (3–6)

Skills: Throwing, dodging, striking

Supplies: Several fleece balls

Formation: Divide the class in half, placing one half on one side of the area and the other half on the other side of the area. Give each half an equal number of balls.

Description: This game is similar to regular dodgeball in regard to throwing balls at the players on the other side, but in this game there are no losers. When a player gets hit, he runs to the other side, joins the other team, and continues to play. The object is for all the players to end up on one side.

■ Cooperative Kickball (3–6)

Skills: Cooperation, kicking, fielding, running

Supplies: A ball

Formation: Divide the class into two teams, a kicking team and a fielding team. No bases are needed, just a ball. The kicking team gets in a single file line, and the fielding team is scattered a distance away.

Description: This is a fun variation on the traditional game of kickball. The first kicker kicks the ball and then begins running around his/her lined-up team. Each time the kicker passes the front of the line, a run is scored. At the same time, a member of the fielding team picks up the ball and all the other fielders line up behind him/ her. They then pass the ball overhead down the line. When the last person gets the ball, s/he yells "Stop." The kicker's turn is up at this point. The kicking team is now the fielding team and the fielding team is now the kicking team.

VARIATION: Have the teams change roles after each member of the kicking team has kicked.

■ The Human Knot (4–6)

Skills: Cooperation, communication, interaction, problem solving, evaluation, decision making

Supplies: None

Formation: Divide the class into groups with six to eight students per group. Have each group form a circle.

Description: This activity is great for developing problem-solving skills and cooperation. It's also fun and provides an opportunity for success. Once the students are in their circles, have them put their hands in the middle and take hold of others' hands. NOTE: You must not take the hand of the person next to you, and you must not give both hands to the same person. Once all have grabbed hands, have them begin. The object is for the group to work together to become unknotted without letting go of hands, ending in a circle. Players may have to step over arms, go under, etc. You may want to have groups knot up again once they have unknotted. Have them continue doing this until all groups have completed the task at least once.

Discuss why some groups finished sooner than others. Discuss what factors were involved (for example, they had one person move at a time, not everyone moving at once; they had one person directing the group, not all members speaking at the same time.) Discuss the need for cooperation to accomplish group tasks.

■ The Multiplying Blob (4–6)

Skills: Cooperation, running, chasing, dodging

Supplies: None

Formation: Two students are chosen to be the blob. These two students join inside hands. The remainder of the class scatters around the area.

Description: The object of this game is for the players that are the blob to attempt to tag the others. Those tagged by the blob join hands with them. When the blob gets four people, they divide in half to make two blobs. This continues until there are two players left. Those two players either become the blob for the next game, or choose two others to be the blob.

■ Cooperative Group Lap Sit (4–6)

Skills: Cooperation

Supplies: None

Formation: Have the class form a tight circle by standing shoulder to shoulder. Have them all turn to their right and take one step toward the center of the circle. Have each player grab the waist of the person in front of him/her.

Description: At a signal, all players, at the same time, try to sit on the knees of the person behind them. The object is to see if the class can make a complete circle, sitting, without falling. If this is accomplished, then while sitting, try to take steps as a group (right, left, and so forth). Then add clapping hands while walking in the lap-sit formation. Ask students to think of other challenges.

■ Group Soccer (4–6)

Skills: Cooperation, dribbling, passing

Supplies: Soccer balls, three soccer goals

Formation: Set up three goals around the playing area. Each goal is defended by two players together as goalies. The class is divided up into teams of three or four players linked together (holding hands or arms around each other). Each group is a playing unit, with each being its own team. There are two fewer balls then there are playing units.

Description: At the signal, the playing units begin dribbling and passing the soccer ball. The units without a ball attempt to steal another group's ball. Each member of a unit must contact the ball before their unit can attempt to score. Any goal can be used by any playing unit. Goalie teams are periodically changed with playing units.

■ Cooperative Basket-Football (4–6)

Skills: Cooperation, throwing, catching, shooting baskets

Supplies: A basketball court, a football

Formation: Divide the class into teams of five players each. Have two teams on the court. The game can begin with a jump ball or with both teams lined up facing each other, with one team hiking the ball.

Description: This game is a combination of basketball and football. The object of the game is to pass the football to all members as you move down the court, and shoot a basket. The other team can attempt to intercept the passes, and the ball becomes theirs at that spot. If a ball is missed or fumbled, it becomes the team's that recovered it. After a designated period of time, have two other teams play. Continue until all teams have had a chance to play.

■ Collective-Score Towel Volleyball (4–6)

Skills: Cooperation

Supplies: Net, standards, ball, towels

Formation: Divide the class in half to form two teams. Each team has its players divide into pairs, with each pair having a towel.

Description: The game begins with a set of partners sending the ball over the net using its towel. A set of partners on the other side of the net catches the ball with its towel. A collective (both teams) point is scored every time the ball goes over the net and is caught by a set of partners on the other side of the net. The ball must be passed at least once to another set of partners on the team's own side before being volleyed over.

■ All-End-Up-On-One-Side Volleyball (4–6)

Skills: Cooperation, volleying

Supplies: Net, standards, beach ball

Formation: Divide the class into teams of five or six players each. The first team sets itself up on one side of the net.

Description: Each player volleys the ball to another player on his team, then goes under the net to the other side. The last player taps the ball over the net and then goes under. The team repeats this process to get back to the other side of the net. The object of this game is to see how many times a team can get to the other side of the net and back without missing the ball. Have the second team go, and continue to do this until all teams have had a chance.

Section 4

Fun With Innovative Fitness Activities

```
┌─────────────────────────────────────────────────────────┐
│                      TEACHING HINTS                       │
│                    FOR CARPET SQUARES                     │
│                                                           │
│  1. Have one carpet square per student. The carpet squares│
│     can often be obtained through donations from carpet   │
│     stores.                                               │
│  2. The suggested grade level is K–3, though carpet square│
│     relays could be done at upper elementary levels.      │
│  3. Carpet squares can be used for movement to music,     │
│     games, and relays. Be creative. Let your students be  │
│     creative.                                             │
│  4. Teach students to stay on the carpet square, not      │
│     allowing it to slip out from under their feet.        │
│                                                           │
└─────────────────────────────────────────────────────────┘
```

■ Activities With Carpet Squares

Skills: Vary according to the activity

Supplies: One carpet square per student, music

Formation: Varies according to the activity

Description: The following activities can be done with carpet squares. This is also a great opportunity for you and your students to create additional activities and games.

TWIST

1. Place the square on the floor carpet side down, and stand on it.
2. Twist from side to side.
3. Twist and move in designated directions (forward, backward, left, right, in a circle, in a square, and so forth).
4. Move any way you wish.

PARTNER TWIST

1. Stand on a square facing a partner.
2. Do hand patterns with your partner (clap left hands, right hands, both hands, for example).
3. Twist.
4. Make up a routine with your partner.

MOVE TO MUSIC

1. Play music and have students move on their squares to the music's beat.
2. Have a student be leader and have the others follow his or her movements.

MUSICAL SQUARES

1. Have the students form a circle with their squares (carpet side up).
2. Have them stand on their squares.
3. Start the music.
4. Direct students to walk clockwise around the circle, stepping on the squares.
5. When the music stops, the students must be standing on a square.
6. Those without a square are out.
7. Repeat until one person is left.
8. Begin a new game.

MARCH

1. Play marching music and give directions.
2. Directions may include: march on your square, march left, march right, step left, step right, and so forth.
3. Have a student lead.

CARPET TRAIN

1. Students sit on squares (carpet side down) in straddle position with hands on waist or shoulders of the person in front.
2. Begin to move as a unit (in groups of six to eight).

RELAY RACES

1. Have students in squads in single-file lines.
2. Use different ways to move on the carpet square to a designated line and back. The carpet should be face down.
3. Some movements are:
   a. Have two squares, one for each foot, and move in a skating motion.
   b. Have one square, with one foot on and one foot off and move like a skateboard.
   c. Kneel on one knee on the square and push with one foot and both hands.
   d. Kneel on both knees on the square and push with both hands.
   e. Stand on one square and twist down and back.
   f. One partner stands or sits and the other partner pulls him or her down and back.
4. Have students come up with different ways to move.

CARPET RACE

1. Each player has two carpet squares.
2. Divide the class into two teams.
3. One team starts at one end of the gym and the other team starts at the other end.

4. At the signal, both teams move on their carpets to the other end.
5. The team whose player crosses the finish line first gets five points.
6. One point is given for each other player who makes it across the line.
7. Any player who slips off his or her carpet must stop in that place.
8. Any player who makes contact with another player must stop.

VARIATIONS

1. Have partners pass a ball back and forth as they move down the floor.
2. Set up an obstacle course and have the students go through it on carpet squares.
3. Play basketball, floor hockey, or other games on carpet squares.
4. Play various games using carpet squares as "shoes."
5. Have students make up a game using carpet squares.
6. Have students make up a dance using carpet squares.

TEACHING HINTS FOR FRISBEES®

1. It is best to have at least one Frisbee® for every two students.
2. Playing Frisbee® can be a lifetime activity and is a lot of fun.
3. The suggested grade levels are 3–6.
4. Frisbee® activities can also be done at the competitive level.
5. This is a good activity to do in the late spring as students gear up for summer vacation.
6. You can have more than one Frisbee® game going at a time, so all students are active.

■ Task Analysis of Frisbee® Skills

THROWING

A. *Backhand*
   1. Hold the Frisbee® with:
      —the thumb on top
      —the index finger under the rim
      —the middle finger extended toward the center
      —the fourth and little fingers curled back against the rim
   2. Extend arm toward the target.
   3. Roll the Frisbee® toward body as arm is brought back.

4. Coil the wrist and forearm.
5. Keep the edge of the Frisbee® toward the target and slightly raised.
6. Bring arm forward and release the Frisbee® with a snap of the wrist and forearm.
   a. Curve
      1. Follow the backhand task analysis steps 1 through 4.
      2. Tilt the Frisbee® in the direction of the desired curve.
      3. Throw in a relaxed and easy manner.
   b. Skip
      1. Follow the backhand task analysis steps 1 through 4
      2. Start with the same motion as for the left curve
      3. Hit the ground on the forward edge of the Frisbee® halfway to the target
      4. Skip the Frisbee® to the catcher
B. *Overhand*
   1. Grip the Frisbee® with:
      —the thumb underneath
      —the other fingers on top
   2. Cock wrist backward.
   3. Keep arm straight and at shoulder level when throwing.
   4. Snap wrist forward at the point of release.
C. *Sidearm*
   1. Grip the Frisbee® with:
      —the two fingers on the underside
      —the thumb on top
   2. Cock wrist backward.
   3. Swing arm downward at about a thirty-degree angle to the body.
   4. Keep the leading edge of the Frisbee® tilted down.
   5. Snap wrist forward at the point of release.

CATCHING

A. *Between the legs*
   1. Move into position to receive the Frisbee®.
   2. Separate legs, lifting one foot off the ground.
   3. Extend catching hand downward and between legs.
   4. Catch the Frisbee®.
B. *Behind the back*
   1. Move into position to receive the Frisbee®.
   2. Turn noncatching side toward the oncoming Frisbee®.
   3. Extend catching arm backward behind the back.
   4. Hold catching hand with palm up.
   5. Catch the Frisbee®.

C. *Behind the head*
 1. Move into position to receive the Frisbee®.
 2. Turn noncatching side toward oncoming Frisbee®.
 3. Extend catching arm over the head.
 4. Bend elbow of catching arm so forearm goes over head.
 5. Position catching hand, palm facing downward.
 6. Catch the Frisbee®.

D. *Finger Catch*
 1. Move into position to receive the Frisbee®.
 2. Extend the catching arm upward.
 3. Extend index finger of catching hand upward.
 4. Catch the Frisbee® underneath the rim with the index finger.

E. *Tipping*
 1. Move into position to receive the Frisbee®.
 2. Extend catching arm upward.
 3. Extend middle finger.
 4. Lightly tip the Frisbee® to the center.
 5. Keep the Frisbee® aloft and in control.

■ Frisbee® Accuracy (3–6)

Skills: Throwing with accuracy

Supplies: Four Frisbees® for each group; a hula hoop (suspended in the air, set on a stand, or held by a student).

Formation: Divide the class into three groups for each hoop area. Have each group line up on one of the 15 yard lines.

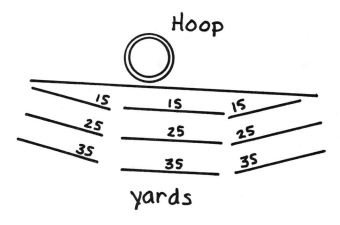

Description: This activity is great for practicing Frisbee® accuracy. After dividing up the class, designate one line as the starting line. The first player in that line gets four turns to throw the Frisbee® through the hoop. A point is scored for each successful throw. Then the first player in the next line throws. After all players have thrown from the 15-yard mark, they move to the 25-yard mark, then the 35-yard mark. Have the groups rotate so they can throw from the three areas. Ask them which area was easiest to make successful throws from, and why.

■ Ship-To-Shore Frisbee® (3–6)

Skills: Throwing with accuracy, cooperation

Supplies: One Frisbee® per team, one pin (or goal) per team.

Formation: Divide the class into teams of four. Give each team member a number from 1 to 4. Set up a pin (you can use plastic liter pop bottles) for each team and give each team a Frisbee®.

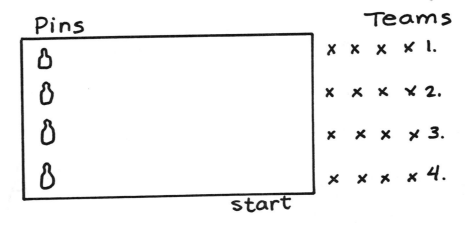

Description: This is a wonderful activity for using cooperation to accomplish a goal. At the signal, the first player on each team tosses the Frisbee® toward his/her pin. The second player on each team runs to where the Frisbee® landed and tosses it from that point. This continues until the pin is knocked down. The team then runs back to the start and sits in a single file line.

If you choose to award points, the scoring is as follows:

1. The team that knocks down the pin in the fewest attempts receives a point.
2. The team that returns to the start and is in a single file line first receives a point.

VARIATION: Play nine-hole-rounds as in golf and see which team has the fewest total number of tosses.

■ Frisbee® Softball (3–6)

Skills: Throwing, catching, teamwork

Supplies: Four bases, one Frisbee®.

Formation: Divide the class into two teams, a batting team and a fielding team. The fielding team sets up as in softball, and the batting team lines up single file.

Description: Frisbee® softball uses softball rules and formation and a Frisbee®. The first player on the batting team throws the Frisbee® and runs the bases. A "batter" is out if:

1. The Frisbee® is caught in the air.
2. The Frisbee® is thrown to the base before the runner gets there.
3. The runner is tagged with the Frisbee® before s/he gets to a base.

Batting and fielding teams switch after three outs OR after everyone on the batting team has "batted."

■ Frisbee® Golf (3–6)

Skills: Throwing with accuracy; throwing for distance

Supplies: A Frisbee® for each player; designated "holes" (such as trees, posts, playground equipment, numbered boxes, or numbered cones)

Formation: "Holes" scattered around the playing area ("golf course"). Each "hole" is designated by a number.

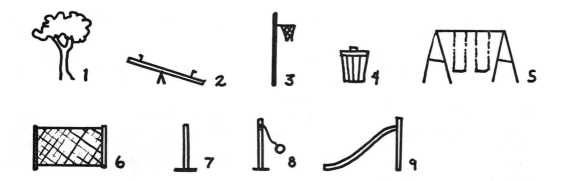

Description: This is a great game for practicing throwing with accuracy at varying distances. Designate a starting point for the first "hole." All other "holes" are started at the "hole" you just completed. Each player counts how many "strokes" (throws) it takes to hit or make it to the "hole." The object of the game is to have the lowest number of total "strokes."

VARIATION: Scramble Frisbee® Golf: Each player in a foursome throws their Frisbee® toward the "hole." The Frisbee® that went the farthest is the spot where all players in the foursome take their next throw from (for example, John's went the farthest. Sue, Tom, and Mary pick up their Frisbees®, take them where John's Frisbee® landed, and they all throw from there for "stroke" number two). Only a team score is kept (number of "strokes" it takes as a group to hit the "hole").

■ Frisbee® Soccer (3–6)

Skills: Throwing, catching, teamwork

Supplies: One Frisbee®, two goals

Formation: Divide the class into teams of six players each. Set up as in soccer (three forwards, two backs, one goalie).

Description: This activity combines six vs. six soccer rules with a Frisbee®. The center forward of one team starts the game by tossing it to one of the side forwards. The object of the game is for the team in possession of the Frisbee® to move it down the field by throwing and catching, to score a goal. The player with the Frisbee® may not move with it, but must toss it to a team member. Any player without the Frisbee® can move around the field in their designated areas.
When a goal is scored, players go back to their original positions and the center forward on the team that did not score starts with the Frisbee®. Periodically rotate forwards with the backs and goalie so all players get an opportunity to score.

■ Frisbee® Tennis Pong (4–6)

Skills: Throwing, catching, scoring

Supplies: Tennis court, net, one Frisbee® for each court

Formation: Divide the class into groups of four players each. Have each group get on a court, two on each side.

Description: This activity allows the students to practice their throwing and catching skills as well as developing strategy to score points.
The four players are set up as in tennis/ping pong doubles with two players on each side of the net. One team serves the Frisbee® by tossing it over the net. The Frisbee® is in play as long as players catch the Frisbee® in the air, and it does not go out-of-bounds. The Frisbee® must be returned from the place it is caught.
Points are scored only by the serving team when an opponent does not catch the Frisbee®, or an opponent throws the Frisbee® out-of-bounds. The serving team loses the serve when they do not catch the Frisbee®, or if they throw the Frisbee® out of bounds. Each time a team wins the serve back, the other team member serves. A game is twenty-one points.

■ Ultimate Frisbee® (4–6)

Skills: Throwing, catching

Supplies: A Frisbee® for each game, cones

Formation: Divide the class into teams of eight players each. Set up as many fields as are needed to accommodate the number of teams. Use four cones for each field. The field size is not set, just set it up with a reasonable amount of space.

Description: Ultimate Frisbee® is a great activity for combining a variety of sports components.

Each team lines up along their respective goal lines. One team begins the game with a throw-off to the other team. As soon as the Frisbee® is released, players may pass their goal line.

The receiving team may catch the Frisbee® or allow it to hit the ground. The rules are:

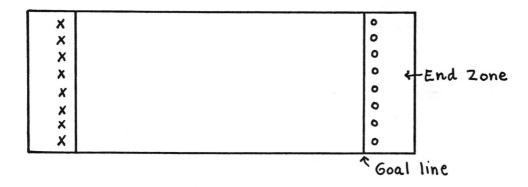

1. If the receiving team touches the Frisbee® but fails to catch it, the throwing team gains possession at that spot.
2. If the Frisbee® hits the ground untouched, the receiving team gets the Frisbee® at that spot.
3. If the Frisbee® goes out of bounds, the receiving team decides whether to have the Frisbee® thrown off again or to take possession of the Frisbee® at the spot where it went out-of-bounds.

The object of the game is to move the Frisbee® into position, by throwing and catching, to score. Players in possession of the Frisbee® may not take steps but can pivot as in basketball. Only one player may guard the player in possession of the Frisbee®.

The defensive team gains possession of the Frisbee® whenever:

1. The offensive team's pass is incomplete.
2. The offensive team's pass is intercepted.
3. The offensive team's pass goes out of bounds.

A goal is scored when an offensive player lands with both feet in the end zone after receiving a pass from a teammate. A player may not run into the end zone. The team that scores receives one point.

```
┌─────────────────────────────────────────────────────────────┐
│                 TEACHING HINTS FOR MOVEMENT                   │
│                                                               │
│  1. Animal walks can be done in relays or as an activity with │
│     tumbling (for example, tumble on the mat, animal walk     │
│     back to the line on the floor).                           │
│  2. Stunts vary with regard to suggested grade level. Many    │
│     can be done at the intermediate level.                    │
│  3. Use mats for stunts.                                      │
└─────────────────────────────────────────────────────────────┘
```

■ Animal Walks (K–2)

Skills: Coordination (hand-eye, foot-eye)

Supplies: None

Formation: Single-file lines or use as a movement to go back to line after performing a tumbling skill on a mat

Description: Each walk is described under its heading.

BEAR WALK

1. Get in position with hands and feet touching the floor.
2. Move the foot and hand on the same side together, then the other side (right hand and right foot, then left hand and left foot).

RABBIT HOP

1. Squat, placing hands on the floor in front of feet.
2. Move the hands first, then move the feet to the hands.

ELEPHANT WALK

1. Bend forward at the waist.
2. Clasp hands together, arms straight to form a trunk.
3. Walk with slow, big steps, keeping the legs straight.
4. Swing trunk from side to side.

GORILLA WALK

1. Bend knees and move trunk forward.
2. Hang arms at side.
3. As each step is taken, touch ground with fingers.

CRICKET WALK

1. Squat with knees apart.
2. Place arms between the knees and grasp the outside of the ankles with the hands.
3. Walk in this position.

SEAL WALK

1. Get in pushup position (straight arms and legs).
2. Walk forward with the hands and drag the feet.

CRAB WALK

1. Squat down and reach back with arms (fingers are pointed away from the body).
2. Touch the floor only with feet and hands.
3. Walk backward.

FROG JUMP

1. Squat down.
2. Place hands on the floor, slightly in front of feet.
3. Jump forward simultaneously with the hands and feet.

WALRUS WALK

1. Get in pushup position with fingers pointing outward to the side.
2. Move forward by moving both hands at the same time.

CAMEL WALK

1. Place one foot in front of the other.
2. Bend at the waist.
3. Clasp hands behind the back.
4. Walk, raising head and chest with each step.

KANGAROO HOP

1. Begin in squat position.
2. Fold arms across chest.
3. Keep body weight over toes.
4. Jump up and forward, landing on toes.

INCHWORM WALK

1. Begin in squat position with hands on the floor.
2. Take short steps with the hands moving forward until the back and legs are straight.
3. Without moving hands, take short steps forward with the feet toward the hands.
4. Repeat.

OSTRICH WALK

1. Bend at the waist.
2. Grab ankles with hands.
3. Walk.

STORK WALK

1. Hold up one foot.
2. Hop on the other foot.

ALLIGATOR WALK

1. Lie on stomach.
2. Move forward by using only arms and hands.

PENGUIN WALK

1. Stand with feet together with legs stiff.
2. Have arms at side with hands out.
3. Walk.

TURTLE WALK

1. Get on hands and feet facing floor.
2. Place feet widely apart.
3. Place hands widely apart.
4. Move with small steps.

■ Stunts (K–3)

Skills: Balance, coordination

Supplies: Mats

Formation: Divide students according to the number of mats available, and have them get in a single-file line behind the mats.

Description: Each stunt is described under its heading. Have one student from each group try the stunt on his or her mat, then go to the end of the line. After each person has had a turn, go to the next stunt.

TURK STAND

1. Stand with arms folded across chest.
2. Cross ankles.
3. Bend knees, going to a sitting position and keeping the back straight.
4. Stand back up.

THE BLOB

1. Sit down and grasp knees with arms.
2. Roll to the right, resting on right knee and arm, then right shoulder, then back, then left shoulder, then left arm and knee, then back to sitting position.
3. Repeat to the left.

COFFEE GRINDER

1. Lie down on your side, legs extended, weight on one extended arm.
2. Keep the extended arm's hand on the floor; hold the other arm up in the air.
3. Pivoting on the hand on the floor, "walk" around in a circle on the sides of the feet.

STORK STAND

1. Fold arms across chest and stand on one foot.
2. Place the other foot against the calf of the supporting leg.
3. Hold.
4. Change supporting legs.
5. Try it with eyes closed.

LEG DIP

1. Stand on one leg.
2. Extend other leg forward, and extend both arms forward.
3. Lower the body to a heel sit and return to a stand without losing balance or touching the floor with any part of the body.

KNEE JUMP TO STANDING

1. Kneel with seat touching heels, toes pointing backward.
2. Using a vigorous upward swing of the arms, try to jump to a standing position.

TOE JUMP

1. Hold left toes with right hand.
2. Jump right foot through without losing the grip on the toe.
3. Jump back again.
4. Try with other foot.

PRETZEL

1. Lie on stomach.
2. Raise head and trunk, arching backward.
3. Bend knees.
4. Bring feet to head.

JACKKNIFE

1. Stand with hands extended at shoulder level, slightly spread apart.
2. Jump up, bringing feet up to touch hands.
3. Feet should come up to hands, not hands down to feet.
4. To get a better start, take a little run and take off on both feet.

HEEL CLICK

1. Stand with feet slightly apart.
2. Jump up and click heels together.
3. Land with feet apart.

TURNOVER

1. Get in a pushup position.
2. Turn over so back is to the floor (body not touching).
3. Keep turning (body straight).

THREAD THE NEEDLE

1. Touch fingertips together in front of the body.
2. Step through arms, one foot at a time.
3. Step back through arms.
4. Try the stunt with fingers clasped.

KNEE WALK

1. Kneel on mat.
2. Reach back and hold both feet up from the mat.
3. Walk on knees.

HEEL STAND

1. Squat, arms at side.
2. Jump upward to leg extension, weight on both heels.
3. While balancing on heels, fling arms out diagonally.

WALL WALK-UP

1. Get in pushup position with feet against a wall.
2. Walk backwards up the wall to a handstand position.
3. Walk down again.

SKIER'S SIT

1. Assume a sitting position with back against wall, legs bent with thighs parallel to the floor.
2. Fold arms across the chest.

WALK THROUGH

1. Assume a pushup position.
2. Walk the feet through the hands until the body is extended with the back to the floor.
3. Reverse to original position.
4. Keep hands in contact with the floor.

FRONT SEAT SUPPORT

1. Sit on floor with legs together and extended forward.
2. Place hands on the floor between the hips and knees with fingers pointing forward.
3. Push down so the hips, legs, and heels come off the floor.
4. Support weight on hands.

SINGLE LEG CIRCLE

1. Squat, with both hands on the floor.
2. Place bent left knee between arms and extend right leg sideward.
3. Swing right leg forward and under lifted right arm, then under left leg and arm, then back to starting position.
4. Do several circles in succession.

TEACHING HINTS FOR PARACHUTES

1. Using the parachute fosters cooperation and is enjoyed by students of all ages.
2. Parachute activities develop muscles and the cardiovascular system.
3. The parachute can be used both indoors and outdoors.
4. Parachute dances are great to use before, after, or instead of a folk dance unit. The parachute adds an extra element of fun to dance.
5. If your school is unable to purchase a parachute, contact a Forestry Service Smokejumpers Unit, the Air Force, or other organization for a donation.
6. Teach a listening position (standing, not touching the parachute) and a ready position (squatting, holding on to the edge of the parachute). Use the words "one, two, three, up" to ensure all students will be lifting the parachute at the same time.

■ Exploring the Parachute

Skills: Cooperation, movement exploration, listening, following directions

Supplies: Parachute

Formation: Class standing around the parachute with an equal amount of space between each student

Description: This is great for a warm-up activity to encourage listening, following directions, and cooperation.

- Grasp the edge of the parachute with your left hand and circle forward to the right (counterclockwise).
- Circle backward to the left (clockwise).
- Move in toward the center of the chute, then move back out.

- Raise and lower the chute while moving around in a circle.
- Make waves using the chute.
- Run in a circle, holding the chute overhead with the right hand.
- Hop around in a circle while gripping the chute, starting on the left foot.
- Grip the chute with both hands and, with arms stretched straight out, raise and lower the chute.
- Raise the chute overhead, let go of it, regrasp it while it is still floating in the air.
- Hold the chute at a high level while you run at a low level.
- Inflate the chute and run to the left (clockwise). Inflate the chute and run to the right (counterclockwise).
- Inflate the chute and hop three steps toward the center and then three steps back out.
- Pass the chute quickly around in a circle without moving your feet.

■ Parachute Exercises

Skills: Muscle development, physical fitness, cooperation

Supplies: Parachute

Formation: Class standing around the parachute with an equal amount of space between each student.

Description: Each exercise is described under its heading.

BEND AND STRETCH

1. Grasp the edge of the parachute with both hands in an overhand grip.
2. Raise the chute to waist level.
3. Bend over and touch the chute to the ground.
4. Come back up and stretch arms overhead.
5. Bring the chute back down to waist level.

BICEP BUILDER

1. Stand around the chute with one leg forward and one leg back.
2. Grasp the parachute with both hands in an underhand then an overhand grip.
3. Lean back holding the chute.
4. Pull the chute toward you on the signal without moving feet.
5. Hold until the teacher signals (six seconds).

WILD HORSE PULL

1. Stand with backs to the chute.
2. Grasp the chute with an overhand grip.

3. Place one foot forward and the other foot back.
4. Lean forward.
5. Hold until the teacher signals.

OCEAN WAVES

1. Hold the chute at waist level.
2. Shake the chute up and down and pull it back.
3. Gradually go faster.

SKY HIGH PULL

1. Hold the chute at waist level with an overhand grip.
2. Spread legs for balance.
3. Lift the chute, with arms stretched high overhead.
4. Using only the arms and shoulders, pull back on the chute and hold tightly.

WRIST ROLL

1. Hold arms straight out in front of you and grasp the chute at waist level with an overhand grip.
2. Roll the edge of the chute slowly toward the center, keeping the chute tight by pulling back before each roll.

PUSHUPS

1. All inflate the chute.
2. Pull the chute to the floor.
3. Get in the pushup position (hands on chute, legs extended back away from the chute).
4. Do pushups until the chute deflates.

■ Parachute Movements

Skills: Muscle development, physical fitness, cooperation

Supplies: Parachute

Formation: Class standing around the parachute with an equal amount of space between each student.

Description: Each movement is described under its heading.

WAVES

1. Stand and hold on to the edge of the parachute.
2. On signal, move the chute up and down.

3. For variety, have every other child alternate the ups and downs, or have half of the chute go up while the other half goes down.
4. Give specific directions (for example, small waves, giant waves, slow waves, fast waves).

CANOPY

1. Grasp the chute with an overhand grip.
2. On the signal "one, two, three, up," lift the chute above heads with arms extended straight up.
3. As the chute comes down, lower arms.

OUTSIDE THE MOUNTAIN

1. Grasp the chute with an overhand grip.
2. On the signal "one, two, three, up," raise arms over head.
3. On the signal "down," bring arms down quickly and hold the edge of the chute tightly to the floor.

INSIDE THE TENT

1. Grasp the chute with an overhand grip.
2. On the signal "one, two, three, up," raise arms over head.
3. On the signal "inside," take one step underneath and pull the chute down.

CAROUSEL

1. Stand with right side to the chute, holding the edge in the right hand with an overhand grip.
2. On a signal, begin to move clockwise. Keep the chute tight so it doesn't touch the floor.
3. On another signal, stop, turn to the opposite direction and change to the left hand.
4. Start walking, then jogging, then running, and so on.

FLOATING CLOUD

1. Grasp the chute with an overhand grip.
2. On the signal "one, two, three, up," raise the chute over head.
3. On the signal "let go," release the chute, put hands at side, and let the chute float.
4. When the chute lands, pick up the edges.

HOT AIR BALLOON

1. Grasp the chute with an overhand grip.
2. On the signal "one, two, three, up," raise the chute over head.
3. On the signal "in," take five steps in toward the center without letting go of the chute.
4. On the signal "out," come back out without letting go of the chute.

■ Parachute Games

Skills: Muscle development, physical fitness, cooperation

Supplies: Parachute, various other items depending on the game

Formation: Class standing around the parachute with an equal amount of space between each student.

Description: Each game is described under its heading.

PARACHUTE TOSS

1. Place an unbreakable doll or stuffed animal on the parachute.
2. Make waves.
3. Watch the doll or stuffed animal fly up in the air.

POPCORN

1. Place a number of fleece balls on the parachute.
2. At the signal, make waves.
3. Watch the balls pop up and down.
4. Try to keep the balls on the chute.

NUMBER EXCHANGE

1. Count off by fours.
2. At the signal, inflate the chute.
3. Call out a number.
4. All those with that number let go of the chute and run underneath it across to the other side.

BEANBAG TOWER

1. Give a beanbag to each student.
2. Count off by fours.

3. Inflate the chute.
4. A number is called out. Those students run under the chute and make a tower with the beanbags.
5. Another number is called, with those players trying to make the tower taller.
6. Continue until all numbers are called.

CAT AND MOUSE

1. Choose two or three students to be "cats" and go on top of the chute (crawling on hands and knees).
2. Choose six students to be "mice" who go under the chute.
3. Others sit around the edge of the chute.
4. The mice move around under the chute trying to avoid being touched by the cats.
5. The students around the chute make small waves to help keep the mice hidden, this adds an extra challenge.
6. When a mouse is touched, that player comes out and another player from the edge of the chute goes in.
7. After a cat catches two mice, that player goes off the chute and another player on the edge comes on.
8. VARIATION: Have one mouse and one cat.

HOT POTATO

1. Hold the chute at waist level.
2. Hand four fleece balls to students in different places around the chute.
3. On the signal, pass the balls from hand to hand around the circle (hold on to the chute with one hand while passing with the other).
4. On the signal "hot potato," inflate the chute and the players holding the fleece balls exchange places under the chute.

PARACHUTE GOLF

1. You need two balls with different markings that will fit through the hole in the center of the chute (if yours has one).
2. Divide the class in half. Have one team on one side of the chute, and the other team on the other side.
3. Both teams have a ball placed on the chute.
4. On the signal, both teams attempt to get their ball in the center hole to score a point. (Ball must be rolled, not thrown.)
5. The team scoring the most points wins.

PARACHUTE DANCES

▪ Dance of Greeting (Danish)

Skills: Strength, rhythm, cooperation

Supplies: Parachute, music for "Danish Dance of Greeting" (Folkcraft 1187)

Formation: Students around the parachute. Boys stand to the left of girl partners.

Description: This is great to use either before or after a folk dance unit. Walk through the steps first without the music.

1. "Lift, lift, bow"—Students make waves with chute, then boys bow to partners and girls curtsey.
2. "Lift, lift, bow"—Students make waves with chute then bow or curtsey to person on the other side.
3. "Stamp, stamp"—Students stamp their right foot, then their left foot.
4. "Turn yourself around"—Turn in place, letting go of the chute with one hand then regripping.
5. Repeat steps 1 through 4.
6. Run to the left for sixteen counts.
7. Run to the right for sixteen counts.
8. Repeat the whole dance.

▪ Pop Goes the Weasel (American)

Skills: Strength, rhythm, cooperation

Supplies: Parachute, music for "Pop Goes the Weasel" (*The Hokey Pokey & Other Favorites*, Melody House MH—33 Folkcraft 1329)

Formation: Students around the parachute, counting off by twos

Description: This is great to use either before or after a folk dance unit. Walk through the steps first without the music.

1. Walk twelve steps to the left while shaking the chute.
2. On "Pop," inflate the chute. The "ones" duck under the chute and come out ahead of the person in front of them.
3. Walk twelve steps shaking the chute.
4. On "Pop," inflate the chute and the "twos" duck under the chute and go to the right of and in front of the person ahead of them.
5. Repeat steps 1 through 4.

▪ Cshebogar (Hungarian)

Skills: Strength, rhythm, cooperation, sliding

Supplies: Parachute, music for "Cshebogar" (Folkcraft 1195)

Formation: Students around the parachute facing the center

Description: This is great to use either before or after a folk dance unit. Walk through the steps without the music first.

1. Merry-go-round to the left, sliding. Face the center for 16 counts, face out for 16 counts (back to chute).
2. Make a slow umbrella (8 counts); pull down fast (8 counts).
3. Make a slow mushroom (8 counts); pull down fast (8 counts).
4. Repeat step 1, except 8 counts IN, 8 counts OUT, 8 counts IN, 8 counts OUT.
5. Repeat steps 2 and 3.
6. Repeat step 1, except 4 counts IN, 4 counts OUT, 4 counts IN, 4 counts OUT, 4 counts IN, 4 counts OUT.
7. Repeat steps 2 and 3.
8. Repeat step 2, except 2 counts IN, 2 counts OUT, etc., to make up 16 counts.

■ La Rapsa (Spanish)

Skills: Strength, rhythm, cooperation, hopping

Supplies: Parachute, music for "La Rapsa" (Folkcraft 1190)

Formation: Students stand around the parachute facing the center. Count off by twos.

Description: This is great to use either before or after a folk dance unit. Walk through the steps without the music first.

1. Holding the chute, do eight *La Rapsa* steps. [The *La Rapsa* step is: Hop on left foot with right heel pointed forward; hop on right foot with left heel pointed forward; hop on left foot with right heel pointed forward; hold. (next time it would be right - left - right - hold.)]
2. Raise chute to make an umbrella (8 counts). Bring it down (8 counts).
3. Repeat step 2.
4. Do eight *La Rapsa* steps.
5. Raise chute to make a mushroom (8 counts). Bring it down (8 counts).
6. Repeat step 5.
7. Do eight *La Rapsa* steps.
8. Make umbrella and the "ones" cross under.
9. Make umbrella and the "twos" cross under.
10. Do eight *La Rapsa* steps.
11. Merry-go-round to the left 16 steps.
12. Mountain, students inside, pull chute down.

■ Schottische (Scottish)

Skills: Strength, rhythm, cooperation, schottische step

Supplies: Parachute, "Schottische" music (*Party Dancing Made Easy,* Epic Stereorama BN 594 Folkcraft 1101)

Formation: Students stand around the parachute facing the center.

Description: This is great to use either before or after a folk dance unit. Walk through the steps without the music first.

1. Teach the *schottische* step (step-step-step-hop). Practice this step to the left (left-right-left-hop) and to the right (right-left-right-hop).
2. Hold the chute with two hands and move to the left, then to the right, then to the left, then to the right (*schottische* step).
3. Stand in place and swing the chute in short, quick moves to the left, to the right, left-right, left-right, left-right.
4. Merry-go-round to the left 16 steps.
5. Repeat *schottische* step as in step 2.
6. Repeat the swing as in step 3.
7. Repeat *schottische* step.
8. Repeat the swing.
9. Make a mushroom (16 counts).
10. Repeat entire routine three times.

TEACHING HINTS
FOR RECREATIONAL DANCE

1. This section gives students an opportunity to be creative. Allow students to work in groups or individually. Have them teach their dances to the class. Keep a book or other record of the dances created by the students.
2. In the area of aerobics, there is a variety of activities that can be used to enhance fitness. Encourage the students to create new activities and to be involved in physical activity outside of p.e. class.
3. When appropriate, allow students to choose their own music. This gives them a sense of ownership.

■ Creative Dance

Skills: Creativity, movement

Supplies: Varies according to activity

Formation: Varies according to activity

Description: There are a variety of activities that can be used for creative dance. Some students may be more receptive to these dances, since the dances focus on creativity in movement rather than on actual dance routines.

BAG OF TRICKS

1. On one set of cards write locomotor movements, such as hop, skip, and jump.
2. On another set of cards write directional instructions, such as forward and backward.
3. A student pulls one card from the bag of locomotor movements and one from the bag of directional instructions.
4. The student does the movements to music, such as hop in a circle.

WHAT'S NEW?

1. Divide the class into groups.
2. Allow each group to pick its own music.
3. Have each group put together a sequence of dance steps and teach the class.

CREATIVE MOVEMENTS

1. All creative movements include one or more of the following elements:
   a. Body awareness (what the body can do)
   b. Qualities (how the body can move)
   c. Spatial awareness (where the body can move)
   d. Relationships (what the body relates to)
2. Examples of creative movement words
   a. Body awareness
      • shapes: curl, stretch, twist, bend, gigantic, circular, crooked
      • balance: standing, sitting, stable, solid, stick, anchor
      • transfer of weight/locomotor movements: stamp, dart, bounce, glide, spring, roll, crawl, slither, spin, rise, sink, expand, contract
   b. Qualities
      • speed: quick, slow, hurried, leisurely, sustained
      • force: strong, light, firm, buoyant, feather-like, stomping
      • flow: free, bounding, traveling, static, jerky
   c. Spatial awareness
      • space: personal, general, cramped, open, limited, etc.
      • direction: forward, backward, sideways, diagonally, down, ascending, slumping
      • levels: high, medium, low, top, deep
   d. Relationships
      • with people: individual, partner, group, away from, mirroring, contrasting, leading
      • with objects: near, away from, over, under, adjacent
3. Suggested lesson structure
   a. Choose a main theme from one of the main elements of movement (for example, locomotor—running and walking).

b. Choose one or more subthemes from the other three elements.

c. Break the lesson down into three stages:
   - introductory activity—vigorous body activity related to the main theme or subthemes
   - theme development—the student needs to explore, discover, and select movements related to the theme
   - final activity—students develop a sequence of movements from the other parts of the lesson

4. Sample lesson plan

   a. Main theme—locomotor skills (running and walking)

   b. Subtheme—change of direction

   c. Introductory activity—Explain that students are to run lightly in any direction without touching anyone else. When the music stops, they are to stop and listen. Repeat these directions.

   d. Theme development—See if you can walk lightly and change directions. Stimulate by asking "Can you move sideways, backward, forward, and turn?" Stop students and ask them to make up their own movement sequence that has three different ways of moving (for example, a walk, a run, and a turn). Stop students and have a few students demonstrate their sequences. Then have everyone try theirs with music.

   e. Final activity—Have students get partners and teach each other their sequences. Have them try their sequences moving together side by side or one in front of the other.

STIMULI

Have students make up creative movements using stimuli such as balloons, fairy tales, pictures, weather, stories, poems, trees, plants, or sports.

■ Aerobic Activities

Skills: Cardiovascular development, a variety of aerobic skills, calculating target heart rate

Supplies: Varies according to the activity

Formation: Varies according to the activity

Description: This provides a variety of different aerobic activities.

COUNTING HEART RATE

1. Find your neck or wrist pulse using your fingertips. (Do not use the thumb, since it has a pulse.)

2. Using a clock or stopwatch, count pulse for ten seconds and multiply by six.

3. Your age-related maximal attainable heart rate is 220 less your age. Thus, if you are ten years old, it would be 220 less 10, which equals 210; your maximum target heart rate is 210 beats per minute.

4. Figure out your target zone area for a safe and beneficial workout:

220 less your age = _____

times _____60%_____

= _____ minimum working heart rate

Your target zone is between:

_____ and _____
minimum   maximum
(× 60%)   (× 80%)

5. Take your pulse after working out for a period of time. Is your working heart rate at minimum or maximum?

6. To get a resting heart rate, take your pulse first thing in the morning for 60 seconds. Do this several times, then find the average.

7. To figure your aerobic heart rate (for maximum safe conditioning):
   a. Maximum target heart rate (MHR) 220 = age = _____
   b. Subtract your resting heart rate (RHR)   − _____
   c. Multiply the answer by 60%   × _____60%_____
                                      = _____
   d. Add your resting heart rate   + _____
   e. This is your aerobic heart rate   = _____

Example: MHR = 220 − 10 = 210
                  Age   = 210
         RHR = 70   − $\underline{70}$
                     = 140
                  × $\underline{60\%}$
                     = 84
                  + $\underline{70}$ (RHR)
Aerobic
Heart Rate $\underline{\underline{154}}$

8. Aerobic activities include: jogging, swimming, cycling, and jump rope.

WARM-UP EXERCISES

- Involves marching, slow jumps, knee bends, kicks, coordination.
- Students stand in a personal space.
1. March in place 24× (L, R, L, R, . . .).
2. Clap hands 2×.
3. Jump spreading both feet apart.
4. Jump bringing both feet together.
5. Repeat steps 1 through 4.
6. Step close, step close, bend, bend (step to right with right foot, bring left foot to right; repeat once more; bend knees twice bringing arms up when knees bend).

7. Repeat step 6 to the left.
8. Repeat step 6 to the right.
9. Clap 2×.
10. Jump with feet apart, then together.
11. Repeat steps 1 through 4.
12. Repeat steps 6 through 10.
13. Repeat steps 1 through 4.
14. Step kick 2×. Step with right foot and kick left foot across and in front of right. Repeat with the left.
15. Jump, jump, turn. Jump with feet together 2×, and on the second jump turn one-quarter turn to the right.
16. Repeat steps 14 and 15 3×.
17. Step kick, step kick, clap, clap, turn (step kick same as step 14, clap 2× and turn one-quarter turn to the right). Repeat 3×.
18. Repeat steps 6 through 10.
19. Repeat steps 1 through 4 2×.
20. Repeat steps 14 and 15.
21. Repeat step 17.
22. March 4×; jump apart, together.

NOTE:
There are actually six sequences:

- The first sequence is steps 1 through 4.
- The second sequence is steps 6 through 10.
- The third sequence is a repetition of the preceding two sequences.
- The fourth sequence is steps 16 and 17.
- The fifth sequence is step 19.
- The sixth sequence is a repetition of the preceding five sequences

FLEXIBILITY EXERCISES

- Involves knee bends, back and leg stretches.
- Students stand in a personal space.
  1. Bend and straighten knees 16×.
  2. Place feet apart; bend and straighten knees 16×.
  3. Alternately stretch right arm and left arm 16×.
  4. Windmills right and left 8×.
  5. Stand with feet together.
  6. Repeat steps 1 through 5.
  7. Bend and straighten knees 8×.
  8. Place feet apart; bend and straighten knees 8×.
  9. Stretch arms 16×.

10. Windmills 8×.
11. Stretch arms 4×.
12. Stand, feet together, and hold.

MODERATE ENDURANCE EXERCISES

- Involves fast walk, hops, jumps, leaps, skips.
- Stand, feet together in a personal space.
  1. Jump and turn one-quarter turn in place 4×.
  2. Hop right, hop left.
  3. Jump with feet apart, then together.
  4. Repeat steps 2 and 3 2×.
  5. Repeat step 1.
  6. Side to side leap: Leap with right foot to right side and tap the left foot next to the right. Then leap with left foot to the left.
  7. Skip 8× in place.
  8. Repeat step 1.
  9. Repeat steps 2 and 3 2×.
  10. Repeat Number Three.

VIGOROUS ENDURANCE EXERCISES

- Involves walking and jogging.
- Stand, feet together in a personal space.
  1. Walk fast.
  2. Jog.
  3. Walk.
  4. Jog (longer period of time).
  5. Walk.
  6. Jog until the end of the music.

STRENGTH EXERCISES

- For each exercise, do as many repetitions as possible in the time allotted.
- Involves sit-ups, trunk twists, leg lifts, shoulder stands, push-ups, spine stretches, arm and leg lifts.
- Start lying down on back.
  1. Sit-ups.
  2. Sit, bend knees, hands behind you, twist knees from side to side, keeping them together.
  3. Lie down, lift both legs in the air, hands under hips, lift hips and lower trunk off the ground and bicycle.
  4. Sit ups.

5. Keeping the body straight, place hands behind you and lift hips and trunk off the floor and lower.
6. Roll over and do push-ups.
7. Stretch four counts and relax: lie on stomach, lift arms and legs as high as possible (arch back).

COOL-DOWN EXERCISES

• Involves walking and stretching.
1. Walk easily, swinging arms and snapping fingers.
2. Walk and bounce (bend knees slightly).
3. Stretch right leg (lunge with right foot forward, left leg extended straight back/ both heels on floor, weight on front leg, pull down and back on back leg).
4. Stretch left leg (same as step 3).
5. Walk.
6. Stretch, reach, tap (step to right and reach both arms up to right side; tap left foot behind right and bring both arms down to the right side). Do this alternately to the left and right.
7. Repeat step 3.
8. Repeat step 4.
9. Walk.
10. Repeat step 6.
11. Stop.

COUNTDOWN

1. Jog five laps, then do two abdominal exercises, ten counts each (for example, V-sits, sit-ups).
2. Jog four laps, then two arm strength exercises, ten counts each (for example, push-ups, clap and catch push-ups).
3. Jog three laps, then two quadricep (thigh) exercises, ten counts each (for example, long sit leg lifts; straddle squats).
4. Jog two laps, then two balance activities, ten counts each (for example, standing scale; yoga stand).
5. Jog one lap, then two flexibility exercises, ten counts each (for example, long sit, touch head to knee; shoulder stand, touch toes alternately to the floor).

EXERCISE WITH MUSIC

1. Have squads in single file lines.
2. Choose popular music.
3. The first person in each line is the leader and leads an exercise a designated number of times. (Each squad can be doing a different exercise.)

4. When it's time to change, the leader jogs to the end of the line and the next person leads an exercise.
5. This continues until all have led their squad in an exercise or the music ends.
6. You can designate the type of exercises (for example, endurance, strength, flexibility, etc.).

ACTIVITY STATIONS

1. Four stations are set up with eight teams.
2. Designate a specific amount of time students will be at the stations.
3. They move from one station to the next and begin immediately.
4. The stations are:
   a. Shooting Baskets—one team versus another team doing lay-ups. Each team has a ball. Each team member goes to the end of the opposite line after shooting. Each team counts its own baskets.
   b. For each team, place two hoops on the floor a distance from each other. One player stands in each hoop. The players in the hoops serve a volleyball to each other, five times each. The player receiving the serve must catch the ball with at least one foot inside the hoop. Count completed serves only. The team scores a point for each completed serve.
   c. Relay—set up two identical obstacle courses for the two teams. A point is given to the team whose player comes in first. (Example: Run through loops, jump over four cones, jump over a stick, go under the table and back.)
   d. Wall Volley—Using a volleyball set, volley the ball to the wall, counting how many volleys are done in a given period of time.

ROLL CALL JOG

Jog around the gym for five minutes. When your name is called give the number of laps completed.

PARTNER JOG

Each student has a partner. One person stands anywhere around the line in the gym. The other person runs around the gym once, then the two partners change places. Do this until each person has run nine times around the gym.

EXERCISE AND JOG

Each student has a partner. One person runs a lap while the other person does the first exercise (have a list of exercises to do). Then switch.

AEROBIC BALL ROUTINE

1. Hold the ball in your right hand and swing your hand forward, back, a small toss, catch in left hand. Repeat with the left hand.
2. Hold the ball in both hands straight overhead. Do a four count side bend to each side 4×.
3. While dribbling the ball, do scissor jumps 16×.
4. Dribble the ball and do sailor jumps 16×. (Dribble with right hand, left hand up to eyebrows. Body is in a semi-lunge—jump and put one foot forward with bent knee; keep back leg straight. Hold two counts. Jump and switch.)
5. Pendulum Jumps—Four step hops, extending free leg to the side (hop on right foot, extend left leg sideward. Repeat hopping on left foot). Eight quick single side to side extensions (step on right foot, extend left leg sideward, step on left foot, extend right leg sideward, etc.). Do this 2×. Dribble the ball in front of you at the same time.
6. Dribble the ball on your right side and skip around 8×; same to the left; then 8× in place.
7. Toss the ball from hand to hand and skip in place 16×.
8. Toss the ball from hand to hand while skipping from side to side 16×.
9. Repeat the routine from step 3 to step 8.

SPECIFIC AEROBIC EXERCISES

1. *Banana Rock and Roll*—Lie on the floor and roll side to side and back and forth.
2. *Roman Soldier*—Get in push-up position; right hand touches left shoulder then back to the floor; left hand to right shoulder; right hand to left shoulder; tap the floor 2× with right hand. Repeat, starting with the left hand.
3. *Flea Hop*—Get in push-up position; jump to the side with feet and hands 3× then do two push-ups. Repeat going the other direction.
4. *Elevator Push-up*—Get in push-up position:
   a. top floor (arms straight) count "one, two, three, four."
   b. second floor (bent elbows) count "one, two, three, four."
   c. bottom floor (all the way down without touching body to floor) count "one, two, three, four."
   d. "going up."
5. *Squat, Slap, Snap*—Squat with knees out; slap knees once; snap fingers 12×; then rest two counts.
6. Run in place and slap knees.
7. *Wall Sits*—Squat with back against wall for two minutes.

TEACHING HINTS
FOR ROPES

1. To find the correct rope length, stand on the center of the rope with both feet. The ends of the rope should reach from armpit to armpit.
2. Suggested guidelines when purchasing ropes:
   a. Primary (K–3): 7 feet to 8 feet
   b. Intermediate (4–6): 8 feet to 9 feet (majority 8 feet)
3. Suggested progression for students:
   a. Try each stunt without a rope.
   b. Try the stunt with the rope.
4. In a 30-minute period:
   a. Warm up using free rope skipping to music.
   b. Teach two to four skills, depending on students' ability.
   c. End with a motivational activity:
      • Speed test (How many jumps in 15 seconds)
      • Endurance test (How long)
      • Number of turns without missing
      • Individual demonstrations
      • Individual routines
      • Partner routines
      • Group routines
5. Though a skill may be task-analyzed starting with the left foot, students may also begin with the right foot.
6. On partner skills the person without the rope (follower) can do the following while jumping:
   a. Perform a quarter, half, three-quarters, or full turn
   b. Juggle
   c. Toss or bounce a ball
   d. Dance
      • Face to face—Schottische; Polka
      • Front to back—Bunny Hop

7. In long ropes there is "front doors" (rope turned toward the jumper) and "back doors" (rope turned away from the jumper). "Front doors" is easier to enter.
8. You can add these to single long rope skills:
    a. Perform a quarter, half, three-quarters, or full turn
    b. Bounce or toss a ball
    c. Twirl hoop
    d. Jump with the hoop
    e. Single rope skills
    f. Partner stunts
    g. Tumbling stunts (cartwheels, round-offs, handsprings)
9. Any short rope skill or long rope skill can be incorporated into the double long rope skills.
10. For conditioning, jump rope to music.
11. For endurance, jump for a certain length of time, then rest. Increase the length of time and the number of repetitions.
12. For strength, try speed skipping, double unders, then rest, jump.
13. The suggested grade level for the following activities is 1–6.

■ Rhythms of Rope Jumping

HALF-TIME RHYTHM

1. Jump over the rope.
2. As the rope continues overhead, take a rebound step.

Jump   Rebound   Jump   Rebound

SINGLE-TIME RHYTHM

1. Jump one step for each turn of the rope.
2. Replace the rebound with a jump over the rope.

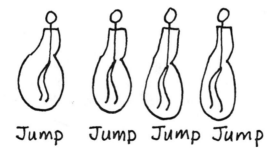

Jump   Jump   Jump   Jump

DOUBLE-TIME RHYTHM

1. Take two steps while the rope makes one turn.
2. Take the second step while the rope is overhead.

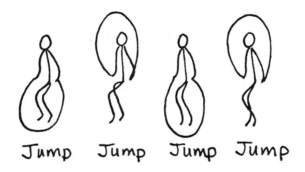

Jump   Jump   Jump   Jump

COMBINED RHYTHM

1. Combine single-time rhythm with half-time foot action.
2. On the odd turns of the rope, do the jump; on the even turns, take the rebound step over the rope.

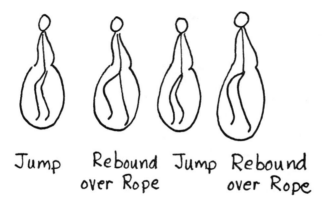

Jump   Rebound   Jump   Rebound
over Rope   over Rope

STOP-TIME RHYTHM

1. Turn the rope at half-time rhythm.
2. Jump as in the half-time rhythm, except eliminate the rebound.
3. In place of the rebound, stop and freeze in the landing position.
4. Hold the freeze position until the rope approaches the feet.

Jump   Freeze   Jump   Freeze

■ Task Analysis of Individual Short Rope Skills

BEGINNING TO JUMP

1. Hold the rope loosely with thumb and index finger.
2. Extend arms sideways with elbows at waist level.
3. Use an outward, downward, and backward rotation of the arms from the shoulders on the first turn only.
4. Use a circular wrist motion to turn the rope after the first turn.
5. Jump on the balls of the feet, with the feet leaving the floor only enough to clear the rope.

SIDE SWING

1. Hold the rope with both hands to one side of the body.
2. Turn the rope on one side of the body.
3. Turn the rope on the other side of the body.
4. Turn the rope alternately from side to side.

ONE-HANDED SIDE SWING

1. Hold both ends of the rope in one hand.
2. Turn the rope on that side of the body.
3. Change hands.
4. Turn the rope on that side of the body.

BEHIND-THE-BACK PASS

1. Hold both ends of the rope in one hand.
2. Pass the rope behind-the-back to the other hand.
3. Hold both ends of the rope in one hand.
4. Pass the rope behind-the-back to the other hand.

UNDER-THE-LEG PASS

1. Hold both ends of the rope in one hand.
2. Raise the opposite leg.
3. Pass the rope under the leg to the other hand.
4. Repeat steps 1, 2, and 3.

COMBINATION

1. Combine the previous four stunts.
2. Perform left side swing; behind-the-back pass; right side swing; under-the-leg pass.
3. Create his/her own pattern.

BASIC BOUNCE

1. Turn the rope and jump, landing on the balls of the feet.
2. Continue to jump without a rebound step.

DOUBLE SIDE SWING AND JUMP

1. Turn the rope on one side of the body.
2. Turn the rope on the other side of the body.
3. Jump over the rope.
4. Repeat steps 1, 2, and 3.

SINGLE SIDE SWING AND JUMP

1. Turn the rope on one side of the body.
2. Jump over the rope.
3. Turn the rope on the other side of the body.
4. Jump over the rope.
5. Repeat steps 1 through 4.

SKIER (SIDE TO SIDE)

1. Jump to one side with feet together on one turn of the rope.
2. Jump to the other side with feet together on next turn of rope.
3. Continue side to side jumping alternating on each turn of the rope.

BELL (FORWARD AND BACKWARD)

1. Jump forward with feet together on one turn of the rope.
2. Jump backwards with feet together on next turn of the rope.
3. Continue forward and backward jumping alternating at each turn of the rope.

SIDE STRADDLE

1. Jump to a straddle position (feet spread shoulder-width apart) on one turn of the rope.
2. Jump, returning to original position on next turn of rope.
3. Continue to jump alternating feet apart, feet together on each turn of rope.

FORWARD STRADDLE

1. Jump to a stride position with one foot forward on one turn of the rope.
2. Jump and reverse foot position on next turn of rope.
3. Continue jumping and reversing foot position on each turn of the rope.

ALTERNATE STRADDLE

1. Jump to a straddle position on one turn of the rope.
2. Jump to a stride position on next turn of rope.
3. Alternate straddle and stride on each turn of the rope.

ALTERNATE BELL AND SKIER

1. Jump forward over the rope with feet together.
2. Jump backwards over the rope with feet together.
3. Jump to the left with feet together.
4. Jump to the right with feet together.
5. Repeat steps 1 through 4.

X MOTION

1. Jump to a straddle position on one turn of the rope.
2. Jump and cross legs on next turn of rope.
3. Continue jumping, alternating between straddle and crossed legs on each turn of the rope.

SWITCHES

1. Jump to cross legs with left over right on one turn of the rope.
2. Jump and switch legs right over left on next turn of rope.

3. Continue jumping, alternating left over right and right over left on each turn of the rope.

WOUNDED DUCK

1. Jump touching toes and knees together, heels spread on one turn of rope.
2. Jump touching heels, toes and knees spread on next turn of rope.
3. Jump, alternating between steps 1 and 2 on each turn of rope.

CRISSCROSS

1. Jump the rope with the basic bounce.
2. Cross arms and jump.
3. Alternate crossing and uncrossing arms as s/he jumps.

CONTINUOUS FORWARD CROSSOVER

1. Cross arms and jump on one turn of rope.
2. Continue to jump with arms crossed on each turn of rope.

SIDE SWING CROSSOVER

1. Turn the rope to one side.
2. Cross arms and jump over the rope.
3. Continue to turn the rope on the same side and jump.
4. Then alternate sides.

JOGGING STEP

1. Step over the rope with one foot.
2. Step over the rope with the other foot.
3. Alternate feet with each turn of the rope.

STRADDLE RUN

1. Step sideways over the rope to the left with the left foot.
2. Step sideways over the rope to the right with the right foot.
3. Alternate sideways steps.

TWIST

1. Jump and rotate hips to the right on first turn of rope.
2. Jump and rotate hips to the left on next turn of rope.
3. Jump and alternate rotating hips left and right.

FORWARD 180

1. Jump forward over the rope and turn the body half way to the right.
2. Rotate the rope from forward to backward position on the half turn.
3. Jump backwards over the rope.
4. Turn the body halfway to the left.
5. Rotate the rope from backward to forward position on the half turn.
6. Jump forward over the rope.

BACKWARD 180

1. Jump backward over the rope and turn the body halfway to the left.
2. Rotate the rope from backward to forward position on the half turn.
3. Jump forward over the rope.
4. Turn the body halfway to the right.
5. Rotate the rope from forward to backward position on the half turn.
6. Jump backwards over the rope.

HEEL TO HEEL

1. Jump, extending one foot forward, touching that heel to the floor.
2. Jump, extending the other foot, and touching that heel to the floor.
3. Alternate heel touches.

TOE TO TOE

1. Jump on left foot and touch right toe next to left heel.
2. Jump on right foot and touch left toe next to right heel.
3. Alternate toe touches.

HEEL-TOE

1. Jump on left foot and touch right heel forward.
2. Jump on left foot and touch right toe next to left heel.
3. Jump on right foot and touch left heel forward.
4. Jump on right foot and touch left toe next to right heel.
5. Repeat the steps 1 through 4.

SHUFFLE (SIDE-STEP, TOUCH)

1. Step sideways to the right and touch the left toe beside the right foot.
2. Step sideways to the left, and touch the right toe beside the left foot.
3. Continue the alternating steps 1 and 2.

KICK SWING

1. Jump on left foot and swing right leg forward.
2. Jump on right foot, and swing left leg forward.
3. Alternate kick swings.
4. Alternate kicks forward, sideways, and backward for a variation.

PEEK-A-BOO

1. Jump on the left foot, extend the right leg sideways, and touch the right toe to the floor.
2. Jump on the right foot, extend the left leg sideways, and touch the left toe to the floor.
3. Alternate toe touches.

DOUBLE PEEK-A-BOO

1. Jump on the left foot and touch the right toe 6 inches sideways.
2. Jump on the left foot and touch the right toe 12 inches sideways.
3. Jump on the right foot and touch the left toe 6 inches sideways.
4. Jump on the right foot and touch the left toe 12 inches sideways.
5. Alternate double toe touches sideways.

LEG SWING

1. Step over the rope on the left foot, and swing the right leg to the right.
2. Step over the rope on the right foot, and swing the left leg to the left.
3. Alternate leg swings, keeping the leg straight and lifting it high.

SIDE STEP AND KICK

1. Step over the rope on the right foot and kick the left leg to the left.
2. Step with the left foot behind the right.
3. Repeat steps 1 and 2, moving to the right.

CONTINUOUS TOE TOUCH

1. Jump on right foot and touch left toe forward.
2. Jump on left foot and touch right toe forward.
3. Continue toe touches alternating forward, sideways, and backward.

CONTINUOUS BACKWARD CROSSOVER

1. Cross arms.

2. Jump backwards.
3. Continue to jump backwards with arms crossed.

DOUBLE UNDER

1. Turn the rope fast to increase the speed.
2. Pass the rope under the feet twice during one jump.
3. Continue to perform the double under after every few jumps or in a continuous manner.
4. Repeat steps 1 through 3 turning the rope backwards.

MONKEY

1. Jump on the right foot.
2. Raise the left leg as left arm reaches under left leg.
3. Continue jumping in this position.

SIDE, CROSS, SIDE, TOGETHER SWING STEP

1. Step over the rope on the left foot and swing the right leg to the right.
2. Jump on the left foot and swing the right leg across in front of the left leg.
3. Jump over the rope on the left foot and swing the right leg to the right.
4. Jump on both feet to prepare for repeating the above, starting with the right foot.

ALTERNATE HEEL AND CROSS TOE

1. Step over the rope on the left foot, touching the right heel forward and to the right.
2. Jump on the left foot and cross over the left foot with the right, touching the right toe to the floor.
3. Jump over the rope on the right foot, touching the left heel forward and to the left.
4. Jump on the right foot and cross over the right foot with the left, touching the left toe to the floor.
5. Repeat steps 1 through 4.

HURDLE JUMP

1. Jump as the rope passes under the feet.
2. Raise the left leg, extending it forward, and raise the right leg, bending it backwards from the knee.
3. Land on both feet.
4. Repeat steps 1 through 3, switching the legs.

BRUSH TAP

1. Step over the rope on the left foot.
2. Swing the right foot forward and to the right, brushing the floor lightly with the foot.
3. Swing the right foot backwards, brushing the floor.
4. Repeat steps 1 through 3 with the left foot.

MONKEY CROSSOVER

1. Jump on the right foot and raise the left leg.
2. Cross arms with the right hand going under the raised leg.
3. Jump the rope.
4. Continue to jump with the arms crossed.

SIDE SWING CROSSOVER 180

1. Perform a side swing on the left side.
2. Perform a half turn to the left.
3. Cross arms and jump the rope backwards.
4. Perform a backward side swing on the left side.
5. Perform a half turn to the left.
6. Cross arms and jump the rope forward.
7. Repeat steps 1 through 6.

CAN CAN

1. Jump on right foot, and lift left knee up.
2. Jump on right foot, and touch left toe to floor.
3. Jump on right foot, and kick left leg out.
4. Perform a basic jump.
5. Repeat steps 1 through 4, starting with the left foot, then alternating right and left.

GRAPEVINE

1. Jump on the right foot.
2. Cross the left foot behind the right foot.
3. Step right on the right foot.
4. Kick the left leg forward.
5. Repeat steps 1 through 4, starting with the left foot.

SHUFFLE-BALL-CHANGE

1. Push off with the right foot, jumping over the rope, standing on the left foot.
2. Brush the sole of the right foot forward, then backward when the rope is overhead.
3. Stand on the right foot momentarily, then stand back on the left foot immediately.
4. Jump from left foot to right foot as the rope passes under the feet.
5. Repeat steps 1 through 4, starting with the left foot.

IRISH JIG

1. Jump on the left foot and cross the right heel in front of the left foot, touching the heel to the floor.
2. Jump on the left foot, cross the right toe in front of the left foot, touching the toe to the floor.
3. Jump on the left foot, touching the right heel to the floor to the right side of the body.
4. Jump on the left foot, touching the right toe to the floor.
5. Repeat steps 1 through 4, jumping on the right foot.

FRONT-BACK CROSSOVER

1. Cross the right arm in front of the body.
2. Cross the left arm in back of the body.
3. Jump the rope.
4. Open the rope and perform a basic jump.
5. Repeat steps 1 through 4.

HEEL CLICK

1. Step over the rope on the left foot.
2. Jump on one foot and click the heels to the right.
3. Land on the left foot.
4. Repeat steps 1 through 3 with the right foot.

ALTERNATE LATERAL TURNS

1. Hold the rope with right hand between legs and left hand above the head.
2. Turn the rope in a circular motion with the hand above the head.
3. Swing the rope backwards under the right leg.
4. Swing the rope forward under the left leg.
5. Swing the left arm downward and across the body, continuing to move the right arm up above the head.
6. Swing the rope forward under the right leg.

7. Swing the rope backward under the left leg.
8. Swing the right arm downward and across the body, continuing to move the left arm above the head.
9. Repeat steps 3 through 8.

WRAP AROUND

1. Hold the rope with the right hand between the legs and the left hand above the head.
2. Swing the rope to the right, backwards under the right leg.
3. Continue turning the rope clockwise until it is wrapped around the body.
4. Turn the rope counterclockwise until it is unwrapped.
5. Swing the rope forward under the right leg.
6. Repeat steps 1 through 5, beginning with the left hand.

VARIATIONS

1. SQUAT JUMP: Jump in a squat position (feet crossed; crossover; partner).
2. Perform a cartwheel, front handspring, front and back walkover, back bend, and then jump.
3. SPEED JUMP: Turn the rope as fast as you can and jump.
4. KNEE JUMP: Using knee pads, jump on knees.

■ Task Analysis of Partner Rope Skills

FACE TO FACE (ONE ROPE)

1. Face partner.
2. Jump with partner as the rope is turned.
3. Turn the rope forward or backward.

FRONT TO BACK (ONE ROPE)

1. Face back to partner's front.
2. Jump with partner as the rope is turned.
3. Turn the rope forward or backward.

SIDE BY SIDE FACING FORWARD (ONE ROPE)

1. Stand side by side with partner.
2. Hold an end of the rope with outside hand.
3. Join other hands together (or arms around shoulders, or arms around waists).

4. Turn the rope and jump with partner.
5. Perform basic short rope skills.

SIDE BY SIDE FACING OPPOSITE (ONE ROPE)

1. Stand side by side with partner.
2. Stand facing forward with partner facing backward.
3. Turn the rope and jump with partner.
4. Jump (one partner jumps forward while the other jumps backwards).
5. Perform basic short rope skills.

INSIDE, OUTSIDE (ONE ROPE)

1. Hold one end of rope while partner holds the other end.
2. Turn own end of the rope and jump while partner turns outside the rope.
3. Take turns going in and out of the rope.

SIDE BY SIDE (TWO ROPES)

1. Stand side by side with partner.
2. Hold one end of own rope and one end of partner's rope.
3. Jump with partner.

VARIATIONS

1. DOWN THE LINE (one rope): Students line up side by side and one starts with a rope and moves down the line and back, jumping with each partner.

2. ROPE EXCHANGE (one rope): Partners face each other and jump. While jumping, the partner turning the rope gives the handles to partner who continues to turn the rope.

3. AROUND THE CLOCK (one rope): Partners face each other and jump. The partner not turning the rope goes around the turner. One way is by jumping to the side of the partner, then behind the partner, then to the other side, and then in front of the partner. Another way is for the jumper to go under the arms of the turner.

4. PIGGY BACK (one rope): One person gets on the other person's back, and the person on the back turns the rope.

5. DOUBLE 180 (one rope): Partners face each other. Partners perform the single rope skills of forward or backward 180 with two people.

■ Task Analysis of Single Long Rope Skills

TURNING

1. Hold one end of a long rope while partner holds the other end.
2. Face turning partner.
3. Use the arm and shoulder for turning the long rope.

ENTERING AND JUMPING

1. Stand by a turner.
2. Watch the rope.
3. Enter the rope when it is at its highest point.

BASKET SHOOT

1. Jump inside a long rope.
2. Attempt to shoot a basket while jumping.

BOUNCE AND JUMP

1. Jump inside a long rope.
2. Bounce a ball and jump at the same time.

CATCH

1. Jump inside a long rope facing a partner.
2. Jump and play catch with partner.

BATON TOSS

1. Jump inside a long rope.
2. Twirl a baton while jumping.
3. Toss the baton and catch it while jumping.

HULA HOOP

1. Jump inside a long rope.
2. Jump a hula hoop inside the long rope.
3. Twirl the hoop while jumping inside the long rope.

PIGGY BACK

1. Place a smaller person on partner's back.
2. Jump inside the long rope with person on the back.

PATTY CAKE

1. Jump inside a long rope facing partner.
2. Perform a hand-clapping sequence with partner while jumping.

THROUGH THE LEGS

1. Jump inside the long rope back to back with partner.
2. Jump three times.
3. Crawl between the straddled legs of the turner partner is facing.

CHASE

1. Jump in the center of a long rope.
2. Stay in the center while another person jumps in and begins to jump around the center person.
3. Stay in the center while a third person jumps in and chases the second person around the center person.

SHORT ROPE/LONG ROPE

1. Take a short rope into a long rope.
2. Face sideways, the direction the rope is turning.
3. Turn short rope the same direction as the long rope; then turn opposite direction.

■ Task Analysis of Double Long Rope Skills

The following activities are for *double dutch* (two ropes and two turners).

TURNING HINTS

1. Hold ends of ropes at waist level, shoulder-width apart, with the thumbs up.
2. Keep elbows close to the body.
3. Turn right arm counterclockwise and left arm clockwise.
4. Have the ropes hit the floor alternately.

JUMPING HINTS

1. Stand by a turner and say "go" each time the back rope hits the floor (rhythm).
2. Run and begin jumping as the back rope touches the floor.
3. Jump in the center of the rope facing a turner.
4. Go out by jumping toward a turner and then run out close to a turner.

BASIC JUMP (FACE SIDEWAYS)

1. Jump on both feet.
2. Land on the balls of the feet.
3. Keep feet, ankles, and knees together.

TURN AROUND (FACE SIDEWAYS)

1. Circle to the left doing the basic jump.
2. Circle to the right doing the basic jump.
3. Circle to the left jumping on the left foot only.
4. Circle to the right jumping on the left foot only.

STRADDLE (FACE SIDEWAYS)

1. Jump to a straddle position.
2. Spread feet shoulder-width apart.
3. Jump to closed legs.
4. Repeat steps 1 through 3.

STRADDLE CROSS (FACE SIDEWAYS)

1. Jump to a straddle position.
2. Jump to crossed-legs position.
3. Repeat steps 1 and 2.

SCISSORS (FACE TURNER)

1. Jump to a stride position with one foot forward.
2. Jump to a stride position, reversing the feet.
3. Spread feet 8 to 12 inches apart.
4. Repeat steps 1 and 2.

HALF SCISSORS (FACE TURNER)

1. Jump to a stride position with one foot forward.
2. Return to basic jump.
3. Jump to stride position with opposite foot forward.
4. Return to basic jump.
5. Repeat steps 1 through 4.

JOGGING STEP (FACE TURNER)

1. Step over the rope with one foot.
2. Step over the rope with the other foot.

3. Continue as if jogging.
4. Circle one direction while doing the jogging step; then the other direction.
5. Jog with knees waist high.
6. Speed skip using the jogging step.

CAN CAN (FACE TURNER)

1. Hop on right foot and lift left knee.
2. Hop on right foot and touch left toe.
3. Hop on right foot and kick left leg.
4. Perform a basic jump.
5. Repeat steps 1 through 3 starting with the left foot.

HALF TURN (FACE SIDEWAYS)

1. Perform a basic jump.
2. Jump and make a half turn facing the opposite direction.
3. Continue making half turns on each jump.

FULL TURN (FACE SIDEWAYS)

1. Perform a basic jump.
2. Jump, making a full turn facing the same direction.
3. Continue making full turns on each jump.

STRADDLE LEAP (FACE SIDEWAYS)

1. Perform a basic jump.
2. Lead to a straddle pike position with straight legs (bend at waist).
3. Touch toes with hands, keeping the back straight.
4. Perform a basic jump.
5. Repeat steps 1 through 4.

BALL TOSSING (FACE SIDEWAYS)

1. Perform a basic jump.
2. Toss the ball and catch it while jumping.
3. Keep eyes on the ball.
4. Continue to jump, toss, and catch.

BALL BOUNCING (FACE SIDEWAYS)

1. Perform a basic jump.
2. Dribble the ball while jumping.

3. Keep the ball at or below waist level.
4. Continue to jump and dribble.

SHORT ROPE/DOUBLE DUTCH (FACE TURNER)

1. Enter the double dutch with a short rope.
2. Decrease the length of rope slightly.
3. Jump the short rope in time with the double dutch rhythm.
4. Continue to jump the short rope.

The following activities are for *double Irish* (two ropes and two turners).

TURNING HINTS

1. Hold ends of the ropes at waist level, shoulder width apart, with thumbs up.
2. Keep elbows close to body.
3. Turn the ropes alternately outward (away from each other) when ropes are above the shoulders.

JUMPING HINTS

1. Run into the ropes with the nearest rope at front doors, and the back rope at back doors.
2. Continue to jump.
3. Perform short rope skills in the double long ropes.
4. Perform long rope skills in the double long ropes.

The following hints are for *egg beater* (two ropes and four turners).

TURNING HINTS

1. Lay the ropes down, crossing them in the center at right angles.
2. Take an end of the rope while the other turners also take an end to form a square.
3. Use arm and shoulder when turning the rope.
4. Turn the two ropes in the same direction.
5. Perform short and long single rope skills in *egg beater.*

■ Jump Rope Dances

Skills: Various jump rope skills

Supplies: A rope for each student

Formation: Varies according to the dance.

Description: Varies according to the dance.

SCHOTTISCHE

1. Students get a partner and form a double circle.
2. The steps moving forward are:
   Step R, step L, step R, hop R
   Step L, step R, step L, hop L
   Step-hop R, step-hop L, step-hop R, step-hop L
3. Move forward on the steps; hop in place; step-hop moving forward.
4. On the step-hops,
   a. Outside person circles to the right on their four step hops. Inside person circles to the left on their four step hops. Partners end up next to each other in their starting position.
   b. Both partners do their step-hops backwards.
5. VARIATIONS: Use the following for the Schottische steps:
   • Skier
   • Swing step
   • Heel-toe
   • Toe-to-Toe
   • Grapevine

BUNNY HOP

1. Students stand in a single file line with space enough so their ropes do not hit.
2. Jump and touch the right heel out and to the right. Jump and touch the right toe next to the left heel. Repeat.
3. Jump and touch the left heel out and to the left. Jump and touch the left toe next to the right heel. Repeat.
4. Jump forward with feet together and hold.
5. Jump backward with feet together and hold.
6. Jump forward three jumps and hold.
7. Repeat steps 2 through 6.

LA RAPSA

1. Students are in a scattered formation facing a partner, with enough space between them so their ropes do not hit.

2. The steps are:
   a. Alternate heel touch—R, L, R, hold
   b. Alternate heel touch—L, R, L, hold
   c. Turn a circle while jumping (Partners are side by side facing opposite directions. They jump and turn a circle together.)

HOKEY POKEY

1. Students form a circle facing the center.
2. Words and actions:
   a. You put your right foot in (extend right leg forward)
      You put your right foot out (extend right leg backward)
      You put your right foot in (extend right leg forward)
      And you shake it all about (and shake).
   b. (Chorus) You do the Hokey Pokey and you turn yourself around, that's what it's all about. (Jump, turning in a circle).
   c. Left foot
   d. Chorus
   e. Right arm (Turn so the right arm is facing towards the center of the circle, then so the right arm is facing away from the center of the circle)
   f. Chorus
   g. Left arm
   h. Chorus
   i. Head (Bend head down then back)
   j. Chorus
   k. Right hip (Turn sideways so hip faces in then out)
   l. Chorus
   m. Left hip
   n. Chorus
   o. Whole self (Jump forward, then backward)
   p. Chorus

TEACHING HINTS
FOR TINIKLING

1. Equipment needed: two 8-foot bamboo poles and two crossbars for the poles to rest on.
2. One striker kneels at one end of the poles with the other striker at the other end.
3. Count 1: Slide the poles together. Counts 2 and 3: The poles are

opened about 15 inches apart, up about 1 inch, and tapped twice on the crossbars (close, tap, tap).

4. A step is done outside the poles on the close (count 1) and two steps are done inside the poles (counts 2 and 3) when the poles are tapped on the crossbars.

5. Steps should be practiced with the poles stationary (may use wands, jump ropes, or lines instead of poles for practice).

6. Always start with the right foot next to the pole unless otherwise stated.

7. The suggested grade level for Tinikling is 4–6.

■ Tinikling Steps

Skills: Tinikling steps, rhythm, cooperation

Supplies: Tinikling poles and crossbars

Formation: Lay out practice stations with two poles and two crossbars each, then divide students evenly according to the number of stations available.

Description: Tinikling is a great activity for developing rhythm and physical fitness. It is also a cooperative activity that focuses on helping each other succeed.

BASIC STEP

1. Have students practice the following pattern with stationary objects.
   Count 1: Step slightly forward with left foot (to get the dance started).
   Count 2: Step with right foot between poles.
   Count 3: Step with left foot between poles.
   Count 4: Step with right foot outside to the right.
   Count 5: Step with left foot between poles.
   Count 6: Step with right foot between poles.
   Count 7: Step with left foot outside to the left.

2. After the students have mastered the basic step, have them:
   a. Move from side to side repeating the pattern.
   b. Have two students moving in opposite directions from side to side.
   c. Have two students moving in the same direction.
   d. Have two students stand holding inside hands, and move from side to side.
   e. Have two students face each other with both hands joined and do the pattern.

REVERSE STEP

1. Step slightly forward with the right foot.
2. Step inside the poles with the left foot by crossing behind the right.

3. Step on right foot between the poles.
4. Step with left foot outside the poles to the right (crossing behind).
5. Step with right foot between the poles.
6. Step with left foot between the poles.
7. Step with right foot outside the poles to the left (crossing behind).

ROCKER STEP

1. Face the poles.
2. Begin with either foot. (This example uses the right foot.)
3. Count 1: Step slightly forward on left foot.
4. Count 2: Step between the poles with the right foot.
5. Count 3: Step between the poles with the left foot.
6. Count 4: Step backwards outside the poles with right foot.
7. Count 5: Step with left foot between the poles.
8. Count 6: Step with right foot between the poles.
9. Count 7: Step with left foot backwards outside the poles.

■ Tinikling Routines

Skills: Tinikling steps, rhythm, cooperation

Supplies: Tinikling poles, crossbars

Formation: Varies according to the routine. The number of poles also varies according to the routine.

Description: Each routine has its own description. This is a great way to put the learned tinikling skills into routines.

LINE OF POLES

1. Set up three or more tinikling sets about six feet apart.

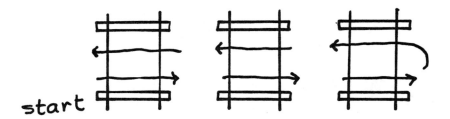

2. The object of the routine is to dance down the tinikling sets, making a circular movement, and return in the opposite direction. The dancer keeps his or her right side to the poles at all times.

3. The dancer does the following:

    a. Measure 1 (three counts): Basic step through the first set of poles, ending on the right side of the poles.

    b. Measure 2 (three counts): Three light running steps to get in position for the second tinikling set.

    c. Measure 3 (three counts): Same as measure 1.

    d. Measure 4 (three counts): Same as measure 2.

    e. Measure 5 (three counts): Same as measures 1 and 3.

    f. Measure 6 (three counts): Circle with three steps to get in position to go through the opposite side.

    g. Repeat measures 1 through 6 on the way back.

CIRCLING THE POLES

1. Stand as in basic step.
2. Measure 1

    a. Count 1: Step slightly forward with left foot.

    b. Count 2: Step between poles with right foot.

    c. Count 3: Step between poles with left foot.

3. Measure 2

    a. Count 1: Step with right foot outside the poles to the right.

    b. Counts 2 and 3: Make a half turn to a position for return movement.

4. Measures 3 and 4

    Return to original position using the same movements as in Measures 1 and 2.

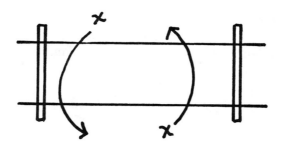

CROSS STEP

1. Stand as in basic step.
2. Count 1: Step across both poles with the left foot (cross step) and hop outside to the right (on left foot).
3. Counts 2 and 3: Hop twice on the right foot between the poles.
4. Count 4: Hop on the left foot outside the poles on the left.
5. Counts 5 and 6: Hop twice on the right foot between the poles.

STRADDLE STEP

1. Count 1: Straddle jump outside the poles.
2. Counts 2 and 3: Two movements of students' choice inside the poles.
3. Repeat steps 1 and 2. The movements can change each time in step 2.

DOUBLE STEP

1. Count 1: Hop on both feet outside the poles (right foot next to pole).
2. Count 2: Hop on both feet between the poles.
3. Count 3: Hop on both feet between the poles.
4. Count 4: Hop with both feet outside the poles, straddling them.
5. Count 5: Hop with both feet between the poles.
6. Count 6: Hop with both feet between the poles.
7. Repeat counts 1 through 6.

HOP STEP

1. Count 1: Hop on left foot outside poles (near side).
2. Count 2: Hop on right foot between the poles.
3. Count 3: Hop on right foot between the poles.
4. Count 4: Hop on left foot outside poles (far side).
5. Count 5: Hop on right foot between the poles.
6. Count 6: Hop on right foot between the poles.

TRIANGLE FORMATION

1. Set up three tinikling sets in a triangle formation.

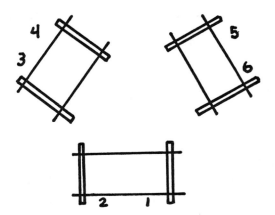

2. Six dancers are positioned as shown in the illustration.
3. The dancers move as follows:
    a. Four hop steps
    b. Four basic steps
    c. Four double steps; on the third double step, dancers 1, 4, and 6 do a half turn clockwise to face their partner
    d. Four hop steps (facing partner)
    e. Four basic steps (facing partner)
    f. Four double steps (facing partner)
    g. Three double steps turning to face outward
    h. Exit out

CROSS FORMATION

1. Set up two tinikling sets in a cross formation.

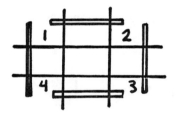

2. Four dancers are positioned as shown in the illustration.
3. The dancers move as follows:
    a. All poles begin rhythm (do twice).
    b. Four each of the basic steps:
        • Dancer 1 does four basic steps (all poles going; other dancers stand)
        • Dancer 2 does four basic steps
        • Dancer 3 does four basic steps
        • Dancer 4 does four basic steps
    c. Hop steps (four each):
        • Dancer 1 does four hop steps
        • Dancer 2 does four hop steps
        • Dancer 3 does four hop steps
        • Dancer 4 does four hop steps
    d. Dancers 1 and 3 do four basic steps.
    e. Dancers 2 and 4 do four basic steps.
    f. Dancers 1 and 3 do four hop steps.
    g. Dancers 2 and 4 do four hop steps.

h. All dancers do four basic steps.

i. All dancers do four hop steps.

j. Basic steps (four each) traveling right one-full circle clockwise around the square:

- Dancer 1 does four basic steps, circling.
- Dancer 2 does four basic steps, circling.
- Dancer 3 does four basic steps, circling.
- Dancer 4 does four basic steps, circling.

k. Basic steps (two each) traveling right:

- Dancer 1 does two basic steps traveling right.
- Dancers 1 and 2 do two basic steps traveling right.
- Dancers 1, 2, and 3 do two basic steps traveling right.

l. All dancers do five basic steps traveling right.

m. All dancers straddle poles facing the center.

WAGON WHEEL FORMATION

1. Set up eight tinikling sets in a wagon wheel formation.

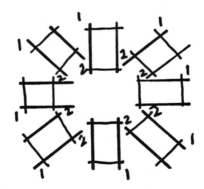

2. The dancers are in positions as shown in the illustration.
3. The dancers move as follows:

a. Poles (no dancers) do rhythm four times.

b. All Dancer 1s do eight basic steps.

c. All Dancer 2s do eight basic steps.

d. All Dancer 1s do eight double steps.

e. All Dancer 2s do eight double steps.

f. All Dancer 1s do eight hop steps.

g. All Dancer 2s do eight hop steps.

h. All dancers do eight basic steps.

i. All dancers do eight basic steps circling clockwise.

j. All dancers do 16 basic steps: All Dancer 1s travel clockwise, all Dancer 2s travel counterclockwise. (Do one basic step at each pair of poles and one basic step between each pair of poles.)

k. All dancers do one double step (home poles).

l. All dancers straddle poles.

Section 5

Individualized Activities For Fitness And Fun

```
┌─────────────────────────────────────────────────────────────┐
│                                                               │
│                      TEACHING HINTS                           │
│                       FOR BALLS                               │
│                                                               │
│  1. Have one 6-foot playground ball per student.             │
│  2. The suggested grade level is K–2.                        │
│  3. Start off the period with the following steps:           │
│      a. Students should each get a ball and find a personal   │
│         space.                                                │
│      b. Allow students to play with their balls in their      │
│         personal spaces without running into people or        │
│         things.                                               │
│      c. When the whistle blows, the students stop, look, and  │
│         listen (balls held still). This indicates that you    │
│         will begin giving directions for their activities.    │
│  4. Go through the individual activities and partner          │
│     activities, then move on to games using balls.            │
│                                                               │
└─────────────────────────────────────────────────────────────┘
```

■ Task Analysis of Basic Ball Skills

Skills: Rolling, throwing, catching, kicking

Supplies: A 6-inch playground ball for every two students

Formation: To practice these skills, the class needs to be divided into pairs. Have each pair find a personal space.

Description: See each skill listed below.

ROLLING

- Stand in a stride position holding the ball with the throwing hand behind the ball and the non-throwing hand in front of the ball.
- Swing your arms backward, keeping your eyes on the ball.
- Bend your knees and swing your arms forward, extending your throwing arm toward the target.

UNDERHAND THROW

- Stand in a stride position with one foot slightly ahead of the other, and hold the ball in both hands.
- Bend your knees slightly and bring the ball back between your knees.
- Bring the ball forward and upward, straightening your knees, and keeping your eyes on the target.
- Release the ball at waist level and follow the direction of the ball with your arm so that the fingers end up pointing at the target.

PITCHING UNDERHAND

- Stand in stride position and hold the ball in your throwing hand.
- Put your weight back on your throwing foot and swing your throwing arm backwards.
- Bend your knees and swing your throwing arm forward. At the same time bring your nonthrowing foot forward and release the ball.

OVERHAND THROW

- Stand in a stride position, then as you swing your throwing arm backwards, transfer your weight back on your throwing foot, keeping your eyes on the target.
- Swing your throwing arm forward and at the same time take a step forward on your nonthrowing foot.
- Release the ball, finishing with your arm extended toward the target.

CATCHING BELOW THE WAIST

- Stand in stride position.
- Cup your hands with fingers spread and held down, little fingers parallel and slightly apart.
- Relax your body, bend slightly forward, and keep your eyes on the ball.
- Extend your arms slightly, relax your body and arms and "give" with the impact of the ball.

CATCHING ABOVE THE WAIST

- Stand in stride position with weight evenly distributed on both feet and body bent slightly forward.
- Hold your hands in front of your chest, fingers spread and pointed up, thumbs slightly apart and pointed at your chest.
- Keep your eyes on the ball and extend your arms slightly.
- Relax your body and arms to "give" with the impact of the ball.
- Grip the ball with your fingers as it rests in the palm of your hands.

PLACE KICKING

- Place your ball on the ground and face the direction your ball will be going.
- Stand in a stride position about one step behind the ball.
- Keeping your eyes on the ball, step forward on your nonkicking foot and swing your kicking foot straight forward, contacting the ball with your toe slightly below the center of the ball.
- Continue forward and upward with your kicking foot.

ROLLING KICK

- Stand in a stride position as you await the ball.
- As the ball is rolled, step forward with your nonkicking foot and swing your kicking foot forward and upward.
- Contact the ball with your toe slightly below the center of the ball and continue forward and upward with your kicking foot.

DROP KICK (punt)

- Hold the ball in both hands, with arms extended and at about waist level.
- Step forward with your nonkicking foot, drop the ball, and swing your kicking foot forward and upward.
- Contact the ball on the top of your foot continuing with a forward and upward movement.

INDIVIDUAL BALL-HANDLING ACTIVITIES

■ Laterality and Directionality

Skills: Laterality, directionality, perceptual motor, ball handling

Supplies: One small ball per student

Formation: Each student in a personal space

Description: This is a great activity for allowing the students to work individually. Read through the "challenges" at a pace that is appropriate for each particular class.

- Hold the ball in front of you with both hands.
- Lift the ball above your head using both hands.
- Hold the ball behind your back.
- Hold the ball on the left side of your body, then on the right.
- Hold the ball in both hands and place it under your chin.
- Hold the ball in your hands between your knees, then let go with your hands and only use your knees.
- Use only your elbows to hold the ball.
- Hold the ball with just your wrists.
- Hold the ball using only the back of your hands, then hold it using the back of one hand and the palm of the other hand.
- Hold the ball using four fingers of each hand, then three fingers of each hand, then two fingers of each hand, then one finger of each hand.

- Hold the ball in your left hand and lift it as high above your head as possible. Then use the right hand.
- Hold the ball as low as possible with your right hand. Then use the left hand.
- Hold the ball out in front of you as far as you can.
- Stand on your right foot as you hold the ball in front of you. Then use the left foot.
- Roll the ball around your body (forehead to nose, mouth, chin, neck, chest, waist, one leg, and so on) without dropping it.
- Hold the ball on your stomach and, keeping it against your body, roll it behind you and around to starting position.

■ Fine Motor Coordination

Skills: Fine motor, laterality

Supplies: One small ball per student

Formation: Each student in a personal space

Description: This is a great activity for allowing students to work individually. Read through the "challenges" at a pace that is appropriate for each particular class.

- Hold the ball with just the fingertips of both hands.
- Make the ball turn with just your fingertips going forward and backward.
- Hold the ball in front of your waist and move it around your waist by changing the ball from one hand to the other.
- Use a different way to move the ball around your waist.
- Hold the ball in both hands and move it in a figure eight in and about between your knees.
- Place the ball on the ground and make a figure eight by rolling it around your feet using only your fingertips.
- Place the ball on the ground, roll it forward, run past it, turn around, and catch it.
- Place the ball on the ground and move it around your space using just your fingers.
- Place the ball on the ground and jump forward and backward over it.
- Place the ball on the ground and go over the ball in a different way without touching it.
- Hold the ball in both hands and, keeping both hands on the ball, step over it forward and backward.
- Hold the ball between your knees and jump like a kangaroo.
- Hold the ball between your knees, jump up and drop the ball from between your knees, and catch it before it hits the ground.
- Stand holding the ball above your head. Slowly sit down and then stand up again keeping the ball above your head.
- Sit on the floor with your knees bent and roll the ball around your body and under your knees.
- Sit on the floor and, using only your feet, lift the ball above your head and back down.

- Hold the ball with both hands behind your neck. Let the ball drop and catch it quickly behind your waist.

■ Eye-Hand Coordination

Skills: Eye-Hand coordination, bouncing, throwing, catching

Supplies: One small ball per student

Formation: Each student in a personal space

Description: This is a great activity for allowing students to work individually. Read through the "challenges" at a pace that is appropriate for each particular class.

- Hold the ball with two hands, drop it, and catch it with your fingers.
- Hold the ball above your head with two hands, drop it, and catch it with your fingers.
- Hold the ball with two hands, bounce it, and catch it with your fingers.
- Bounce and catch the ball ten times, counting to yourself.
- Bounce the ball, clap your hands, and catch the ball.
- Toss the ball above your head, let it bounce, and catch it.
- Toss the ball above your head, turn around, and catch the ball on the first bounce.
- Bounce the ball under your right leg (then left) and catch it.
- Bounce the ball high, jump, and catch it.
- Bounce the ball high and forward, run after it, and catch it on the first bounce.
- Toss the ball above your head, stand still, and catch it in the air.
- See how straight above your head you can throw the ball.
- Toss the ball above your head and reach as high as you can to catch it.
- Toss the ball above your head and catch it as low as possible.
- See at how many different levels you can catch the ball.
- Toss the ball above your head, stoop down and catch it. Then jump up and toss the ball while you are still in the air.
- Toss the ball above your head, clap, and catch the ball.
- Toss the ball above your head, touch your knees, and catch the ball.
- Toss the ball, take four steps, and catch the ball.
- Toss the ball to a wall, let it bounce once, and catch it.
- Toss the ball to a wall, let it bounce once, clap your hands, and catch it.
- Toss the ball to a wall, let it bounce once, jump, and catch it.
- Toss the ball to a wall, let it bounce once, touch the floor, and catch it.
- Toss the ball to a wall, let it bounce once, turn around, and catch it.
- Toss the ball to a wall, let it bounce once, clap hands behind back, and catch it.
- Toss the ball to a wall, let it bounce once, sit down, and catch it.

■ Dribbling

Skills: Dribbling, locomotor movements

Supplies: One small ball per student

Formation: Each student in a personal space

Description: This is a great activity for allowing students to work individually. Read through the "challenges" at a pace that is appropriate for each particular class.

- Keep the ball bouncing without catching or stopping it. (This is dribbling.)
- Stand in one place and use both hands to dribble the ball softly.
- Use one hand to dribble the ball in place, hard enough to keep the ball waist high.
- Keep dribbling the ball without letting it get away from you.
- Stand dribbling the ball with one hand, sit down without stopping the dribbling, and then stand up again.
- Dribble the ball high then low, using your fingertips to push the ball downward.
- Dribble the ball with one hand, dribble forward a few steps, and then dribble backward a few steps.
- Dribble the ball with your right hand, then switch to your left without stopping.
- Look at my hand. It is your target. Keep looking at it and dribble without looking down.
- Close your eyes and dribble.
- Dribble the ball under each leg without stopping the dribble.
- Balance on one foot and dribble.
- Hop forward a few steps while dribbling.
- Dribble the ball with your hands, your elbows, your head, your wrists, your feet.
- Dribble forward, backward, sideways, in a circle, and in other ways.
- Watch your target (my hand) and dribble in the direction I point. Change hands whenever I say "left hand" or "right hand."
- Walk and dribble.
- Skip and dribble.
- Run and dribble.
- Sit and dribble.
- Lie on your stomach and dribble.
- Lie on your back and dribble.
- Go from sitting, to kneeling, to standing while dribbling.

■ Foot Dribble and Hand Volley

Skills: Dribbling, trapping, kicking, volleying

Supplies: One small ball per student

Formation: Each student in a personal space

Description: This is a great activity for allowing the students to work individually. Read through the "challenges" at a pace that is appropriate for each particular class.

FOOT DRIBBLE, TRAP, AND KICKING

- Grip the ball between your feet and walk in a circle without losing the ball.
- Tap the ball back and forth between your feet without losing it. (This is dribbling.)

- Dribble the ball using just the inside of your feet.
- Dribble around in a small circle.
- Dribble with your feet and stop the ball with your feet. (This is trapping.)
- Dribble around the area and trap the ball when I signal. Repeat.
- Kick the ball forward a short distance, run up to it, trap it with your foot, and dribble it back to your starting place.
- Kick the ball so it travels on the ground.
- Kick the ball so it travels in the air.
- Hold the ball with two hands, drop it, and kick it before it hits the ground.

HAND VOLLEY

- Hold the ball in a palms-up position with fingers pointing forward. Use your fingers to tap the ball up in front of you.
- Tap the ball in the air as many times as you can without losing control.
- Throw the ball up in the air and catch it above your head with just your fingertips, keeping elbows out to the side.
- Toss the ball in the air, tap it once with your fingers, and keep fingers spread to make a pocket with your thumbs close.
- Volley (tap) the ball two times above your head. Then catch it.
- Volley (tap) the ball as high as you can.
- Volley (tap) the ball above your head as many times as you can. Count them silently.
- Hit the ball to the floor with your hand.
- Hit the ball to the floor with your fist.
- Toss the ball in the air and hit it underhand.
- Toss the ball in the air and hit it overhand.

PARTNER ACTIVITIES

■ Eye-Hand Coordination

Skills: Rolling, throwing, catching

Supplies: One small ball for every two students

Formation: Divide the class into pairs, give each pair a ball, and have each pair find a personal space.

Description: This is a great activity for allowing students to work with a partner on ball skills. Read through the "challenges" at a pace that is appropriate for each particular class.

- Sit facing your partner and roll the ball back and forth.

- Sit facing your partner and roll the ball to your partner using only one hand.
- Stand facing your partner, step forward on your left foot, and roll the ball with your right hand to your partner. Then use your right foot and left hand.
- Bend your knees and roll the ball softly and smoothly to your partner.
- Use an easy way to throw the ball to your partner.
- Stand facing your partner and, using both hands, throw the ball underhand to your partner.
- Step forward with your left foot and use only your right hand to throw the ball underhand to your partner.
- Throw the ball to your partner with a high underhand throw.
- Hold the ball at waist level and throw the ball to your partner. Throw it lower each time until you reach foot level.
- Walk around with your partner, playing catch as you walk.
- Hold the ball with both hands, fingers pointing up, and throw to your partner. (This is an overhand throw.)
- Hold the ball against your chest with an overhang grip and push-throw it to your partner. (This is a chest pass.)
- Hold the ball in an overhand grip, thumbs close together and fingers spread wide. Bring the ball against your chest, step forward with your left foot, and throw it to your partner.
- Hold the ball above your head using two hands and throw it to your partner. (This is an overhead pass.)
- Place your hands behind the ball and push it down toward the floor and forward to your partner. (This is a bounce pass.)
- Chest passs the ball to your partner, who catches it and bounce passes it. Then you bounce pass it and your partner chest passes it, and so on.
- Pass the ball back and forth with your partner in different ways.

■ Kicking, Volleying, Serving

Skills: Kicking, trapping, volleying, serving

Supplies: One small ball for every two students

Formation: Divide the class into pairs, give each pair a ball, and have each pair find a personal space.

Description: This is a great activity for allowing students to work with a partner on ball skills. Read through each "challenge" at a pace that is appropriate for each particular class.

KICKING

- Have your partner kick the ball to you and trap it.
- Have your partner roll the ball to you and you kick it back to him/her.
- Use only the sides of your feet as you pass the ball back and forth with your partner.

- Move around while passing with your partner.
- Kick the ball back and forth with your partner, increasing the distance.
- Kick the ball back and forth with your partner, trapping it each time.
- Kick the ball back and forth with your partner while running.

VOLLEYING

- Toss the ball above your head, and using your fingertips with thumbs close together, tap the ball to your partner (volley).
- Volley the ball back and forth with your partner, keeping the ball in the air and not catching it.
- Toss the ball in the air and use your head to hit it to your partner.
- Have your partner toss the ball to you and you head it back to your partner.

SERVING

- Drop the ball on the ground and using one or two hands, hit it to your partner so he can catch it.
- Drop the ball and use the fingers of both hands to hit the ball to your partner.
- Drop the ball and use the flat of your hand to hit the ball to your partner with your palm and fingers.
- Bounce the ball once, using the flat of your hand, and hit the ball to your partner with your palm and fingers.
- Hold the ball in one hand, palm up, and hit it from your hand to your partner with the palm of your other hand.
- Hold the ball in the palm of one hand and hit from your hand to your partner with the fist of your other hand.

■ Wastebasket Basketball

Skills: Throwing with accuracy

Supplies: A wastebasket and a ball for each team

Formation: Teams in single file lines. A foul line is marked. A basket is placed a distance away from the foul line.

Description: This is a fun alternative to Basketball. The first player in each line attempts to make a basket, retrieves the ball, gives the next person in line the ball, and goes to the end of the line. Each player on the team gets a turn.
Scoring is 1) One point if the ball bounces in and then out. 2) Two points if the ball bounces in and stays in. 3) Five points if the ball goes in without bouncing. You can add up points scored as a team, or have individual points.
If used as a relay have each student throw until they make it in.

■ Quick Reactions (1–3)

Skills: Tossing, catching, timing

Supplies: A ball for each circle

Formation: Divide the class into small groups (6-8). Have each group form a circle with one player in the center with the ball. This player is "It." All other players stand with their hands behind their back.

Description: The object of the game is for the player who is "It" to attempt to trick the other players in the circle. The player who is "It" either tosses the ball to a player or pretends to toss it. If the ball is tossed, the player moves his hands to catch the ball. If the player who is "It" pretends to toss the ball, the player must keep his hands behind his back. When a player makes an error (ie. Misses the ball, or moves his hands when "It" pretends to toss the ball), he turns his back toward the group. When the next player makes an error, he turns his back toward the group and the first player rejoins the game. Periodically change the player who is "It."

BALL GAMES

▪ Circle Call Ball (K–2)

Skills: Throwing, catching, reaction time

Supplies: A ball for each circle

Formation: Divide the class into groups of eight to ten players each. Have each group form a circle with one player in the center holding the ball. Have each player in each circle number off.

Description: This game is good for working on reaction time and retention, as well as the skills of throwing and catching. The center player tosses the ball straight up in the air and calls out a number. The player with that number runs to the center and tries to catch the ball in the air or on the first bounce. That player now becomes the tosser (or the tosser could change after everyone's number has been called). This continues until everyone has had a turn to toss and catch. For an added challenge, see how fast students can toss and catch while keeping in control.

▪ Hoop Ball (1–2)

Skills: Throwing with accuracy and speed

Supplies: Two basketball hoops or backboards, several balls of all shapes and sizes, two hula hoops.

Formation: Divide the class into two teams. Line up one team on one sideline and the other team on the other sideline. Number each team. Place all the balls in the center of the floor. Hang a hoop from each basket. Designate a hoop for each team.

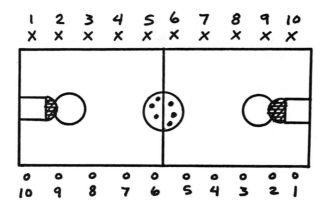

Description: This is a great game of modified basketball. The object is to see how many balls students can get through the hoop in a designated period of time. The teacher calls out a number, the player with that number on each team runs to the center, picks up one ball at a time and attempts to throw it through their hoop. This continues for 30 seconds. Each ball that goes through the hoop scores a point. After 30 seconds is up, the players gather the balls, put them in the center, and go back to their places. Another number is called. This continues until all players have had a turn.

■ Throw It and Run (1–2)

Skills: Throwing, catching, fielding, tagging, dodging, running

Supplies: A ball for each group, two cones for each group, jump ropes to outline the field areas

Formation: Divide the class into teams with two or three players on each team. Set up about six fields with two teams at each field (throwing and fielding teams).

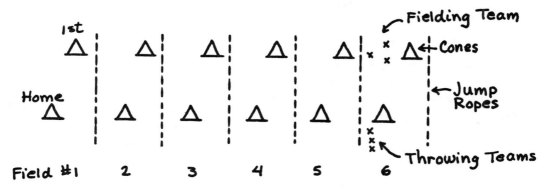

Description: This game is an all-time favorite for several reasons. First of all, it provides an opportunity for all students to be active most of the time. Second, the game is played with a small number of players which also provides for more participation. Third, it provides an opportunity for students to practice a variety of skills. Fourth, it introduces a modified game of softball. Last, it can be adapted to kicking and batting. Have the throwing teams line up single file by their home bases, thrower on the throwing team throws the ball, runs to first base and home. The fielding team attempts to get the runner out by: (1) Catching the ball in the air, (2) Tagging the runner with the ball, (3) Tagging the base the runner is running to. After all players on the throwing team have thrown, they trade places with the fielding team.

VARIATIONS:

- *Kick It And Run:* Rules are the same, but students kick the ball rather than throw it. Use a stationary ball first, then a pitched ball.
- *Bat It And Run:* Rules are the same, but students use a whiffle ball and plastic bat. Have the students hit the ball off the cone.

■ Knee Kickball (2–4)

Skills: Shooting, timing

Supplies: A playground ball or foam ball for every two players

Formation: Divide the class into pairs, and give each pair a ball. Have each pair find a personal space. One partner has the ball, and the other partner stands about 5 feet to 8 feet from him/her and extends the arms to form a circle in front of his body with clasped hands.

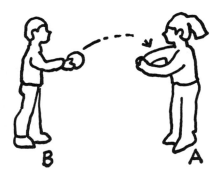

Description: This activity is great for practicing basketball-type skills along with timing, and it is a fun warm-up activity. Looking at the diagram, player B attempts to throw the ball through player A's circled arms. Player A anticipates player B's throw and attempts to use his knee to hit the ball out through his circled arms before the ball goes through and hits the floor. Player A receives a point if he "knees" the ball out. Player B receives a point if the ball goes through A's arms and hits the floor. Player B gets five turns to shoot and then trades places with Player A.

■ Ball Four (4–6)

Skills: Kicking, receiving, shooting, running

Supplies: A foam football, volleyball net and standards, basketball hoop, home plate, two cones

Formation: Divide the class into two teams. One team is the kicking team and the other team is the fielding team.

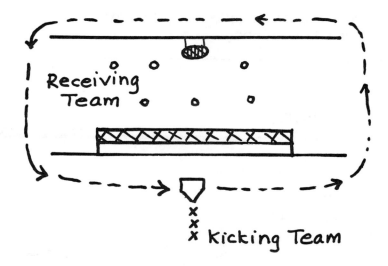

Description: This is a great indoor game that uses equipment and skills from three sports. It is a fun and different way to practice skills and is sure to liven up a gloomy day.

Have the kicking team line up behind home plate with the football. Have the fielding team scatter between the net and the basketball hoop. The first player on the kicking team kicks the ball then runs around the court and back to home plate. At the same time, the fielding team gets the ball and attempts to make a basket before the runner gets home. A run is scored each time the runner crosses home plate before a basketball is scored. After each player has kicked, the kicking and fielding team trade places.

VARIATIONS: Have the fielding team pass the ball to each member of the team rather than shoot a basket. Have the team at home plate throw the ball instead of kick it.

TEACHING HINTS
FOR BEANBAGS

1. Have one beanbag per student. Beanbags can be made or bought.
2. The suggested grade level is K–2.

---

3. Start off the period with the following steps:
    a. Students should each get a beanbag and find a personal space.
    b. Allow students to play with their beanbags in their personal spaces without running into people or things.
    c. When the whistle blows the students stop, look, and listen (beanbags held still). This indicates that you will begin giving directions for their activities.
4. Go through the individual activities and partner activities, then move on to games using beanbags.

INDIVIDUAL ACTIVITIES

■ Balance and Body Awareness

Skills: Balance, body awareness

Supplies: A beanbag for each student

Formation: Each student in a personal space

Description: This is a great activity for practicing beanbag skills individually. It provides an opportunity for maximum involvement.

- Hold the beanbag high in one hand.
- Hold the beanbag low in one hand.
- Touch your chin with the beanbag.
- Touch the beanbag to your nose, right ear, chest, left hip, right ankle, left elbow, and so forth.
- Balance the beanbag on your head.
- Balance the beanbag on your foot, shoulder, wrist, knee, elbow, back of hand, and so forth.
- While balancing the beanbag on your head, sit down and stand up.
- Rotate your head in a circle without moving your feet or dropping the beanbag.
- Hold the beanbag between your elbows, wrists, knees, ankles.
- Place the beanbag on the floor. Build a bridge over it using four parts of your body touching the floor, three parts, five parts. Make a long bridge, high, low, wide, narrow.
- Balance the beanbag on top of your foot and swing your foot back and forth without dropping it.
- Hold the beanbag in your right hand with arm straight out in front. Kick each leg up, one at a time, touch toes to right hand. Do the same thing holding the beanbag in the left hand.

• Sit on the floor and hold the beanbag between your feet. Lift legs upward, rock backwards, and touch beanbag to the floor in back of your head. Rock back to sitting position.

• Same as above except when you rock back, place the beanbag on the floor behind your head; rock to sitting position, rock back and pick up the beanbag with your feet; rock back to sitting position.

■ Locomotor Movements

Skills: Walking, jumping, leaping, crawling, skipping, galloping, sliding

Supplies: A beanbag for each student

Formation: Each student in a personal space

Description: This is a great activity for practicing beanbag skills individually. It provides an opportunity for maximum involvement.

• Place the beanbag on the floor and creep around it on your hands and knees.
• Jump forward, sideways, and backward over the beanbag.
• Hop over the beanbag on one foot, then the other.
• Run and leap over the beanbag.
• Move around the beanbag. You may slide, gallop, skip.
• Move quickly around the beanbag. Then move slowly.
• Place one hand on the beanbag, with the other extended away from the beanbag. Move around the beanbag like a coffee grinder.
• Hold the beanbag between your ankles and jump.
• Hold the beanbag between your ankles, jump, release the beanbag, and catch it with your hands.
• Balance the beanbag on your head and walk.
• Balance the beanbag on one foot and hop on the other foot.
• Get in a crab-walk position. Place the beanbag on your stomach and do the crab walk.

■ Speed and Agility

Skills: Speed, agility

Supplies: A beanbag for each student

Formation: Each student in a personal space

Description: This is a great activity for practicing beanbag skills individually. It provides an opportunity for maximum involvement.

• Quickly pass the beanbag around your waist, passing it from one hand to the other.
• Pass the beanbag around your head, behind neck and under chin, changing hands.
• Pass the beanbag from one hand to the other around your knees in a figure-eight pattern.

- Stand on one foot and pass the beanbag from one hand to the other around your raised knee.
- Place the beanbag on your head, bend backwards until the bean bag falls on the floor, bend forward, reach between your legs and pick up the beanbag.

■ Throw and Catch

Skills: Throwing, catching

Supplies: A beanbag for each student

Formation: Each student in a personal space

Description: This is a great activity for practicing beanbag skills individually. It provides an opportunity for maximum involvement.

- Toss the beanbag upward and catch it with both hands.
- Toss the beanbag upward and catch it with right hand, left hand.
- Toss the beanbag upward with one hand and catch it with the other hand.
- Toss and catch in the following progression: both hands, right hand, left hand, opposite hand.
- Flip the beanbag up and over (like flipping a pancake), catching it with both hands, palms up. Repeat, catching it with one hand; then on the back of the hands.
- Toss the beanbag back and forth across your body from one hand to the other.
- Toss the beanbag overhead from one hand to the other.
- Toss the beanbag above your head, jump, and catch it at the highest possible point.
- Toss the beanbag upward, turn, and catch it.
- Toss the beanbag upward, bend down, touch the floor, catch the bean bag in the air.
- Toss the beanbag upward, clap hands, catch the beanbag. See how many times you can clap before catching the beanbag.
- Toss the beanbag upward, clap hands behind the back, catch the beanbag.
- Toss the beanbag forward, run and catch it.
- Place the beanbag on your foot, kick the beanbag upward with your foot, and catch it with your hands.
- Toss the beanbag upward and catch it with your eyes closed.
- Toss the beanbag upward and catch it on top of your head (no hands).
- Toss the beanbag overhead and catch it with hands behind back.
- Stand, toss the beanbag in the air, sit down and catch it. Reverse.

■ Throwing with Accuracy

Skills: Throwing with accuracy

Supplies: Beanbags, targets (taped square on the wall, wastebasket, bike tires, hula hoops)

Formation: Students in single file lines

Description: The following are a few ideas you can use to practice throwing with accuracy. Use your imagination and the students' imaginations to create other ways. You can set up several stations.

- Throw the beanbag over the goal line.
- Throw the beanbag at the target on the wall.
- Throw the beanbag through the hoop held by another student.
- Throw the beanbag into each hoop.
- Throw the beanbag into the wastebasket.

PARTNER ACTIVITIES

Skills: Hand-eye coordination, throwing, catching, cooperation

Supplies: A beanbag for every two students

Formation: Each set of partners finds a personal space

Description: Here is a great variety of partner activities that work on skills, and provide students with challenges and fun.

- Toss the beanbag to your partner with an underhand toss, overhand toss.
- Toss the beanbag high to your partner, low.
- Play catch with your partner using only the right hand, left hand.
- Play catch with your partner alternating hands for throwing and catching (throw with right; catch with left).
- Play catch with your partner, each telling the other which hand to catch with after or as the beanbag is tossed.
- Play catch with your partner, clapping hands before catching the beanbag.
- Kick the beanbag to your partner using the foot or toe.
- Toss the beanbag to your partner with elbow, head, or knee.
- Toss the beanbag in various directions so that your partner is forced to move to catch it.
- One partner stands still while the other partner runs around him/her. Partners play catch while doing this.
- Stand facing your partner. One partner holds the beanbag at arm's length while the other partner holds one hand above the beanbag. As the beanbag is released, the partner tries to catch it before it hits the floor.
- Partners stand back to back. One partner passes the beanbag between his legs to the other partner who returns it overhead to his partner.
- Partners stand back to back and pass one beanbag around their bodies exchanging it from hand to hand.
- Partners stand back to back (4 feet to 5 feet apart) and toss the beanbag by twisting the trunk to one side then the other.

- Partners stand back to back (4 feet to 5 feet apart) and toss the beanbag overhead to their partner.
- Partners face each other with their beanbag on the floor between them. The teacher calls out "Right," "Left," or "Both." The players try to grab the beanbag with that hand. The object of the game is to see who can grab the beanbag first using the correct hand.

BEANBAG GAMES

■ Beanbag Freeze (K–2)

Skills: Balance, movement, cooperation

Supplies: A beanbag for each student

Formation: Students are scattered and have their beanbags on their heads.

Description: Beanbag freeze is a wonderful way to motivate students to help each other. Each student places a beanbag on his/her head and moves around the area. If a player's beanbag falls off his/her head, s/he must freeze until someone else picks up the beanbag and places it back on his/her head. If the helper's beanbag falls off while helping, the helper too must freeze.

Discuss with students what they can learn from this activity that can be used in the classroom, on the playground, or at home (helping others, for example). Discuss how it feels when someone helps you and how it feels when you help someone else. Discuss the difference between the kinds of feelings (When someone helps you: makes you feel good; makes you feel like someone cares; makes you feel important. When you help someone else: makes you feel good; makes you feel like you've done something nice for someone else; gives you a sense of satisfaction and worth).

■ Leader Beanbag (K–3)

Skills: Tossing, catching, keeping track of points (optional)

Supplies: A beanbag for each group

Formation: Divide the class into groups of five or six students each. Have each group find a space and line up side by side with one player as the leader who faces them and has the beanbag.

Description: The leader stands about 10 feet away from the players. The object of the game is to move up to the leader's spot by not making any bad throws or missing catches. The leader tosses to each student (starting on the left) who must catch the beanbag and toss it back to the leader. Any player who makes a throwing or catching error goes to the end of the line at the leader's right, and the line moves up. If the leader makes a mistake, s/he goes to the end of the line and the student at the front of the line becomes the new leader. If a leader stays in that position for three rounds, s/he scores a point and then goes to the end of the line and the next student becomes the leader.

A variation that focuses on the positive would be awarding points for good tosses. This encourages students to make accurate tosses. The leader gets a point for each person who catches the beanbag. The receivers each get a point for each person who catches the beanbag. The receivers each get a point if they toss it back and the leader catches it. Points can also be awarded for catching the beanbag. After the leader has tossed to everyone, the next student in line becomes the leader. This approach also avoids emphasizing mistakes.

■ Beanbag Quoits (K–2)

Skills: Tossing with accuracy

Supplies: Two beanbags for each player, two hoops for each group

Formation: Divide the class into groups of two or four students each. Make a court with 20 feet between circles for each group of players.

Description: This is a great adaptation of horseshoes. The object of the game is to get one or both beanbags in the circle or closer to the circle than the other team. The game starts with one player who stands behind a circle and tosses both beanbags, one at a time. Then the other player tosses. Points awarded are: 3 points for beanbag in the circle, 1 point for the beanbag closest to the circle. The player with the most points from the previous toss goes first. The game is 11, 15, or 21 points.

TEACHING HINTS
FOR HOOPS

1. Have one hula hoop per student. These can be made with plastic PVC pipe.
2. The suggested grade level is K–2.
3. Start off the period with the following steps:
   a. Have each student get a hoop and find a personal space.
   b. Allow students to play with their hoops in their personal spaces without running into people or things.
   c. When the whistle blows, the students stop, look, and listen (hoop held still). This indicates that you will begin giving directions for their activities.
4. Go through the individual activities and partner activities, then move on to games using hoops.

INDIVIDUAL ACTIVITIES

■ Stationary Hoop (1-3)

Skills: Balancing, jumping, hopping

Supplies: A hoop for each student

Formation: Each student in a personal space

Description: This is a great activity for allowing the students to work individually. Read through the "challenges" at a pace that is appropriate for each particular class.

- Place the hoop on the floor, stand in the center of it, and balance on your right foot.
- Stoop low while balancing on one foot.
- Stretch tall while balancing on one foot.
- Balance on one foot and one hand.
- Balance on three parts of your body.
- Balance on five parts of your body.
- Balance with two parts of your body on the inside of the hoop and two parts on the outside of the hoop.
- Stand inside the hoop and jump five times, making each jump a little higher.
- Stand inside the hoop, jump forward out of the hoop, and backwards into the hoop.
- Jump out of the hoop and then back into the hoop in another way.
- Jump as far as you can out of the hoop.
- Jump forward around the hoop, keeping one foot inside the hoop and the other foot outside the hoop. Do the same thing backwards.
- Keeping your feet together, jump around the hoop alternating inside and outside (zigzag).
- Hop around the outside of the hoop on one foot, then around the other way on the other foot.
- Hop around the hoop on one foot, alternating inside and outside.
- Move around the hoop in another way.
- Hold the hoop in both hands and lift it high above your head.
- With the hoop above your head, pretend you are driving around a mountain curve.
- Hold the hoop on end and spin it. As it spins low to the ground, jump in and out of it without stopping it.
- Use the hoop like a jump rope.

■ Stationary Hoop with a Ball (1-3)

Skills: Rolling, bouncing, throwing, catching, dribbling

Supplies: A hoop and a ball for each student

Formation: Each student in a personal space

Description: This is a great activity for allowing the students to work individually. These activities have an added challenge with the use of a ball along with the hoop. Read through the "challenges" at a pace that is appropriate for each particular class.

- Stand inside the hoop and roll the ball around the inside edge of the hoop.
- Stand outside the hoop, bounce and catch the ball inside the hoop.
- Stand outside the hoop, bounce the ball inside the hoop, clap your hands, and catch the ball.
- Stand outside the hoop, toss the ball in the air, let it bounce inside the hoop, and catch it.
- Stand inside the hoop, toss the ball in the air, and catch it.
- Stand inside the hoop, toss the ball in the air, slap your knees, and catch the ball.
- Kneel inside the hoop, toss the ball in the air, stand up, and catch it.
- Stand inside the hoop, toss the ball in the air, turn around, and catch it.
- Walk around the hoop with one foot inside the hoop and the other foot outside the hoop. Toss the ball in the air and catch it as you walk. Do this backwards.
- Stand inside the hoop, and dribble the ball inside the hoop.
- Stand inside the hoop, and dribble the ball outside the hoop.
- Walk around the outside of the hoop and dribble the ball in the center of the hoop.

■ Movement (1–3)

Skills: Space and body awareness, agility, movement

Supplies: A hoop for each student

Formation: Each student in a personal space

Description: This is a great activity for allowing the students to work individually. Read through the "challenges" at a pace that is appropriate for each particular class.

- Throw the hoop in the air, and catch it before it hits the floor.
- Roll the hoop on the floor using a back spin so it rolls back to you.
- Roll the hoop on the floor using a back spin, run out and go through the hoop before it comes back to you.
- Roll the hoop forward moving along with it so it doesn't fall over.
- Roll the hoop with another part of your body.
- Roll the hoop and run around it as it rolls, without touching it.
- Spin the hoop around one arm.
- Make the hoop move up and down your arm as you spin it around your arm.
- While spinning the hoop around one arm, change it to the other arm without stopping it.

- Make the hoop spin around your neck.
- Make the hoop spin around your waist.
- Make the hoop spin around your knees.
- Balance on one foot and spin the hoop around your ankle.
- Make the hoop travel from your waist to your knees without losing control.
- Walk forward while making the hoop spin around your waist.

PARTNER ACTIVITIES

Skills: Rolling, tossing, catching

Supplies: A hoop for each student

Formation: Each set of partners in a personal space

Description: This activity presents a great opportunity for partners and small groups to work together. Read through the "challenges" at a pace that is appropriate for each particular class.

- Face a partner and exchange hoops by rolling yours and catching theirs.
- Use only one hoop and play catch with your partner.
- While tossing and catching with your partner, catch the hoop on one arm and start spinning it.
- Using two hoops, play catch with your partner.
- Find other ways to exchange hoops with your partner.
- Get in small groups, set up hoop patterns to jump and hop through.
- With your small group, make an obstacle course using your hoops.

HOOP GAMES

■ Hoop Tag (K–3)

Skills: Running, chasing, dodging

Supplies: Several hoops

Formation: Lay the hoops randomly around the area with space between them. Choose one student to be "It." The other students scatter around the area.

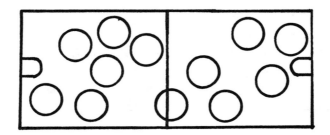

Description: Hoop Tag adds a fun twist to the traditional game of tag. As in tag, the object is for the person who is "It" to tag the other players. In Hoop Tag, a player is safe while standing with both feet inside a hoop. Only one player can be in a hoop at a time; a player may only stand in a hoop for ten seconds; when one player enters the hoop, the other must leave. Players tagged outside the hoop must freeze, and they can tag people as they go by as long as they do not move their feet. The last person tagged can choose to be "It" or choose someone else to be "It."

■ Hoop Horseshoes (1–3)

Skills: Tossing with accuracy

Supplies: Four hoops and two cones for each set of partners or foursome

Formation: Divide the class into pairs or groups of four, and have each group find a space to set up the game.

Description: This game is an adaptation of horseshoes. The object is for the players to get the hoops over the cone. Players stand at the cone and toss both their hoops, one at a time, at the other cone. After both players have tossed, points are added up: 3 points if the hoop goes over the cone; 2 points if the hoop leans against the cone; 1 point for the hoop that is closest to the cone. A game is 21 points.

■ Hoop Lasso (3–5)

Skills: Hand-eye coordination

Supplies: A hoop, rope, and box for each team. Tie the rope to the hoop.

Formation: Divide the class into teams of five or six players each. Have each team line up single file behind a designated line.

Description: This game is great for a "Western Day" or just to liven up a slow time of year. The object of this game is to lasso the box and drag it back across the line in one minute. At the signal, the first player in each line attempts to lasso the box and drag it back across the line. If s/he is successful, the team receives a point. When one minute is up it is the next player in line's turn. This continues until all players on each team have had a turn.

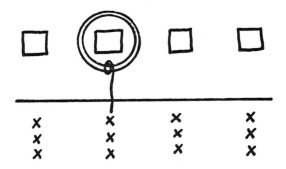

■ Hoop Goal Ball (3–6)

Skills: Throwing, catching, striking, coordination, teamwork

Supplies: Four pins, twelve hoops, one ball

Formation: Divide the class into two teams. Six players from each team play in the game at one time. Set up the game as follows:

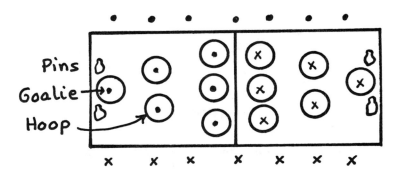

Description: This is a fantastic game that is both fun and challenging. Each player must move around the area inside the hoop without stepping out of it. The object of the game is for the players to pass the ball to teammates to get in position to toss the ball and knock down their pins. The goalie guards the pins. Players may shuffle while holding the ball, but may only hold the ball for three seconds. Knocking down one pin is a goal and scores a point. The pin stays down until the other pin is hit, then they are both set back up. After a goal is scored (one pin knocked down) the teams go back to their original positions and the team that did not score starts with the ball at the center.

Penalties include: (1) If the goalie steps out of his hoop, the opposing team gets a free shot from 10 yards away. (2) If any other player steps out of his hoop, the ball is given to the other team.

The winner is the team with the most points at the end of the designated time period (if you choose to keep score).

TEACHING HINTS
FOR RHYTHM STICKS

1. Have two rhythm sticks per student. These can be made by cutting dowels in 12-inch lengths.
2. The suggested grade level is K–2.
3. Begin the period with the following activities:
   a. Each student gets a pair of rhythm sticks and sits in the circle.
   b. Allow students to play with their rhythm sticks where they are sitting.
   c. When the whistle blows, the students stop, look, and listen (holding their rhythm sticks still). This indicates that you will begin giving directions for their activities.
4. Allow students to use their creativity to make up games, routines or both.

TASK ANALYSIS FOR TWO STICKS

The following are rhythm stick movements:
- Cross Tap: cross hands and tap upper ends to the floor.
- End Tap: tap ends on the floor.
- Flip: toss stick in air and catch.
- Partner tap: tap partner's stick (right to right, left to left, left to right, right to left).
- Pass: lay stick on floor and pick up partner's stick.
- Side tap: tap upper ends to side.
- Tap Together: hold sticks parallel and tap together.
- Toss Right: toss right-hand stick to partner's right hand, while at the same time receiving partner's right-hand stick (can do on left side).
- Toss Right and Left: toss right to right and left to left at the same time.
- Vertical Tap: tap upright (vertical) sticks to the floor.

INDIVIDUAL ACTIVITIES

■ One Rhythm Stick

Skills: Perceptual motor, agility, balance/body awareness, eye-hand coordination, rhythm

Supplies: One rhythm stick per student

Formation: Each student in a personal space

Description: These activities are great for providing students with the opportunity to work individually. The following activities touch on a variety of motor development skills.

PERCEPTUAL MOTOR

- Hold the stick vertically with one hand, using only your fingers. Move the stick in a circular direction. Try this with the other hand.
- Hold the stick in a horizontal position with one hand, using only your fingers. Move it forward in a circular direction, then backward.
- Hold the stick vertically in one hand, using only your fingers. Move your fingers up and down the stick.
- Hold onto the stick in the middle with your fingers. Twirl the stick in front of you, then at the side of your body.
- Sit on the floor, place the stick on the floor in front of you, and spin it clockwise and counterclockwise.
- Sit on the floor with knees bent. Place the stick on the floor under your knees and roll the stick around your body and under your knees while changing hands.

AGILITY

- Hold the stick in one hand, pass it around your body clockwise, changing the stick to the other hand. Then pass it around your body counterclockwise.
- Make a figure eight around your knees using the stick.
- Hold the stick horizontally in front of you with one hand on each end. Step over the stick with one foot, then the other while holding the stick. Then step backwards over it, one foot at a time.

BALANCE/BODY AWARENESS

- Balance the stick using four fingers of one hand, then three fingers, then two fingers, then one finger.
- Balance the stick on different parts of your body—forehead, nose, shoulder, knee, chin, and so forth.
- Hold your hand out with palm up and balance the stick vertically on the palm of your hand, then on your fingers.
- While balancing the stick on a part of your body, walk forward, then backward, then sideways.

EYE-HAND COORDINATION

- Hold the stick in one hand and toss it back and forth from one hand to the other.
- Lift the stick above your head with one hand, let go of it, and catch it with the same hand.

- Flip the stick in the air so it turns once. Then catch it.
- Flip the stick in the air so it turns twice or more. Then catch it.
- Hold the stick horizontally in front of you with one hand on each end. Raise the stick to eye level, let go, and catch it with one hand.
- Hold the stick horizontally with one hand, raise it to eye level, let go, and catch it below waist level with the same hand.
- Hold the stick near the top with one hand in a vertical position, raise it above your head on the same side of your body, let go, use your other hand to reach across your body, and catch it.
- Sit on the floor, hold the stick in a vertical position in one hand, bounce it on the floor, and catch it with the same hand.
- Sit on the floor, hold the stick horizontally across the fingers of both hands, hold your arms close together and straight out, let the stick roll across your hands and arms to your shoulders, and then back down to your fingers.

RHYTHM

- Hold the stick in one hand, tap the end on the floor, flip the stick in the air so it makes one turn, and catch it with the same hand. Repeat.
- Continue with the pattern of tap, flip, and catch several times.

■ Two Rhythm Sticks

Skills: Perceptual motor, balance/body awareness, eye-hand coordination, rhythm

Supplies: Two rhythm sticks per student

Formation: Each student in a personal space

Description: These activities are great for providing students with the opportunity to work individually. These activities add a challenge to the previous skills because they involve two sticks.

PERCEPTUAL MOTOR

- Hold one stick in each hand vertically with your fingers. Move both sticks in a circular clockwise direction, then in a counterclockwise direction.
- Hold one stick in each hand horizontally with your fingers. Move them forward and backward in a circular direction.
- Hold one stick in each hand vertically with your fingers. Move your fingers up and down the sticks.
- Hold each stick in the middle with your fingers. Twirl the sticks.

BALANCE/BODY AWARENESS

- Balance one stick on each shoulder and walk in different patterns (for example, circle, square, or figure eight). Balance the sticks on other body parts (for example, wrists, back of hands, and behind the ears).

- Balance both sticks on the floor about one inch apart. Walk a figure eight pattern in and around your sticks.
- Make a letter *T* with your sticks and jump over it. See if you can make any other letters or numbers with your sticks.
- Hold one stick vertically in one hand, balance the end of the other stick on top of it.

EYE-HAND COORDINATION

- Hold a stick in each hand horizontally in front of you with palms down. Hit the ends of the two sticks together, hitting them through your fists. Turn your palms up and hit the ends together.
- Holding one stick in each hand, lift the sticks above your head, let them go, and catch them with the same hands.
- Holding one stick in each hand, flip both sticks in the air so that they turn over once, and then catch them.
- Holding one stick in each hand, flip both sticks in the air so that they turn over twice or more, and then catch them.
- Hold one stick in each hand, toss them, and catch them in the opposite hands.

RHYTHM

- As a leader taps out a rhythm pattern with two sticks, repeat the same pattern with your sticks. Repeat with different leaders each time.
- Tap the sticks on the floor in front of you, then tap them together. Repeat in rhythm with the class.
- Tap the sticks on the floor, tap them together, flip them once in the air, and then catch them. Repeat in rhythm with the class.
- Tap the sticks on the floor, tap them together, flip them once in the air, catch them, and then tap the ends on the floor. Repeat in rhythm with the class.
- Tap the sticks on the floor ("front"), tap them together ("together"), flip once in the air ("flip"), catch them, tap ends on the floor ("down"), tap one stick on each side of your body ("side"), and then cross arms and tap sticks on the floor ("cross").
- Repeat the previous rhythm using just the verbal cues of: "front," "together," "flip," "down," "side," and "cross." Repeat in rhythm with the class.
- Make up your own patterns. Then teach the patterns to a partner, group, or class.

INDIVIDUAL AND PARTNER ACTIVITIES

Skills: Striking, hand-eye coordination, blocking

Supplies: Two rhythm sticks per student, one tennis ball per student

Formation: Each student or each set of partners in a personal space

Description: These activities provide an added challenge involving a ball, together with the sticks.

INDIVIDUAL

- Tap the ball back and forth between your sticks.
- Bounce the ball using one stick.
- Bounce the ball using alternate sticks.
- Pick up the ball using only your sticks.
- Pick up the ball with your sticks, release it, and catch the ball with your sticks after it bounces once.

PARTNER

- Sit facing partner with a few feet between you. Hit the ball back and forth using your sticks and keeping the ball on the floor. Move farther apart as it gets easier to hit the ball.
- Set up one stick on end between you for a target. One player starts with the ball. Using a stick s/he attempts to hit the ball at the target and knock it over. Then it's the other partner's turn.
- Each player sets up one stick in front of his/her body for a target. One player starts with the ball and uses the other stick to attempt to knock over his partner's target. Players may try to block the ball with their sticks.

■ Rhythm Stick Games

Skills: Rhythm stick movements, rhythm, patterning, sequencing

Supplies: Two rhythm sticks per student

Formation: Partners facing each other sitting cross-legged

Description: Putting learned skills into games is the next step for practicing skills in a specific pattern.

PEASE PORRIDGE HOT

Words	*Action*
Pease porridge hot,	Floor, together, partner tap
Pease porridge cold,	Floor, together, partner tap
Pease porridge in the pot,	Floor, together, tap right, together, tap left
Nine days old.	Floor, together, partner tap

Have the students make up movements to go with other rhymes.

STRIKING STICKS

The rhythm background is 1-2-3-4 and may be played on a drum.

Position 1: Heads of sticks rest on the floor. Strike heads of sticks on the floor (1-2-3). Strike together with partner (4). Repeat four times.

Position 2: Stand sticks upright. Strike sticks on the floor (1-2-3). Strike together with partner (4). Repeat four times.

Position 3: Rest heads of sticks on the floor. Strike sticks on the floor (1-2). Strike crossed sticks (3). Strike sticks with partner (4). Repeat four times.

RHYTHM STICK ROUTINES

Skills: Rhythm stick movements, rhythm, patterning, sequencing, cooperation

Supplies: Two rhythm sticks per student

Formation: Partners facing each other sitting cross-legged

Description: Routines are a great introduction for getting students to use their creativity to come up with their own routines. They can teach their new routines to others, write them out and compile them in a booklet, and perform them for others.

SAMPLE ROUTINE 1

Count 1: Hit own sticks on the floor.
Count 2: Hit own sticks together at waist level.
Count 3: Partners hit right sticks together.
Count 4: Hit own sticks together at waist level.
Count 5: Partners hit left sticks together.
Count 6: Hit own sticks together at waist level.
Count 7: Partners hit both sticks together.
Count 8: Hit own sticks together at waist level.
Repeat.

SAMPLE ROUTINE 2

The following can be used as one long routine, as each being a separate routine repeated four times, or by combining various parts to create a new routine.

1. Vertical tap, tap together, partner tap right.
   Vertical tap, tap together, partner tap left.
2. Vertical tap, tap together, pass right stick.
   Vertical tap, tap together, pass left stick.
3. Vertical tap, tap together, toss right stick.
   Vertical tap, tap together, toss left stick.
4. Repeat 1 through 3, with the addition of an end tap and flip to the beginning of the stated movement.
5. Vertical tap, tap together, toss right and left.
6. End tap, flip, toss right and left.
7. Cross hand tap, cross hand flip, uncross arms, vertical tap.

8. Right flip at side, left flip in front, vertical tap, partner tap right.
9. End tap in front, flip, vertical tap.

Tap together, toss right, toss left.

10. Vertical tap, tap together, right stick to partner's left hand, tossing your left stick to your own right hand. Repeat. (This is the circle throw.)

TEACHING HINTS FOR SCOOPS

1. Scoops can be made out of large bleach or duplicating fluid containers by cutting out the top part and part of the bottom. The handle of the bottle is the handle for the scoop.

2. Whiffle balls work best with the scoop.
3. You can make up relays and games to go with the scoops.
4. Some of the games are similar to traditional sports except for the use of scoops (Scoop Volleyball—Volleyball; Scoop Golf—Golf; Scoop Softball—Softball; Scoop Goalball—Soccer, Floor/Field Hockey). You could use these as variations in the appropriate sports units.

■ Task Analysis of Scoop Skills (1–6)

Skills: Throwing, catching

Supplies: Scoops, whiffle balls

Formation: Divide the class into pairs. Have each pair find a personal space.

OVERHAND THROW

- With the ball in the scoop, bring your throwing arm back by rotating your shoulder.
- Thrust the scoop forward over the head and follow through making sure the ball leaves the scoop before the downward motion.

UNDERHAND THROW

- Start by bringing the scoop backward then bring the scoop forward, keeping your arm straight.
- Flick the scoop with your arm and wrist, releasing the ball at waist level.

SIDEARM THROW

- Hold the scoop in a forehand grip.
- Bring your throwing arm back, rotating your body away from the direction of the throw.
- Swing your arm forward, keeping your arm straight, and release the ball off the tip of your scoop.

BACKHAND THROW

- Hold the scoop in a backhand grip.
- Bring your throwing arm back, rotating your body away from the direction of the throw.
- Swing your arm forward in a sideward and backhand motion, releasing the ball off the tip of the scoop.

SNAP THROW

- Hold the scoop at head height and extended in front of your body.
- Without moving your arm, snap your wrist and flex the scoop sharply. This will release the ball with speed.

OVERHAND CATCH (to field high balls)

- Hold the scoop vertically.
- Catch the ball at the tip of the scoop and let it roll along the curve of the scoop.

UNDERHAND CATCH (to field slow, looping fly balls)

- Hold the scoop parallel to the ground.
- Let the ball drop into the scoop.

COVER RETRIEVING (to retrieve a "dead" ball)

- Hook the tip of the scoop over the ball, and draw the ball toward you.
- Twist the scoop with a flip of the wrist so the scoop is now under the ball.

SIDE RETRIEVE (to field a rolling ball)

* Approach the ball with the scoop on its side (open side toward the ball).
* Receive the rolling ball into the scoop.
* Get rid of the ball with a sidearm throw.

■ Individual Activities (K–2)

Skills: Throwing, catching

Supplies: A scoop and ball for each student

Formation: Each student in a personal space

Description: This beginning activity is a good warm-up as you enter into some relays and games using scoops. Read each of the following "challenges" at a pace that is appropriate for each particular class.

* Put the ball on the floor and pick it up with the scoop.
* Throw the ball in the air and catch it with the scoop.
* Put the ball in the scoop, toss the ball in the air, and catch it with the scoop.
* Throw the ball against the wall and catch it with the scoop.
* Throw the ball against the wall with the scoop and catch it with the scoop.
* Throw the ball against the wall with the scoop, switch the scoop to the other hand, and catch the ball.
* Throw the ball in the air, do a stunt (for example, heel click or turn), and catch the ball with your scoop.

SCOOP GAMES

■ Scoop Six Circles (–3)

Skills: Throwing with accuracy while increasing distance

Supplies: A scoop and ball for each group, six hoops for each group (or make six circles with tape or rope)

Formation: Divide the class into as small a number of groups as you have equipment for. Each group needs to have a playing area set up as diagrammed (You may want fewer circles or to have the circles closer together for the younger children.)

Description: The object of this game is to challenge the students to throw with accuracy while increasing distance. The first player in each line throws the ball with the scoop from the throwing line, attempting to get it in the nearest hoop. The player then goes to the end of the line, and it is the next player's turn. This continues until all have had a turn. The next time through the line, those who made it into the first hoop attempt the second hoop, and those that did not make it try to make it into the first hoop. The winner is the first person to make it into the last hoop. Any players who have a chance to tie the winner may attempt their throw. If there is a time, the players throw three times to the last hoop, and the player making the most, wins. If you choose not to have "winners," do not address the issue of winning, just challenge your students to try to make it in all hoops.

VARIATION: A player who makes it into the first hoop continues on to the next ones until s/he misses; then it is the next player's turn.

■ Scoop Golf (2–4)

Skills: Throwing with accuracy

Supplies: A scoop and ball for each player

Formation: Divide the class into small groups to fit the wall space available. Set up each area as diagrammed below:

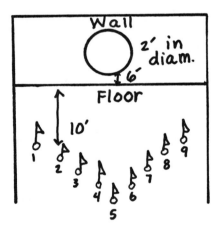

Description: This game adds an aspect of fun as well as challenge to the skill of throwing with accuracy. Have the players line up behind hole 1. The first player throws the ball at the circle on the wall. If s/he succeeds in hitting it, s/he moves to hole 2. If s/he fails to hit it, he goes to the end of the line and waits for his next turn. Players keep track of their own attempts at each "hole" and add them up for the final score. As in golf, the player with the lowest score wins.

■ Scoop Softball (2–4)

Skills: Throwing, catching, batting, fielding

Supplies: A scoop for each player in the field, a whiffle ball, a whiffle bat, four bases

Formation: Divide the class into two teams, a fielding team and a batting team.

Description: Add a new twist to softball by playing Scoop Softball. The rules are the same as softball except the fielding team has scoops to catch with rather then gloves, and a whiffle ball and bat are used. The fielding team must field, catch and throw with the scoop. Pitching is also done with the scoop using an underhand motion.

■ Scoop Volleyball (2–4)

Skills: Throwing, catching, teamwork

Supplies: A scoop for each player, a ball, a net

Formation: Divide the class in half, and place six players from each team on the floor to play, as in volleyball.

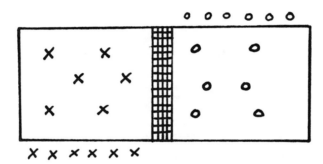

Description: This game uses volleyball rules and a volleyball net, but uses scoops and a ball for the game. The scoop is used for serving, throwing, and catching. When a player receives the serve, s/he must toss the ball to a teammate or toss it over the net. The serving team scores a point when the receiving team fails to return the ball or throws it out of bounds. The receiving team wins the serve when the serving team does not get the serve over the net, when they fail to return the ball, or when they throw the ball out of bounds. Teams rotate when they get the serve. A game can be 15 or 21 points.

■ Scoop 500 (3–4)

Skills: Throwing, catching, batting

Supplies: A scoop for each player, a ball and bat for each group

Formation: Divide the class into small groups to fit the space available.

Description: This game is a fun variation of the game 500. One player bats and the others are in the field. The batter tosses the ball up and hits it into the field. The fielders attempt to catch the ball with their scoops. Points are awarded as follows: 100 points for catching a fly ball; 75 points for catching a ball on the first bounce; 50 points for catching a ball on the second bounce; 25 points for catching a rolling ball. When a player receives 500 points, s/he becomes the new batter.

■ Scoop Goalball (3-6)

Skills: Throwing, catching, intercepting, scoring, goaltending, teamwork

Supplies: A scoop for each player, a ball for each game, two sets of goals for each game

Formation: Divide the class either in half or into teams of six players each. There are six players who play on a team at a time.

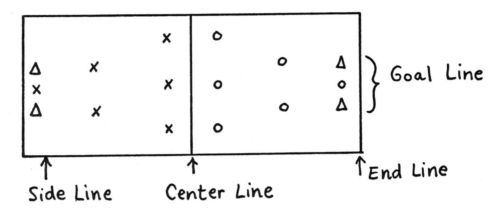

Description: This game is an adaptation of 6 versus 6 Soccer and floor/field hockey. One team starts the game with the center player tossing the ball to a teammate. The object of the game is for the offensive team to move the ball down the field by tossing it to teammates, and to throw it through the goal. At the same time, the defensive team attempts to intercept the tosses to gain possession of the ball. Players may only hold the ball for five seconds, and may only take three steps when in possession of the ball. If the ball goes out of bounds, it is thrown in by the other team. When a goal is made, play starts at the center by the defending team.
The position responsibilities are as follows:

1. The three front players can move all over the field, and their job is to attempt to score goals.
2. The two back players can only go on their half of the field, to the center line. They toss the ball to the front players, and help block the goal.
3. The goalie stays in the goal area to block the attempted goals.

TEACHING HINTS
FOR STREAMERS

1. The streamer ribbon activities can be done with students in grade K-6, but is most enjoyed at the K-2 level.

2. You can either buy commercial streamers, or you can make them. To make them, take a dowel about 12 inches long and tape a strip of crepe paper around one end (3 feet to 5 feet long).

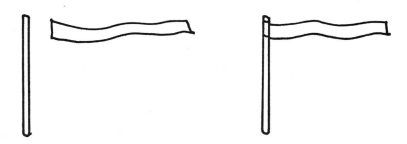

3. As you move the dowel around in patterns, the crepe paper streamer floats through the air.
4. Teach the basic movements first, then do the routines, then have students create their own movements and routines. Write them down and teach them to others.
5. Other ideas:
    a. Move the streamer around as you do locomotor movements.
    b. Move the streamer as you do nonlocomotor movements.
    c. Use the streamer with basic dance steps (waltz, polka, schottische).
    d. Have the students make numbers, letters, and shapes with their streamers.
6. Many activities begin with the right hand. Students may start with their left hands; change the directions accordingly.

BASIC STREAMER MOVEMENTS AND ROUTINES

■ Task Analysis of Basic Streamer Movements

Skills: Fine and gross motor coordination, creativity, sequencing, patterning, agility, flexibility, balance, strength, control

Supplies: A streamer for each student

Formation: Each student in a personal space

Description: Streamers are a fun and inexpensive addition to your rhythms unit. Each movement is described under its heading. Have the students put movements together to make a routine and have them set it to music they choose. Then have them teach the routine to the class.

BACKSTROKE

- Hold the streamer in one hand. Alternate extending the arms in a backstroke (R, L, R, L).
- Attempt different rhythm patterns (for example, slow, slow, quick, quick, slow).

OVERHEAD WHIP

- Stand with one foot slightly ahead of the other foot. Cast the streamer back overhead, whip it forward, and pull it back toward your chest.

ARC AND PULL

- Extend the right arm in a high arc overhead.
- Allow the right arm to continue downward to chest level, then pull the right arm across the chest from left to right.

CIRCLING

LASSO:
Circle the streamer overhead.

TORNADO:
Circle the streamer in front of the ankles.

INSIDE CIRCLE:
Extend arms and bring them up above the head, and continue to circle outward meeting at chest level.

OUTSIDE CIRCLE:
Extend arms and move them outward in a circle to meet overhead.

BACKWARD WHIP

- Whip the streamer downward and backward on your left side twice, then bring the streamer forward and whip it downward and backward on the right side twice.

HORSE AND BUGGY

- Bend your arms and hold your hands at shoulder level.
- Cast your arms forward in front of your chest, then pull your arms back to the starting position.

FIGURE EIGHT

- Move your arm from right to left horizontally outlining a figure eight. Do this overhead, at waist level, low to the floor, and on both sides of your body.

FLAME

- Rapidly shake the streamer from side to side in front of your body, making the streamer dance like flames.

ARM CROSS AND UNCROSS

- Extend your arms and cross them at waist level, then uncross them bringing them out to the side.

SIDE-TO-SIDE SWAY

- Extend your streamer overhead and move it from right to left and left to right, in a slow swaying movement.

CROSS AND UNCROSS OVERHEAD

- With arms extended overhead, cross and uncross your arms.
- Attempt different rhythm patterns (for example, cross–slow, uncross–slow, cross–quick, uncross–quick, cross–slow).

SIDE PADDLE

- Move both arms down and backward on the left side then the right side.
- Try a combination movement—arm cross and uncross twice, paddle twice on left side, arm cross and uncross twice, paddle twice on the right side.

UNDERHAND PITCH

- Step forward on your left foot, and at the same time make an underhand pitch with the right arm (streamer arm).
- Bring your right toe to the back of the left foot on the pitch.
- Step backward on the right foot, and bring the right arm backward in an underhand motion.

SHOULDER-KNEE

- Holding the streamer in the right hand, cast the streamer over your left shoulder then downward by the right knee.

SHAKE IT DOWN

- Hold your streamer arm straight overhead, then shake the streamer downward keeping your arm straight.

SIDE STRETCH

- Stand in straddle position with arms extended straight down.
- Swing arms to shoulder level and stretch right to left and left to right.

DOWN AND UP

- Begin with elbows bent at waist level.
- As you lower your body in four counts by bending your knees, twist from side to side moving the streamer from right to left and left to right. Come back up the same way in four counts.

KNEE WHIP

- Whip the streamer down and behind your knees, bending your knees at the same time.

TWIST

- Stand in a straddle position with arms extended forward at chest level.
- Twist left on both feet and shake the streamer on the left side twice, then twist right and shake it on the right side twice.

SWEEP UP-DOWN

- Stand with arms extended at your side, sweep both arms up and down.

WAVES

- Make a series of upside down *V*s to the right and left.

WINDSHIELD WIPER

- Hold your bent elbows at chest level and move the streamer from right to left and left to right. As you do this movement, cross and uncross your arms.

■ Streamer Routines

Skills: Patterns, sequencing, rhythm, movement

Supplies: A streamer for each student, music

Formation: Each student in a personal space

Description: These routines combine various streamer movements. This is the next step in streamer activities. After students have the experience of performing routines, have them create their own routines to teach to the class.

JIVE MOVING

1. Arm cross and uncross 8x.
2. Backward whip 4x.
3. Sweep up-down 4x.
4. Shake it down 4x.
5. Repeat steps 1 through 4.

CREATIVE MOVEMENT

As the music starts, the teacher begins to call out things to make with your streamer. Then ask for student ideas. The object is to use streamers to make the "thing" however the students visualize it—there is no wrong way.

- Clouds
- Flames
- Ocean Waves
- Falling leaves
- A ballet dancer
- A kite flying in the sky
- A merry-go-round

WESTERN ROUND-UP

1. A figure eight at waist level 4x.
2. Whip the streamer on your left side, then whip it in front of you, then whip it on your right side. Repeat this 4x.
3. Overhead whip 4x.
4. Horse and buggy 4x.

SLOW SWAY

1. Side-to-side sway 4x.
2. Sweep the streamer along the floor from side to side 4x.
3. Inside circle 4x.
4. Outside circle 4x.
5. Twist 4x.
6. Repeat steps 1 through 5.

THE RAIN IS FALLING

1. Figure eight above your head then shake it down. Repeat this pattern 4x.
2. Figure eight at waist level 4x.
3. Sweep up-down 4x.
4. Repeat steps 1 through 3.

A HOT SATURDAY NIGHT

1. Sweep up-down 4x.
2. Arm cross and uncross 4x.
3. Tornado 4x.
4. Shoulder-knee 4x.
5. Windshield wiper 4x.
6. Repeat steps 1 through 5.

TEACHING HINTS FOR WANDS

1. Wands are dowels approximately ½ inch to 1 inch in diameter and 3 feet long. They can be purchased at hardware stores.
2. Wands are recommended for grades 3 through 6.
3. Teach safety, and make sure students hold the wand still or place it on the floor while directions are being given.
4. Wands do break, so be prepared for that possibility.

EXERCISES, ACTIVITIES, AND STUNTS

■ Wand Stretching Exercises

Skills: Stretching, flexibility

Supplies: One wand for each student

Formation: Each student in a personal space

Description: These exercises are a great warm-up activity which add a change of pace to traditional warm-ups.

SIDE BENDING

- Stand with feet shoulder width apart, holding the wand horizontally, with arms extended overhead.
- Bend sideways, keeping arms and legs straight, return to a standing position, then bend to the other side.

TWIST

- Stand with feet shoulder width apart, place the wand behind neck, and drape arms over the wand from behind.
- Rotate upper body to one side then the other, keeping feet and hips in position (twist at waist only).

TWIST TO KNEE AND TOUCH

- Stand with feet shoulder width apart, place the wand behind neck and drape arms over the wand from behind.
- Rotate the upper body to one side, touching the end of the wand to the opposite knee, return to a stand, and twist to the other side.

SHOULDER TWIST

- Grip the wand at both ends and extend arms overhead.
- Rotate the wand, arms and shoulders going backwards until the wand touches the back of the legs (keep arms straight).

TOE TOUCHERS

- Grip the wand with hands shoulder width apart, and bend forward.
- Reach down as far as possible without bending knees. Return to a stand, then repeat.

LEG STRETCH

- Sit and flex knees.
- Place the wand under the toes, rest it against the middle of the arches, and grip the wand just outside your feet.
- Slowly extend legs forward, pushing against the wand.

■ Wand Challenge Activities

Skills: Flexibility, balance, reaction time, movement

Supplies: One wand for each student

Formation: Each student in a personal space

Description: After the wand stretching exercises, these challenge activities are a good step before doing the individual and partner stunts. Read each challenge at a pace that is appropriate for your class.

- Reach to the floor and pick up your wand without bending your knees.
- Balance your wand on different parts of your body.
- Hold the wand against the wall, move under it and over it.
- Spin the wand.
- Move different ways around your wand while it is on the floor.
- Put one end of the wand on the floor and hold on to the other end. See how many times you can run around the wand without getting dizzy.
- Hold the wand vertically, release your grip and catch the wand before it hits the floor.
- Have a partner hold a wand horizontally above the floor. Jump, leap, or hop over the wand, gradually raising the height.

■ Individual Stunts

Skills: Agility, flexibility, balance, coordination

Supplies: One wand for each student

Formation: Each student in a personal space

Description: The challenge in these activities raises the level of motivation and enthusiasm for participation with wands.

CATCH THE WAND

- Stand the wand on end and hold it with fingers on top.
- Bring one foot over the wand, let go of it, and catch it before it hits the floor.
- Bring one foot behind the wand, let go of it, and catch it before it hits the floor.
- Do this with the right and left foot, inward and outward.

TWO-FOOT BALANCE

- Lie on your back, hold the wand above your head, and place feet under the wand.
- Release your hands, extend your legs upward keeping the wand balanced, then lower your legs to starting position.

THREAD THE NEEDLE (lying down)

- Lie on your back with your knees bent, and hold the wand in front of and above your body.
- Pass your feet up and under the wand, then return to your original position.

THREAD THE NEEDLE (standing)

- Hold the wand horizontally with both hands.
- Step between your arms and over the wand one leg at a time.
- Return to your original position by stepping backwards over the wand one leg at a time.
- Repeat the first two steps, but return to original position by bringing the wand up your back, then overhead to the front of your body.

WAND WHIRL AND CATCH

- Stand the wand on end, let go of it, turn around, and grasp it before it falls.
- Do this with right and left hands.
- See if you can turn more than once before catching the wand.

UNDER-ARM TWIST

- Stand the wand on end and grasp the top of the wand with one hand.
- Twist under that arm without letting go of the wand or lifting it off the floor.
- Try this with your other arm.

DIZZY IZZY

- Stand the wand on one end, bend forward and place your forehead on the top of the wand.
- Place your hands behind your back and walk around the wand using a crossover step without letting it fall to the floor.

JUMP OVER THE WAND

- Hold the wand horizontally with your hands on either end of the wand, and slightly bend your knees.
- Jump up and over the wand between your arms without letting go, then jump backwards over the wand.

WAND BACKBEND

- Stand with your feet shoulder width apart and grasp the wand at one end with the other end pointing toward the ceiling.
- Bend backwards, placing the wand on the mat behind you, and walk your hands down the wand.
- Walk your hands back up and return to a standing position.

GRAPEVINE STEP

- Hold the wand horizontally in front of you.
- Step with your right foot around your right arm, bringing your foot over the wand and inward toward your body.
- Pass the wand backwards over your head and right shoulder until you are standing straight with the wand between your legs.
- Reverse the process to get back to your original position.
- Try to do this with your left foot.

DOWN THE BACK

- Hold the wand horizontally in front of you with arms crossed and palms facing up.
- Bend your elbows, put the wand over and behind your head, and pass the wand down your body from shoulders to heels.
- Step backwards over the wand to get back to original position.

■ Partner Stunts with Wands

Skills: Tossing, catching, jumping, timing, agility, flexibility, cooperation

Supplies: Some stunts require one wand per student, some a wand for every two students.

Formation: Divide the class into pairs and have each pair find a personal space.

Description: These activities are great for focusing on cooperation and for challenging the students. After completing these stunts, you may want to have students create some of their own ideas for stunts.

PARTNER WAND CATCH

- Face your partner with about 5 feet between you.
- One partner holds the wand in his right hand, and tosses it to his partner.
- Partners toss and catch, alternating hands.

PARTNER WAND EXCHANGE

- Face your partner with about 5 feet between you.
- Stand your wand on end and hold on to the top of the wand.
- At the signal, run to your partner's wand and catch it before it falls.

DISHRAG TURN

- Face your partner, both grasp the wand, holding it horizontally.
- Raise one pair of arms (right for one person, left for the other person) and turn under that pair of arms (turning the same direction).

• Continue a full turn until you are back in your original position.
• See how many consecutive turns you can make.

PARTNER BALANCE AND CARRY

• Face your partner, place the wand horizontally with one end on each partner's forehead, and move around the area.
• Try holding the wand between other body parts.

WAND DROP AND CATCH

• Face your partner and have one partner hold the wand horizontally.
• Have the other partner hold his/her hand above the wand, palm facing down.
• The partner holding the wand drops it and the other partner tries to catch it before it hits the floor.
• Change roles with your partner.

Section 6

Lead-Up Games For Super Sports

TEACHING HINTS
FOR BASKETBALL

1. Suggested grade level for basketball is 4–6, but if you choose to teach basic skills to younger students, I would suggest:

   a. Use a foam basketball or playground ball for grades 1 and 2.

   b. Use wastebaskets on chairs for the baskets for 1–2 (unless you have baskets that raise and lower in height).

   c. Through grade 3, use junior size basketballs and modify the game: Hitting the backboard - 1 point; rim - 2 points; basket - 3 points.

   d. Use select lead-up games (for example, Line Basketball).

2. A few hints for skills:

   a. Passing

      1. Be accurate.

      2. Follow through with arms and body, stepping forward on one foot.

      3. Shift ball quickly from receiving position to passing position.

   b. Dribbling

      1. Push the ball toward the floor by bending the wrist and contacting the ball with the fingertips.

      2. Dribble with both hands, alternating after several consecutive dribbles.

      3. Dribble on the opposite side of where your opponent is (keep yourself between the ball and your opponent).

3. You do not have to teach all the suggested skills or all the regulation game rules—adapt to best suit your situation.

4. Teach the rules and teach students how to call their own rule infractions so they can learn to be independent of constant teacher intervention. This allows for more than one game to go on at a time, which then provides for maximum student involvement. This also teaches students to be honest about their "mistakes."

5. If you choose to play regulation basketball, I would suggest it for grades 4–6 only. Teach man-to-man defense to grades 4–6 and zone defense to grade 6.

6. If possible, have more than one game going on at a time so that all students can be active.

GLOSSARY OF BASKETBALL TERMS

Charging: a foul committed by an offensive player running into the defensive player

Double dribble: when a player dribbles with both hands or stops dribbling and begins again

Dribbling: controlled bouncing in any direction and at various speeds to advance the ball

Field goal: a goal scored when a player puts the ball through the basket during the game (two points)

Foul: called by the referee when body contact occurs

Free throw: a shot made from a set line and awarded because of a foul by an opponent (one point)

Guarding: the act of playing defense

Jump ball: an action that puts the ball into play; is used to begin the game and after a held ball; throw ball up between two opposing players who attempt to tip it toward a teammate

Lane: area in the court from underneath the goal to the free-throw line which an offensive player can be in no more than three seconds during play and from which players are excluded during a free throw

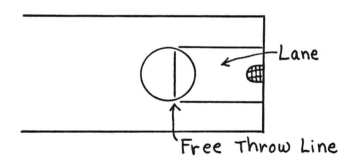

Passing: moving the ball from one player to another from a stationary or moving position

Pivoting: act of turning on a given point (one foot stationary)

Post: player who is stationary

Shooting: means used for scoring

Traveling: moving with possession of the ball but without dribbling it

Suggested Basketball Skills Sequence

GRADE 3	GRADE 4	GRADE 5	GRADE 6

DRIBBLING
Drills
  Whistle Dribble
  Line Dribble
  Cone Dribble
	DRIBBLING
	Drills
	  Whistle Dribble
	  Line Dribble
	  Cone Dribble
	  Direction Dribble
		DRIBBLING
		Drills
		  Cone Dribble
		  Weave Dribble
		  Dribble Contest
		  Dribble, Pivot,
		    Pass
			DRIBBLING
			Drills
			  Weave Dribble
			  Dribble Contest
			  Dribble, Pivot,
			    Pass

PASSING
  Chest
  Bounce
  Overhead
	PASSING
	  Chest
	  Bounce
	  Overhead
		PASSING
		  Chest
		  Bounce
		  Overhead
		  Baseball
			PASSING
			  Chest
			  Bounce
			  Overhead
			  Baseball
			  Hook

Drills
  Partner Pass
  Circle Pass
	Drills
	  Circle Pass
		Drills
		  Circle Pass
		  Triangle Drill
			Drills
			  Triangle Drill
			  Think Pass
			  Three Player
			    Weave

SHOOTING
  Set Shot
	SHOOTING
	  Set Shot
	  Jump Shot
		SHOOTING
		  Set Shot
		  Jump Shot
		  Lay-Up
		  Overhead
			SHOOTING
			  Set Shot
			  Jump Shot
			  Lay-Up
			  Overhead
			  Hook

		OFFENSE/DEFENSE
		Drills
		  One-On-One
			OFFENSE/DEFENSE
			Drills
			  One-On-One
			  Offense/Defense
			  Drill With Post

		OTHER
		  Basketball Station
		    Tasks
			OTHER
			  Basketball Station
			    Tasks

	RELATED SKILLS
	  Guarding
	  Jump Ball
		RELATED SKILLS
		  Guarding
		  Jump Ball
		  Pivoting
		  Rebounding
			RELATED SKILLS
			  Guarding
			  Jump Ball
			  Pivoting
			  Rebounding

	RULES
	  Traveling
	  Double Dribbling
	  Out-Of-Bounds
	  Scoring
		RULES
		  Traveling
		  Double Dribbling
		  Out-Of-Bounds
		  Scoring
		  Positions
		  Fouls
			RULES
			  Traveling
			  Double Dribbling
			  Out-Of-Bounds
			  Scoring
			  Positions
			  Fouls

Suggested Basketball Skills Sequence (Cont.)

GRADE 3	GRADE 4	GRADE 5	GRADE 6
LEAD-UP GAMES	LEAD-UP GAMES	LEAD-UP GAMES	LEAD-UP GAMES
Basket-O-Rama	Basketball Flag	End Ball	End Ball
Basketballbowl	Dribble	Basketball	Three On Three
Basketball Relay	Basketballbowl	Baseball	Line Basketball
Line Basketball	Five Passes	Line Basketball	
	Basketball Relay		
	Line Basketball		

TASK ANALYSIS OF BASKETBALL SKILLS

CHEST PASS

1. Stand with both feet together.
2. Hold the ball at chest level with fingers spread and thumbs close together.
3. Flex elbows and hold them close to the body.
4. Step forward on one foot, extending arms and releasing the ball in a pushing action off fingertips.

BOUNCE PASS

1. Stand with both feet together.
2. Hold the ball at waist level with fingers spread and thumbs close together.
3. Flex elbows and hold them close to the body.
4. Step forward on one foot, extending arms, push downward to a spot on the floor (a little more than halfway between two players) and release the ball.

BASEBALL PASS

1. Stand with both feet together.
2. Hold the ball in front of body, with elbows bent and fingers spread around the sides of the ball.
3. Bring arms back and transfer ball to throwing hand when it is behind shoulder and at ear level.
4. Step forward, rotating body, and release the ball with a snap of the wrist and fingers.

OVERHEAD PASS

1. Stand with feet together and knees slightly bent.
2. Hold the ball above the head with thumbs under the ball and fingers spread on the side of the ball pointed up.
3. Have elbows and wrists slightly flexed.
4. Step forward on one foot, shifting arms forward and releasing the ball at about head level with a snap of wrists and fingers.
5. Follow through with hands to eye level.

HOOK PASS

1. Stand with nonpassing shoulder toward the receiver.
2. Extend passing arm to the side.
3. Hold the ball with hand under it, palm up.
4. Raise passing arm sideways so it crosses passing shoulder and over head.
5. Release ball; hand is directed downward (palm is down after release).

DRIBBLING

1. Stand with knees flexed and head up.
2. Relax wrist and spread fingers.
3. "Push" ball to floor with fingertips and flexed wrist.
4. Move fingers, wrist, and arm backward on the rebound.

TWO-HAND SET SHOT

1. Stand with one foot slightly ahead of the other, flexed knees, and weight evenly distributed.
2. Hold the ball with fingers spread and thumbs close together, elbows close to side.
3. Simultaneously straighten knees and extend arms and body upward and forward.
4. Release the ball with snap of wrists and fingers.
5. Follow through with palms facing basket.

ONE-HAND SET SHOT

1. Stand with shooting foot slightly forward, knees slightly bent.
2. Hold the ball with both hands opposite the chin and above shooting foot.
3. Simultaneously straighten legs, release nonshooting hand, and extend shooting arm upward and forward.
4. Release ball with snap of wrist and fingers.

JUMP SHOT

1. Stand square toward basket.
2. Jump upward looking at basket.
3. Place shooting hand under the ball and nonshooting hand on the side of the ball.
4. Bring the ball slightly above and in front of head.
5. Cock wrist and point elbow toward basket.
6. Release the ball at the top of jump.
7. Follow through in direction of basket.

TWO-HAND OVERHEAD SHOT

1. Stand with knees slightly flexed, feet shoulder width apart.
2. Place thumbs under the ball with fingers on the side pointing up and back.
3. Raise ball overhead.
4. Swing ball forward and upward.
5. Extend arms and legs as body weight shifts forward.

LAY-UP

1. Approach the basket at a 45-degree angle.
2. Place shooting hand on top and slightly behind the ball, and nonshooting hand in front and under ball.
3. Shift weight to inside foot (nonshooting foot) and lift body by bringing up outside knee (shooting leg).
4. Carry ball to shoulder height and push off nonshooting foot.
5. Release nonshooting hand as shooting arm directs ball up to the backboard.
6. Follow through with palm of shooting hand in direction of backboard.

HOOK SHOT

1. Stand with back to basket holding the ball in both hands.
2. Step with nonshooting foot and turn toward the basket.
3. Place shooting hand under the ball.
4. Bring shooting arm upward to an overhead arc.
5. Turn head and fix eyes on backboard as ball is crossed over body.
6. Raise free arm (nonshooting) with elbow bent to help protect the ball.
7. Release ball with snap of the wrist when arm is extended.
8. Follow through in the direction of the basket.

FREE THROW

1. Stand with knees slightly bent and body loose with shooting foot pointed at basket.
2. Pull shooting elbow in above the hip.

3. Hold the ball in both hands.
4. Raise the ball to the level for sighting over the top (ball obscures most of net) and cock wrist.
5. Begin thrust from legs and move up through the body as the arm is extended.
6. Release the ball so it rolls off three fingers (thumb, index, middle).
7. Follow through with arm fully extended in a straight line.

PIVOTING

1. Stand with weight evenly distributed on both feet.
2. Hold ball in both hands with elbows out to protect ball.
3. Keep pivot foot in contact with the floor.
4. Turn in any direction on pivot foot.
5. Move nonpivoting foot in any direction.

GUARDING

1. Stand in stride position with weight on balls of feet.
2. Flex ankles, knees, and hips (slightly crouched position).
3. Keep head up.
4. Place one hand high to defend shot and one hand low to defend pass; both hands low to guard against dribbler.
5. Stay between opponent and basket.
6. Keep eyes on opponent's midsection.

JUMP BALL

1. Stand with flexed knees.
2. Keep eyes on the ball at all times.
3. Push off from toes and arch back.
4. Extend body.
5. Tip the ball with one hand.
6. Land on balls of feet, flexing ankles and knees.

REBOUND

1. Stand with feet apart.
2. Push off from toes with both hands reaching up.
3. Pull the ball out of the air.
4. Land with feet apart and parallel.

MAN-TO-MAN DEFENSE

1. Keep eyes on player s/he is guarding, not on the ball.
2. Stay at arm's length distance from person being guarded.
3. Guard only this person.

ZONE DEFENSE

1. Stand in designated area.
2. Move with the offense and the ball.
3. Stay in area.

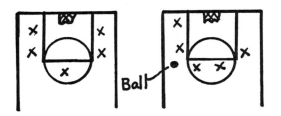

BASKETBALL DRILLS

■ Dribbling Drills

Skills: Dribbling

Supplies: One basketball per group

Formation: Varies according to the drill

Description: Each drill is described individually

ONE-KNEE DRIBBLE

1. Have players kneel on one knee and dribble the ball with the same hand as the kneeling knee.
2. VARIATIONS:

   a. Move the ball backward and forward while kneeling.

   b. Move the ball around the front of the opposite leg and change hands.

   c. Move the ball under your leg and change to the other hand.

DIRECTION DRIBBLE

1. The teacher stands in front and directs the class.
2. Give various directions: "Dribble right," "Dribble left," "Dribble forward," "Dribble any direction."

WEAVE DRIBBLE

1. Have each squad spread their line out.
2. The first player dribbles around each player and back to original place.

3. The ball is given to the next player and the first player goes to the end of the line.
4. Repeat until all have had a turn.

WHISTLE DRIBBLE

1. First player in each line has a ball.
2. First player begins dribbling at the single whistle blow.
3. At the double whistle blow, the player stops and dribbles in place.
4. VARIATIONS:
   a. Use hand signals instead of a whistle (hand up—dribble; hand down—stop). This forces player to keep head up.
   b. Use hands to have players stop and pivot by extending arm to the right or left to indicate pivoting.

LINE DRIBBLE

1. Have squads stand single file, each with a ball.
2. Set up a cone a distance away from the line.
3. One at a time, each player dribbles to the cone, around and back to the line.

CONE DRIBBLE

1. Have each squad line up single file with a ball.
2. Set up three or more cones in front of each line about 5 feet apart.
3. One at a time, each player dribbles down weaving in and out of the cones and back.

Note: When dribbling, the player should always be between the ball and the cone, changing hands to dribble.

DRIBBLE, PIVOT, PASS

1. Have squads line up in single file lines, each with a ball.
2. The first player dribbles to a designated line, stops, pivots, passes to the next person in line (pivots to face squad).
3. The first player goes to the end of the line.
4. Continue until all have had a turn.

DRIBBLE CONTEST

1. Divide the class into four teams, each with a ball.
2. Each team forms a line in a corner of the gym.
3. At the signal, the first player in each line dribbles around the rectangle and back to his line.
4. Continue until all have had a turn.

■ Passing Drills

Skills: Passing, catching

Supplies: One basketball for each group

Formation: Varies according to the drill

Description: Each drill is described under its heading.

PARTNER PASSING

1. Have two squads facing each other.
2. Give the first player in one line a ball.
3. After teaching them how to pass, have them practice the pass.
4. Player 1 in one line passes the ball to player 1 in the opposite line.
5. Player 1 who has just received the ball passes it to player 2 in the first line.
6. Continue passing and catching down the two lines.

TRIANGLE DRILL

1. Divide class into groups of four to eight players each.
2. Each group has a ball.
3. The players line up single file, and two players go out to form a triangle.

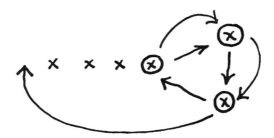

4. The ball begins at the head of the line.
5. The player with the ball passes it to the player who is straight across from him/her (shown by dotted arrows).
6. As each player passes, s/he moves to the spot to which s/he passed (shown by solid arrows).
7. Continue until all players have had a turn at each position.

THREE-PLAYER WEAVE

1. Three players are lined up side by side with space between them.
2. The center player is given a ball.
3. All players start running forward.

4. The center player passes the ball to one of the other players.
5. Always go behind the player to whom you threw the ball.

6. As soon as you've gone behind and around the player, go diagonally across the floor until you receive a pass.
7. Continue down the court and back; then the next three people go.

THINK PASS

1. Have each squad stand side by side with one player a distance away facing them with a ball (passer).
2. The passer begins by using a chest pass to each player in the group.
3. Then the teacher calls out another kind of pass and the passer must alternate the passes.
4. The teacher keeps adding passes and the passer must follow the sequence.
5. When the passer makes the wrong pass, a new passer comes out and the game starts over.

CIRCLE PASS

1. Have each group form a circle with space between each player.
2. The teacher calls out the type of pass to practice.
3. Players pass to anyone in the circle, trying not to exclude anyone.

■ Shooting Drills

Skills: Shooting

Supplies: One basketball for each group

Formation: Varies according to the drill

Description: Each drill is described under its heading.

BASKET SHOOTING

1. Divide the class into as many groups as you have baskets.
2. Have the groups line up single file behind the free throw line with one player at the end line under the basket.
3. The first player in line dribbles toward the basket and attempts a shot.

4. At the same time, the player on the end line moves forward to guard the basket.
5. Both players attempt to get the rebound.
6. Whoever retrieves the ball passes it to the next player.
7. The end line player goes to the end of the shooting line and the shooter goes to the end line.

SET SHOT

1. Divide the class into as many groups as you have baskets.
2. Have each group form a semicircle facing the basket.
3. One player (leader) stands under the basket with a ball.
4. The leader passes the ball to the first player in the semicircle who attempts a set shot.
5. The leader recovers the ball and passes to player 2.
6. This continues until all players in the semicircle have shot.
7. Change leaders and repeat.
8. Change type of shot if you choose.

LAY-UP

1. Arrange two lines at angles to the basket and behind the free throw line.
2. One line is the shooting line, and one line is the retrieving line.
3. The first player in the shooting line dribbles toward the basket and attempts a lay-up.
4. At the same time the first player in the retrieving line moves to retrieve the ball and passes it to the next player in the shooting line.
5. Retriever goes to the end of the shooting line and the shooter goes to the end of the retrieving line.

FILE AND LEADER

1. Divide the class so there are two groups at each basket.
2. The first player in each group goes out to be the leader.
3. The first player in line has the ball and is the shooter. The shooter passes the ball to the leader and then moves to a shooting spot (anywhere).
4. The leader passes the ball back to the shooter who then shoots the ball.
5. The leader goes to the end of the shooting line and the shooter becomes the leader.
6. Continue until all have had a chance to be the shooter and leader.

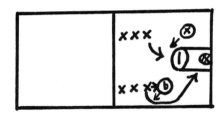

■ Offensive and Defensive Drills

Skills: Guarding, pivoting, dribbling, passing

Supplies: One basketball for each group

Formation: Varies according to the drill

Description: Each drill is described under its heading.

ONE ON ONE

1. Have two lines face each other.
2. One line has the ball.
3. The first player in the line with the ball begins dribbling.
4. The first player in the opposite line moves out to attempt to steal the ball.
5. Players go to the end of the opposite line.
6. The ball is returned to the line that started with the ball.
7. Repeat until all players have had an opportunity to dribble and attempt to steal the ball.

GROUP DEFENSIVE DRILL

1. Class is scattered on the court facing the leader.
2. The class assumes defensive position.
3. The leader will call out commands (right, left, forward, backward), and the players move accordingly.
4. The leader has a ball and dribbles moving forward, backward, and side to side. The defensive players move accordingly.

OFFENSE-DEFENSE DRILL WITH POST

1. Divide the class up according to how many baskets are available.
2. The drill consists of an offensive player, defensive player, and a post player.
3. The post player is stationary and receives the ball from and passes to the offensive player.
4. The offensive player tries to move around the defensive player and shoot.
5. After a shot has been attempted, rotate players.

■ Basketball Station Tasks

Skills: Passing, catching, dribbling, shooting

Supplies: One basketball for each station; at the wall pass station have one ball per student

Formation: Divide the class into four groups and assign each group a station to start at.

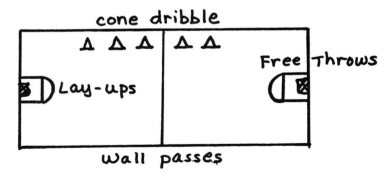

Description: This is a great independent activity to do after practicing skills and before lead-up games. Explain the tasks for each station. Assign each group a station and have them begin. After a designated period of time have them move to another station. Continue until all students have been at each station.

BASKETBALL LEAD-UP GAMES

■ Basketball Flag Dribble

Skills: Controlled dribbling

Supplies: A basketball for each student, a flag for each student

Formation: Divide the class into groups of eight to ten players each. Have as many groups play at a time as space will allow. The players have a ball and have a flag tucked in at the waist. Players start in a personal space.

Description: This is a great activity for practicing controlled dribbling. At the signal, the players begin to dribble. The object of the game is for the players to eliminate the other players by pulling their flags. A player is eliminated if s/he loses control of the ball (traveling, double dribbling, and so forth). When only one player is left, the next group comes in.

■ Basket Baseball

Skills: Passing, catching, shooting, teamwork

Supplies: Basketball, four bases, one basket

Formation: Divide the class in half. One team is the batting team, and one team is the fielding team. Each team is numbered consecutively.

Description: This is a fun game for practicing teamwork as well as shooting under pressure. Player 1 on the batting team throws the ball and runs all the bases. Player 1 on the fielding team gets near the basket. The rest of the fielding team is spread out on their half of the floor.
The fielding team retrieves the ball and passes it to their player 1 who attempts to shoot a basket. If the fielder makes a basket before the batter gets home, the batter

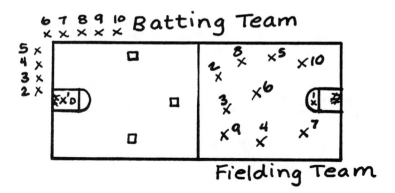

is out. If the batter makes it home before the fielder makes a basket, s/he scores a run.

Continue with the remaining players on both teams. After all players have gone, the teams change sides.

■ Basket-O-Rama

Skills: Shooting, rebounding

Supplies: A basketball for every two students at each basket

Formation: Have two groups at each basket. Students are paired up and each pair is given a ball.

Description: This is a fantastic activity for developing your students' ability to perform in a game situation. There will be four students at each basket. The first two players shoot as rapidly as possible using any type of shot. The player who makes five baskets is the winner and their game is over. The next two players do the same thing. Have each group play several games.

VARIATION: Focus on specific shots for each game (jump shots, lay-ups, and so forth).

■ Basketball Bowl

Skills: Rolling with accuracy, passing, catching, shooting

Supplies: A basketball per team; Indian club or bowling pin per team.

Formation: Divide the class into four teams and set them up as diagrammed. Two teams play against each other, so there are two games going on at one time.

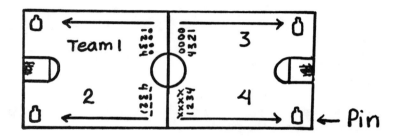

Description: This game adds a different twist to practicing the skills of passing and shooting. The first player on each team rolls the basketball toward his/her pin. The first player to knock down the pin begins shooting baskets, while the opposing player retrieves his ball, goes to his/her team and makes a chest pass to each of the team members. Then they sit down. When this is done, the player shooting baskets stops. Two points are scored for each basket made.

If both players miss the pin when they roll the ball, they retrieve it, run back to their line and roll it again. They keep doing this until one of them knocks the pin down. Then it is the second player's turn. This continues until all players have had a turn.

■ Five Passes

Skills: Passing, catching

Supplies: A basketball

Formation: Divide the class into groups of five players each. Have two teams spread out on the floor. Have two opposing players start the game with a jump ball.

Description: This game is great for focusing on passing with accuracy. The object of the game is to make five complete passes in a row. There is no dribbling or moving with the ball. When the passes begin, they must be counted out loud. The ball may not be thrown back to the player who just passed it. A great cooperative way to play is to have each person on a team receive a pass so that each person gets the ball during the five passes. If the pass is intercepted or missed, the count begins again with the team that gained possession of the ball.

■ End Ball Basketball

Skills: Passing, catching, intercepting, guarding

Supplies: Two basketballs, one for each team

Formation: Divide the class in half. Choose four to six players from each team to play in the end zone, with the rest of the players spread out on the floor.

Description: This game is great for practicing passing with accuracy. The object of the game is for each team to pass their ball to one of its end zone players, while the other team tries to intercept the passes.

The game starts with one of the end zone players on each team in possession of the ball. The end zone players try to pass it to a fielder. Fielders work the ball down the court using passing to get it to one of their end zone players. If an end zone player catches the ball in the air in the end zone, a point is scored. After every five points, the end zone players rotate with the fielders.

■ Basketball Relay

Skills: Passing, catching, shooting

Supplies: Two basketballs, two baskets

Formation: Divide the class in half and place one team side by side along one sideline, and the other team along the other sideline. Each team is assigned a basket. Two balls are placed in the center.

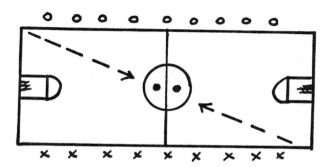

Description: This game is great for practicing quick, yet accurate passes as well as controlled dribbling and shooting. At the signal, the first player in line from each team runs to the center, gets a basketball, dribbles back to his line and chest passes to each player on his team. When he gets to the last player, he dribbles to his basket and shoots until he makes a basket. Once he has made a basket he dribbles the ball back to the center, sets the ball down, and goes to the end of his line. Then the next player in line does the same thing. This continues until all players on the team have had a turn. The team that finishes first wins.

■ Three-On-Three Basketball

Skills: Passing, catching, dribbling, guarding

Supplies: A basketball for each basket

Formation: Divide the class into groups of three players each. Set the groups up according to how many courts you have available.

Description: This game is great for practicing basketball skills in small groups. It is an activity that provides more opportunity for participation.
The offensive team on each half of the court lines up at the center line facing the basket they will be shooting at. The defensive team lines up near the free throw line. The "waiting" teams line up behind the end out-of-bounds line.

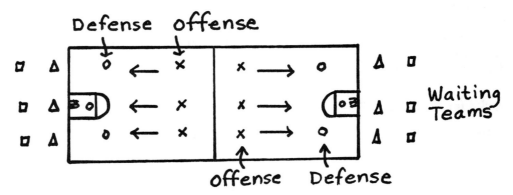

The game starts with the center player on each offensive team in possession of the ball. The object of the game is for the offensive team to move the ball down the court and attempt to score, while the defensive team attempts to steal the ball. The scrimmage is over when the offensive team scores or when the defensive team steals the ball.

In rotating, the defensive team becomes the offense; the offensive team goes to the end of the "waiting" line; the first waiting team becomes the defense. This continues until all teams have had a turn at offense and defense.

■ Line Basketball

Skills: Passing, catching, dribbling, shooting, teamwork

Supplies: A basketball

Formation: Divide the class in half and line each half up along the two sidelines. Have each side count off consecutively.

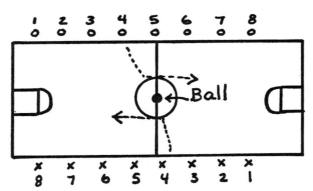

Description: Adding one player at a time is a great way to build on the use of skills in a game situation. With one on one only dribbling and shooting are used. As more players enter the game, passing is added. The object of the game is to use individual skills, and later teamwork to get the ball down the court and score.

A number is called, and the player with that number from each side runs out and tries to gain possession of the ball. Whoever gains possession of the ball begins dribbling toward his/her basket and attempts to score. The opposing player attempts to steal the ball and dribble toward the other basket. When a basket is made, the ball goes back to the center and the players go back to their places. This continues until all players have had a turn.

After calling one number at a time, call two numbers at a time and make the rule that players must pass with their teammates before they can attempt to score. Then call three numbers at a time. Continue this until you have done four numbers at a time. Then move on to regulation basketball.

TEACHING HINTS
FOR FLOOR/FIELD HOCKEY

1. I suggest Floor/Field Hockey for grades 3–6, but it can be adapted to grades 1 and 2 by teaching basic skills and playing such select lead-up games as Line Hockey.
2. Floor hockey is played indoors with hockey sticks and a puck. Field hockey is played outdoors with hockey sticks and a whiffle ball.
3. A few hints for skills:
   a. Dribbling
      1. Use short, controlled taps with one side of the stick (stand to the side of the puck/ball) or both sides of the stick (stand facing the puck/ball so it is in line with the middle of the space between your legs).
      2. Keep your stick between the puck/ball and your opponent.
   b. Passing and receiving
      1. Hit the puck/ball just so it gets to your teammate (not too hard, not too soft).
      2. If a pass is coming fast and hard, contact the puck/ball with your stick and "give" with the stick (bring it slightly back after contact).
4. Teach no high-sticking (not lifting the stick above waist level—preferably not above knee level).
5. When doing lead-up games, have as many games going as possible. The more games, the more active the students will be.
6. Teach students the rules and how to call their own rule infractions so they can learn to be independent of constant teacher intervention. This allows for more than one game to go on at a time, which then provides for maximum student involvement. This also teaches students to be honest about their "mistakes."
7. See the soccer chapter for additional lead-up games adaptable to hockey.

GLOSSARY OF FLOOR/FIELD HOCKEY TERMS

Dodging: a means of evading a tackler while maintaining control of puck/ball.

Dribbling: controlled means of moving the puck/ball along the ground with hockey stick.

Driving: used to pass a moderate or long distance and for shooting goals.

Face-off: method of putting ball/puck into play at the start of the game and after a goal has been scored.

Fielding: receiving and gaining control of the puck/ball.

Goalkeeping: the act of guarding the goal.

Grip: holding the stick properly; a fundamental hockey skill.

High-sticking: a violation; bringing the stick above waist level.

Passing: a short, quick hit to send the puck/ball to a teammate.

Scoop shot: used to lift the ball slightly off the ground to dodge an opponent, pass, or shoot ball into corner of goal.

Tackling: a means of taking the puck/ball away from an opponent.

Suggested Floor/Field Hockey Skills Sequence

GRADE 3	GRADE 4	GRADE 5	GRADE 6
DRIBBLING Use one side of the stick	DRIBBLING Use one side of the stick Introduce using two sides of the stick	DRIBBLING Use two sides of the stick	DRIBBLING Use two sides of the stick
Drills Single Dribble Obstacle Dribble	*Drills* Single Dribble Obstacle Dribble	*Drills* Forward, Left, Right Dribble Speed and Controlled Dribbling	*Drills* Forward, Left, Right Dribble Speed and Controlled Dribbling
PASSING *Drills* Partner Goal Pass Put Dribble and Pass Together	PASSING *Drills* Partner Goal Pass Partner Quick Pass Partner Dribble and Pass	PASSING *Drills* Partner Quick Pass Moving Pass Pass, Field, Dribble Partner Dribble and Pass	PASSING *Drills* Partner Quick Pass Moving Pass Pass, Field, Dribble Partner Dribble and Pass

Suggested Floor/Field Hockey Skills Sequence (Cont.)

GRADE 3	GRADE 4	GRADE 5	GRADE 6
DODGING *Drills* Shuttle Dodge			
	DODGE & TACKLE *Drills* Shuttle Dodge One vs. One Tackle	DODGE & TACKLE *Drills* One vs. One Tackle Two vs. Two Tackle	DODGE & TACKLE *Drills* One vs. One Tackle Two vs. Two Tackle
SHOOTING *Drills* No-Goalie Shooting	SHOOTING *Drills* One vs. One	SHOOTING *Drills* Two vs. One	SHOOTING *Drills* Two vs. One
		OTHER Positioning	OTHER Positioning
LEAD-UP GAMES Circle Keepaway Hockey Circle Race Line Hockey	LEAD-UP GAMES Line Hockey Cooperative Hockey	LEAD-UP GAMES Line Hockey Sideline Hockey Cooperative Hockey	LEAD-UP GAMES Line Hockey Sideline Hockey Cooperative Hockey

TASK ANALYSIS OF FLOOR/FIELD HOCKEY SKILLS

GRIP AND CARRY

1. Grasp the stick in the middle with preferred hand.
2. Grasp the top of the stick with nonpreferred hand, thumb pointing down to the blade.
3. Place the blade on the floor.
4. Carry the stick with the blade close to the ground while running.
5. Keep the stick at or below waist level.

DRIBBLING

1. Give a series of short taps in the desired direction.
2. Dribble slightly to the right or left of the feet.

3. Make this movement come from the shoulders rather than the wrists.
4. Rotate wrists, rather than change grip when dribbling with both sides of the stick.

DRIVING

1. Move hands closer together on stick when approaching puck/ball.
2. Point nonpreferred shoulders in desired direction of puck/ball.
3. Keep head over puck/ball.
4. Swing arms back.
5. Bring arms forward and downward.
6. Contact ball off nonpreferred foot.
7. Follow through low and in direction of hit.

SCOOP SHOT

1. Lean forward with preferred foot in front.
2. Tilt stick back.
3. Place stick under puck/ball.
4. Make a strong lifting, shovel-like action with preferred arm.

FIELDING

1. Place the stick at a right angle to the direction of the oncoming puck/ball.
2. Loosen grip slightly as the puck/ball impacts the stick to absorb the impact of the puck/ball.
3. Contact the puck/ball as far away from body as possible to allow the force to be absorbed over the greatest distance.
4. Gain control of the puck/ball.

TACKLING

1. Move toward opponent with eyes on ball.
2. Lean body forward.
3. Have weight evenly distributed on both feet.
4. Keep the blade of the stick held low to the ground.
5. Place the blade of stick against puck/ball when it is off opponent's stick.
6. Quickly dribble or pass puck/ball in the direction of the goal.

DODGING

1. Attempt to move ball past opponent.
2. Push the ball to one side of the opponent.
3. Run around to the other side.

4. Pick up own pass.
5. Time the pass so as to prevent the opponent from gaining possession.

FACE-OFF

1. Stand on one side of the puck/ball with opponent on the other side.
2. Place the blade of stick on the ground.
3. Lift stick at same time as opponent and touch sticks above puck/ball.
4. Touch the ground next to ball.
5. Repeat steps 3 and 4 three times.
6. Play the puck/ball after the third hit.

GOALKEEPING

1. Stand in front of the goal line and move between goal posts.
2. Move in front of the puck/ball when it is hit toward the goal.
3. Block the puck/ball with any part of body.
4. Gain control of the puck/ball.
5. Pass the puck/ball to a teammate immediately.

FLOOR/FIELD HOCKEY DRILLS

■ Dribbling Drills

Skills: Dribbling
Supplies: A puck/ball per group, a hockey stick per group
Formation: Varies according to the drill
Description: Each drill is described under its heading.

SINGLE DRIBBLE

1. At the signal, the first player in each line dribbles to a designated line and back.
2. This is repeated until each player has had a turn or the teacher signals the end of the drill.

FORWARD, LEFT, RIGHT DRIBBLE

1. At the signal, the first player in each line dribbles to a designated line and back.
2. Give directions as the player dribbles forward; to the right; to the left.
3. Repeat until all have had a turn.

OBSTACLE DRIBBLE

1. Set up three to five cones in front of each squad line with some distance between each cone.
2. At the signal, the first player begins dribbling, weaving in and out of the cones and back.
3. Repeat until all have had a turn.

SPEED AND CONTROLLED DRIBBLING

1. At the signal, the first player will begin walking then jogging, then running while dribbling to a designated point and back.
2. If player loses control, s/he should slow down.
3. This is repeated until all have had a turn.

■ Passing and Fielding Skills

Skills: Passing, fielding

Supplies: A puck/ball for each group, a hockey stick for each group, cones, targets

Formation: Varies according to the drill

Description: Each drill is described under its heading.

TARGET PASS

1. Put up a target on a wall for each squad.
2. At the signal, the first player passes the puck/ball and attempts to hit the target.
3. The player runs down, picks up the puck/ball, and runs it back.
4. The player gives the equipment to the next player in line.
5. This continues until all have had a turn.

PARTNER QUICK PASS

1. Divide each squad in half, having them line up in single file lines facing each other.

X X X   X X X

(Shuttle Formation -   5   3   1   2   4   6)

2. At the signal, player 1 passes to player 2 who fields it and immediately passes back to player 1.
3. Emphasize an immediate pass after the field.
4. Players 1 and 2 go to the end of their lines.
5. Continue drill with remaining players.
6. For an added challenge, have students make as many passes as they can in a limited time.

PARTNER GOAL PASS

1. Divide the squads in half, having them line up in single file lines facing each other.

× × ×   × × ×

(Shuttle Formation -   5 3 1   2 4 6) ▲

× × ×   × × ×

(5 3 1 ▲ 2 4 6)

2. Set up a goal between each squad half.
3. At the signal, player 1 passes the puck/ball between the cones (goal) to player 2.
4. Player 2 passes between the cones (goal) to player 1.
5. Players 1 and 2 go to the end of their lines.
6. Continue with remaining players.

MOVING PASS

1. Divide the squads in half, having the two halves stand side-by-side with distance in between them.

X X X — — — — —

X X X ↓ ↑ ↓ ↑ ↓

2. At the signal, the first two players in line begin moving the puck/ball down the floor to a designated line by passing only.
3. They do the same coming back then go to the end of their lines.
4. This is repeated until all partners have had a turn.

PASS, FIELD, DRIBBLE

1. Have squads stand in the same way as in the moving pass drill.
2. At the signal, the first two players in line begin moving down the floor with partners passing, fielding, dribbling, passing.
3. They repeat the same coming back, then go to the end of their line.
4. This is repeated until all partners have had a turn.

■ Dodging and Tackling Skills

Skills: Tackling, dodging

Supplies: Pucks/balls, hockey sticks, cones

Formation: Varies according to the drill

Description: Each drill is described under its heading.

SHUTTLE DODGE

1. Divide the squads in half and have them line up single file, facing each other.

2. At the signal, player 1 dribbles to the cone (simulated defensive player), dodges around it and passes to player 2.
3. Player 1 goes to the end of player 2's line.
4. Player 2 dribbles to the cone, dodges around it, and passes to player 3.
5. This continues until all have had a turn or teacher signals the end of the drill.
6. VARIATION: Have a player stand in place of the cone.

ONE vs. ONE TACKLE

1. Divide the squads in half and have them line up in shuttle formation.
2. Player 1 dribbles toward player 2 who attempts to tackle.
3. Player 1 goes to the end of player 2's line, and player 2 goes to the end of player 1's line.
4. This continues until all have had a turn or teacher signals to stop.

TWO vs. TWO TACKLE

1. Divide squads in half and have them line up single file, side-by side.
2. Have one squad line up facing another.

```
      5  3  1      1  3  5
      X  X  X.    X  X  X
  offense
      X  X  X      X  X  X
      6  4  2      2  4  6
```

3. At the signal, players 1 and 2 in the offensive line (line with the ball) begin moving the puck/ball by dribbling and passing.
4. Players 1 and 2 in the defensive line attempt to take the puck/ball away.
5. Then the players that were playing offense go to the end of the defense line, and defense players go to the end of the offense line.
6. This continues until all have had a chance to be offense and defense.

■ Shooting Skills

Skills: Shooting

Supplies: Pucks/balls, hockey sticks, cones

Formation: Varies according to the drill

Description: Each drill is described under its heading.

NO-GOALIE SHOOTING

1. Have each squad get in a semi-circle facing their goal.

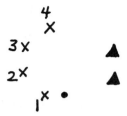

2. At the signal, player 1 starts with the ball and attempts to shoot it through the goal.
3. Player 1 retrieves the ball and gives it to player 2 who does the same as player 1.
4. This continues until all have had a turn at shooting.

ONE vs. ONE

1. Squads in single file line, each with a goal, and goalie.

2. At the signal, player 1 dribbles the puck/ball toward the goal and attempts to shoot a goal.
3. Player 1 becomes the goalie, and the goalie goes to the end of the line.
4. Player 2 repeats steps 2 and 3.
5. This continues until all players have had a chance to shoot and be goalie.

TWO vs. ONE

1. Divide the squads in half and have them stand in single file lines side-by-side facing their goal.

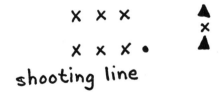

shooting line

2. One line is designated as the shooting line.
3. Partners dribble and pass toward their goal and then the player from the shooting line attempts to shoot a goal.
4. Rotation: Player who shot becomes the goalie; partner (one who didn't shoot) goes to the end of the shooting line; goalie goes to the end of the nonshooting line.
5. This continues until all have shot and been goalie.

FLOOR/FIELD HOCKEY LEAD-UP GAMES

■ Circle Keepaway

Skills: Passing, fielding

Supplies: A puck/ball for each group, a hockey stick for each player

Formation: Divide the class into groups of six students each. Have each group form a circle with one player in the center.

Description: This game is great for passing and fielding skills. The object of this game is to keep the player in the center from touching the puck/ball. At the signal, the puck/ball is passed back and forth among team members with emphasis on accurate passing and controlled fielding skills. The player in the center attempts to intercept the puck/ball. If the center player touches the puck/ball, the player who last passed the puck/ball, takes the place of the center player. Continue this for a designated period of time. NOTE: This game can be used as a drill for passing and fielding skills.

■ Hockey Circle Race

Skills: Controlled dribbling

Supplies: A hockey stick and a puck/ball for each group

Formation: Divide the class into groups of six students each. Have each group form a circle.

Description: This game emphasizes speed and control. The object is to dribble the puck/ball around the circle as quickly as possible and yet with control. At the signal, the first player dribbles the puck/ball around the outside of the circle and back to his/her place. S/he then gives the stick and puck/ball to player 2 who does the same. This continues until all have had a turn to dribble. NOTE: This game can be used as a drill for dribbling skills.

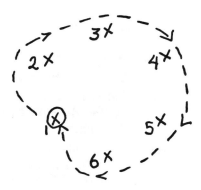

■ Line Hockey

Skills: Dribbling, passing, shooting, dodging, tackling, fielding, teamwork

Supplies: A puck/ball, hockey sticks, four cones for goals

Formation: Divide the class in half and have each half line up along a sideline. The puck/ball and hockey sticks are laid in the center (Two sticks for one vs. one; four sticks for two vs. two; six sticks for three vs. three; and eight sticks for four vs. four). Number students in each half and assign each half a goal and a color of stick.

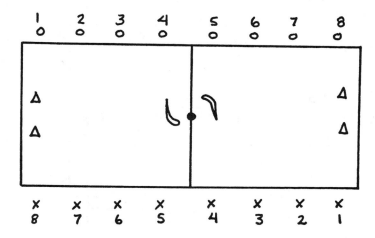

Description: This activity is great for building on skills. Begin with one versus one. When you call a number, the player from each half with that number runs out, picks up a stick, and dribbles toward his/her goal. The opposing player attempts to steal

the puck/ball. When a goal is scored, the equipment goes back to the center, and the players go back to their lines. Then call two numbers at a time (players must dribble and pass with teammates before they can attempt to score). When you call three and four numbers at a time, the last number you call goes to the goal as goalie. The remaining players are forwards who use teamwork to score.

■ Sideline Hockey

Skills: Dribbling, passing, fielding, dodging, tackling, shooting, teamwork

Supplies: A puck/ball, a hockey stick for each player, four cones for goals

Formation: Divide the class in half and have each half line up along a sideline. Have four players from each team go out on the floor on their half. These are the active players. The sideline players help by passing the ball/puck to their active players.

Description: This game is a way to use all players, yet with only a few on the floor at a time. This focuses on total teamwork. The game is started with a face-off in the center, and there is a face-off after each goal. The active players change after each goal or after a designated period of time.

■ Cooperative Hockey

Skills: Dribbling, passing, shooting, tackling, dodging, fielding, teamwork

Supplies: A puck/ball, twelve hockey sticks, four cones for goals

Formation: Divide the class into teams of six players each. There are one center forward and two side forwards who can go everywhere and attempt to score goals; two backs who can only go to the center line and help guard the goal and pass to their forwards; and one goalie who can use any part of his/her body to stop the puck/ball from going in the goal.

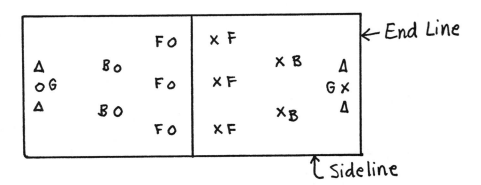

Description: This game is a favorite because it focuses on teamwork. All forwards on a team must dribble and pass with each other before they can attempt to score. All players on a team must score for a team to win.

The game begins with a face-off between the two center forwards. When a goal is scored, the puck/ball goes back to the center for a face-off. Some rules:

1. If the puck/ball goes out of bounds at the sideline, the team who did not hit it out, hits it in. (You do not need to use sidelines for floor hockey if you have a small gym.)
2. If the puck/ball goes out on the end line the goalie gets it and hits it in. (You do not have to use this rule if the gym is small.)
3. The stick must stay at least below waist level (Encourage below knee level). If a player brings it above waist level it is a penalty and the player must sit out for one minute while the team plays short-handed.

Change front and back players after a designated period of time so all players have an opportunity to score.

TEACHING HINTS
FOR FOOTBALL

1. Football is recommended for 4–6 grades only.
2. Use junior size footballs.
3. Play flag football rather than touch football.
4. Play with smaller teams so that each student has a greater opportunity to have contact time with the ball.
5. Rotate all positions frequently so each player can experience the skills required for each position.
6. For sidelines use jump ropes to mark the boundaries; for the end lines use cones.
7. If you are forced inside due to inclement weather, use foam footballs. You can practice the skills in relay formation and some of the lead-up games for indoors (Touchdown Keepaway and Deflagging Game, for example).
8. A few hints on skills:
   a. Passing and receiving
      1. Place the throwing hand on the football with the fingers slightly spread, contacting the laces with the fingers (this varies from person to person).
      2. Decide whether you throw best with your hand in the middle of the ball or nearer the point closest to your ear.
      3. When you receive the ball, catch with two hands and "give" with your body.
   b. Punting
      1. Hold the ball so the laces are on top.

2. You can hold the ball with:
   a. Two hands, one on each point of the football.
   b. Two hands, thumbs side-by-side on one point of the football.
   c. Two hands, one on one side of the football near the point closest to you, and the other hand on the other side of the ball near the lower point of the ball.
   d. One hand near the point closest to you.
3. Contact the ball with the top of your foot.

9. You do not need to use all the regulation rules; adapt them to suit your situation.
10. Teach the rules and have students learn to call their own rule infractions so they can be independent of constant teacher intervention. This allows for more than one game to go on at a time, providing for maximum student involvement. This also teaches students to be honest about their "mistakes."
11. Set up more than one field so that all students can be active.

Suggested Football Skills Sequence

GRADE 4	GRADE 5	GRADE 6
PASSING 　Forward Pass 　Centering	PASSING 　Forward Pass 　Lateral Pass 　Centering	PASSING 　Forward Pass 　Lateral Pass 　Centering 　Pass Patterns
Drills 　Pass and Receive 　Run, Turn, and Pass 　Target Pass	*Drills* 　Same as grade 4, plus: 　Center, Pass, Receive, 　　and Hand Off 　Center, Pass, Receive, 　　and Defend	*Drills* 　Same as grades 4 and 　　5, plus: 　Pass Patterns
PUNTING *Drills* 　Punt and Receive	PUNTING *Drills* 　Punt and Receive 　Center, Punt, Receive, 　　and Run	PUNTING *Drills* 　Same as grade 5
BALL CARRYING AND DEFLAGGING *Drills* 　Deflagging Drill	BALL CARRYING AND DEFLAGGING *Drills* 　Ball Carry and Defend	BALL CARRYING AND DEFLAGGING *Drills* 　Same as grade 5

Suggested Football Skills Sequence (Cont.)

GRADE 4	GRADE 5	GRADE 6

RULES
  Kick-Off
  Downs
  Off Sides
	RULES
	  Kick-Off
	  Downs
	  Line of Scrimmage
	  Off Sides
	  Blocking
	  Safety
		RULES
		  Kick-Off
		  Downs
		  Off Sides
		  Line of Scrimmage
		  Safety
		  Blocking
		  Positions and Plays

LEAD-UP GAMES
  Touch Down Keepaway
  Quick Pass
  Punt and Catch
  Three Man Football
  Four vs. Four Football
  One Down Football
	LEAD-UP GAMES
	  Same as grade 4, plus:
	  Kickoff Football
	  Football Softball
		LEAD-UP GAMES
		  Same as grades 4 and
		  5

GLOSSARY OF FOOTBALL TERMS

Ball carrier: the person who has possession of the ball.

Blocking: act of impeding the progress of a player.

Centering: passing the ball from the ground to the quarterback to initiate play. (Offensive player is called the center.)

Deflagging: to deflag the ball carrier and stop the offensive play.

Down: a method of starting play after a ball has been stopped.

Fake: a movement designed to deceive the opponent.

First down: first play in a series. A team must gain 10 yards in four or fewer plays to be awarded a first down.

Forward pass: a pass thrown in the direction of the opponent's goal.

Fumble: to drop a ball unintentionally.

Goal line: the line at the end of the field which must be crossed in order to score.

Illegal use of hands: holding or pushing by offensive players.

Interception: to catch a pass intended for a player on the opposing team.

Interference: illegally preventing a pass receiver from catching the ball.

Kickoff: the method of putting the ball into play at the start of the game.

Lateral pass: a pass made sideways or backward. The passer is in front of the receiver.

Offside: when any part of the player's body is ahead of the ball before it is kicked or centered.

Pass: throwing the ball to a teammate during play.

Play: a method conceived by the offensive players to score a touchdown or gain yardage.

Punt: to hold ball in hands, drop it, and kick it before it hits the ground.

Receiver: any player who receives a pass, punt, or kickoff.

Safety: when a defensive player touches the ball carrier in the latter's end zone. This scores two points for the defensive team.

Scrimmage line: the line on which each down begins.

Touchback: when a punted or kicked ball goes into the end zone, or when an intercepted pass is recovered in the end zone by the defense.

Touchdown: occurs when a team has possession of the ball in the end zone of the defending team (six points).

TASK ANALYSIS OF FOOTBALL SKILLS

GRIPPING THE BALL

1. Place the first joint of the middle finger between the first and second cross laces.
2. Place the ring finger on or over the third and fourth laces.
3. Comfortably spread the little finger.
4. Form a "V" with the thumb and index finger.
5. Grip the ball firmly but not too tightly.

FORWARD PASS

1. Stand with weight evenly distributed on both feet, opposite foot to throwing arm forward and pointing in the direction of the throw.
2. Hold the ball with both hands.
3. Shift the ball back past the ear, guiding it with the nonthrowing hand, and rotate the body away from the throw.
4. Keep the elbow of the throwing arm high and away from the body.
5. Extend the nonthrowing hand out for counterbalance just before the beginning of the pass.

6. Stride forward with the front foot as the ball starts forward and shoulders and hips are rotated.
7. Lead with the elbow on the throw.
8. Snap the wrist and fingers forward and outward on the release.
9. Follow through in the direction of the intended flight.

LATERAL PASS

1. Stand with feet spread apart.
2. Hold the ball with two hands at about stomach level.
3. Shift the ball to the opposite side of the intended throw.
4. Bring the ball across the body and release it about waist high.
5. Pass the ball sideways or backwards with an underhand toss.
6. Follow through with arms and body in the direction of the throw.

CENTERING

STANCE AND GRIP

1. Place the ball on the ground ahead of the shoulders.
2. Stand in a wide straddle with knees bent and body weight forward.
3. Place the dominant hand on the ball as in passing.
4. Place the nondominant hand on the opposite side of the ball toward the rear tip.
5. Extend the arms and elbows straight.

HIKING

1. Move the ball with a short slide backward, lifting the ball with a simultaneous rotating of the wrists (turns ball one-half revolution).
2. Keep elbows straight and swing ball upward using the wrists (top hand is power hand, lower hand is guide).
3. Snap the ball so it smacks into the upper receiving hand of the quarterback.
4. Move with both hands going forward to block.

QUARTERBACK'S RECEIVING POSITION

1. Stand with feet shoulder width apart.
2. Place the top of throwing hand against the center's crotch with fingers extended.
3. Fit the lower hand into the curvature of throwing-hand thumb.
4. Receive the snap and bring the ball to stomach.
5. Prepare to run, hand off, pitch out, or pass.

CATCHING

1. Focus eyes on ball and "look" the ball into hands.

2. Position hands together so that:
   a. little fingers are together, fingers pointed down for low balls, up for high balls.
   b. thumbs together, fingers pointed up for ball coming directly at receiver.
3. Give with hands and arms as ball is caught.
4. Tuck the ball into body gripping the end tightly, placing the forearm on the outside of the ball, and forcing the other end of the ball toward the armpit.
5. Carry the ball in the arm away from the opponent.

STANCE

THREE-POINT STANCE (Offensive Position)

1. Stand with feet shoulder width apart, knees slightly bent with the toe of one foot even with the heel of the other.
2. Place the hand on the side of the foot that is back, forward, with fingertips pressed lightly on the ground.
3. Keep head up with eyes focused straight ahead.

FOUR-POINT STANCE (Defensive Position)

1. Stand with feet shoulder width apart, knees slightly bent, with the toe of one foot even with the heel of the other.
2. Extend the right arm in line with the right foot and the left arm in line with the left foot.
3. Extend the fingers of both hands to contact the ground.

PUNTING

1. Stand with kicking foot slightly forward and weight evenly distributed over both feet.
2. Hold the ball at waist level, laces up, with the kicking-side hand to the rear and side, and with the nonkicking-side hand forward and to the side.
3. Take a short step with kicking foot and natural stride with nonkicking leg.
4. Drop the ball as kicking leg starts forward, toes pointed toward ground and inward.
5. Contact the ball with the top and slightly outer side of the foot, with the kicking leg extended at contact.
6. Extend arms sideways to assist balance.

BLOCKING

1. Stand on his/her feet.
2. Set his/her shoulder against the opponent's shoulder or upper body.
3. Hold hands near the chest with elbows out.
4. Do not use hands when blocking.

HANDOFF

1. Keep eyes straight ahead, maintain proper body angle, while quarterback makes a one-step pivot.
2. Raise inside arm (closest to quarterback) with elbow near shoulder level.
3. Position outside arm at waist level with palm of hand to the inside.
4. Allow the quarterback to give him/her the ball.
5. Squeeze the ball as it hits stomach.
6. Move the ball into carrying position, keeping eyes straight ahead.

POSITION RESPONSIBILITIES

DEFENSIVE POSITIONS

Ends: play on the line. They rush; put pressure on the quarterback; and prevent a runner from going between the end and the sideline.

Tackles: determine whether the play is a pass or a run. If a pass, they backpedal. If a run, they meet the ball carrier at the line of scrimmage to stop the play there.

Cornerbacks: responsible for deep outside part of the field. Stay between the player and the goal.

Safety: covers all deep receivers.

Linebackers: physical and strategic leaders of defense.

OFFENSIVE POSITIONS

Running Backs: block the defense.

Tight End; Tackle; Guards; Split End; Center: offensive linemen; are hard-charging forward wall that blocks the defense.

Quarterback: calls the plays; either passes, runs, or hands off the ball.

FOOTBALL DRILLS

■ Passing Drills

Skills: Passing, receiving, running

Supplies: Footballs, playground balls, cones

Formation: Divide the class into squads of approximately 6 students each.

Description: Each drill is described under its heading.

PASS AND RECEIVE

1. Player 1 passes the ball to player 2, who receives it.
2. Player 2 passes the ball back to player 1, who receives it.
3. Both players 1 and 2 go to the end of their line.
4. This pattern continues until each has had a turn or the teacher signals the class to stop.
5. VARIATION: Challenge students by asking them to pass and receive as many times as they can, without missing, for one minute.

RUN, TURN, AND PASS

1. At the signal, the first player in each squad runs to the designated line, turns around and throws it to the next player.
2. That player catches the ball then does as player 1 did (runs to designated line, turns, and throws it).
3. This continues until all have had a turn.

TARGET PASS AND HIT

1. Player 1 takes the playground ball and moves out to the second cone.
2. Player 2 has the football.
3. Player 1 tosses the playground ball straight up, high in the air, while Player 2 attempts to hit it with the football by throwing a pass.
4. Player 1 goes to the end of the line. Player 2 goes out to toss the playground ball.
5. This continues until all have had a chance to pass and toss.

CENTER, PASS, RECEIVE AND HAND OFF

1. Player 1 takes the ball, moves out to center it (hike it) to the QB Player 2 person behind him/her in line).
2. After player 1 centers the ball, s/he runs out to receive the pass from the quarterback.
3. Player 1 tucks the ball into his body and runs back to his line handing off to player 2 and then goes to the end of the line.
4. Continue the drill until all players have had a chance to play both positions.

```
                    Cone      cone
                     •          •
   X  X  X  X  X  X                    Diagram 1



               QB
   X  X  X  X  X     X - - →            Diagram 2
   6  5  4  3  2      1
```

CENTER, PASS, RECEIVE AND DEFEND

1. The center snaps the ball to the quarterback.
2. As soon as the quarterback has the ball, the receiver runs forward and tries to catch a pass.
3. The defender moves at the same time and tries to intercept the pass.
4. Rotate positions, and continue until all players have played every position.

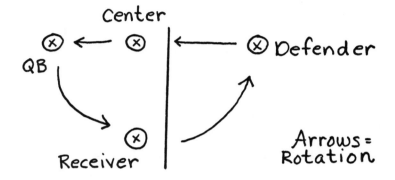

PASS PATTERN PRACTICE

1. Player 1 centers the ball to the player behind him/her and then runs out for a pass, following the designated pass pattern.
2. Player 1 runs the ball back handing off to Player 2 and then goes to the end of the line.
3. This continues until all have tried the pattern; then a new pattern is tried.

PASS PATTERNS

BUTTON HOOK

Run out fast and turn to the: (1) inside; (2) outside.

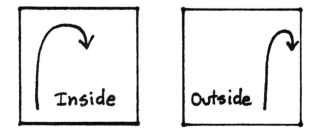

SQUARE OUT

Run straight and then cut sharp left or right, going toward the sideline.

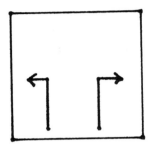

POST PATTERN

Run down 8 yards to 10 yards, then break for the goal.

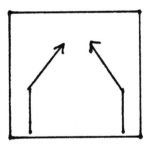

LOOK IN

Take a few steps toward your defender, then cut sharp (45 degrees) toward the center.

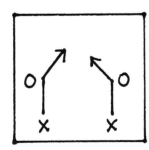

Z-PATTERN (Z Out)

Run straight, then run to the inside, then out.

Z-PATTERN (Z in)

Run straight, then run to the outside, then in.

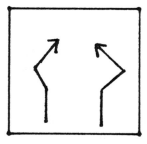

SQUARE OUT AND GO

Run straight, turn toward the sideline, then cut upfield.

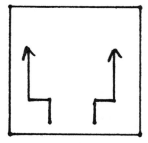

DOWN AND ACROSS

Run straight and then make a sharp turn to the inside.

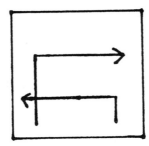

■ Punting Drills

Skills: Punting, receiving, centering, running, dodging, deflagging

Supplies: Footballs, flags

Formation: Varies according to the drill

Description: Each drill is described under its heading.

PUNT AND RECEIVE

1. Divide the class into groups of six students each. Have each group get in a single file line, then have them divide in half (shuttle formation) having their single file lines facing each other.
2. Player 1 punts the ball to player 2 who moves to receive the punt.
3. Player 2 punts to player 1, who moves to receive the punt.
4. Players 1 and 2 go to the end of their lines.
5. This continues until all players have had an opportunity to punt and receive.

CENTER, PUNT, RECEIVE AND RUN

1. Divide the class into groups of five students each. Give each group a football. Position and rotate them as diagrammed (Positions: E=End, K=Kicker, C=Center, R=Receiver).

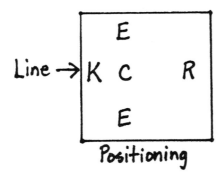

Positioning

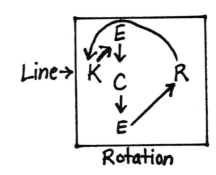

Rotation

2. The object of this drill is for the receiver to catch a punted ball and run to the designated line, while the ends attempt to deflag him/her.

3. The center hikes the ball to the kicker who punts the ball down to the receiver.

4. As soon as the receiver has the ball, the ends start after the receiver to deflag him/her (this gives the receiver a chance).

5. Rotate positions, and continue until all players have played every position.

■ Ball Carrying and Deflagging Drills

Skills: Handoffs, ball carrying, dodging, deflagging

Supplies: Footballs, flags, cones

Formation: Varies according to the drill

Description: Each drill is described under its heading.

HANDOFF

1. Player 1 has the ball, runs with it to player 2 and hands off.
2. Player 1 goes to the end of player 2's line.
3. Player 2 runs to player 3 and hands off.
4. Player 2 goes to the end of player 3's line.
5. This continues until all players have had an opportunity to hand off and receive a handoff.

DEFLAGGING DRILL

1. The first player in each half of each squad line attempts to deflag the player s/he is facing.
2. Once one of the partners has been deflagged, it's the next set of partners' turn.
3. VARIATIONS:

   a. Do in small groups (five or six) with each player acting as an independent trying to deflag all other players. Players are eliminated after being deflagged.

   b. One player attempts to run with the ball to a designated line while the partner tries to deflag the ball carrier. If the ball carrier makes it to the line without being deflagged, s/he gets a point. If the ball carrier is deflagged before s/he gets to the line, his/her partner gets a point.

BALL CARRY AND DEFEND

1. Divide the class into groups of four students each. Have each group set up as diagrammed below.
2. The ball carrier stands at the starting line and three defensive players are stationed in zones marked by cones, facing the ball carrier.
3. The defensive players attempt to deflag the ball carrier while in their zone.

4. After the ball carrier has completed the run, s/he goes to the end of the defender line, rotating into the defending position; the first defender becomes the ball carrier.

5. This continues until all players have had an opportunity to carry the ball.

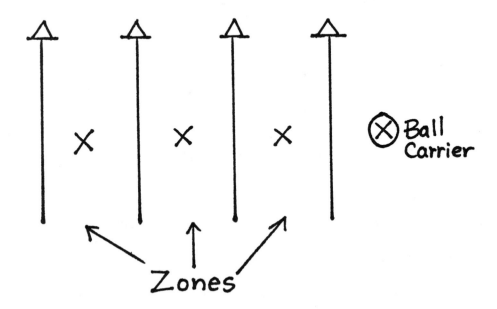

FOOTBALL LEAD-UP GAMES

■ TOUCHDOWN KEEPAWAY

Skills: Passing, receiving, moving to an open space, teamwork

Supplies: One football per game, field markers

Formation: Divide the class into groups of six students each. Have two teams per field. One team is on one half of the field along its goal line, and the other team is on the other half along its goal line. This is the starting position for the beginning of the game and after a touchdown is scored.

Description: This is a fun game which focuses on accurate passing and receiving without running with the ball. Both teams line up side by side along their goal line. One team starts with the ball at its goal line and tries to move across the field past the opposite goal line using passing. A player may not move when in possession of the ball, but must pass, then move. The defensive team attempts to intercept the passes and move the ball toward its goal line. Any ball that touches the ground is dead and goes to the team that recovers it at that spot. Once a touchdown is scored, the players go back to their places, and the game begins again with the team that did not score in possession of the ball. If you have more then one game going on at a time, rotate teams after a designated period of time.

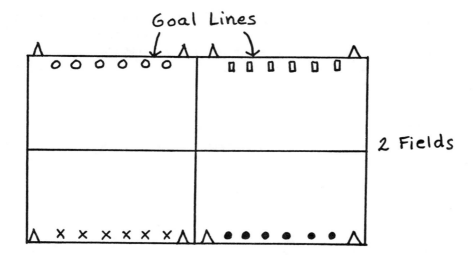

■ Football Basketball

Skills: Passing, receiving, shooting

Supplies: Two footballs

Formation: On a basketball court divide the class in half with one half along one sideline and the other half along the other sideline.

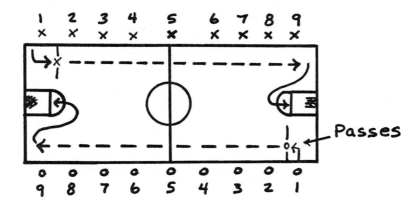

Description: If you are forced indoors due to inclement weather, this game adds a fun twist to practicing passing and receiving skills. One player on each team is the passer and begins moving down his/her line of teammates passing to each player. When s/he gets to the end of the line, s/he takes the football and shoots a basket. After making the basket, the passer passes to the next player on the sideline, and this player repeats the same process. This continues until all players have been the passer. NOTE: The line will need to shift a space each time so the students do not get bunched up. The passer always goes to the end of the line after his/her turn is over.

VARIATION: When shooting a basket, a player gets three tries. As soon as they make it they throw the ball to the next player in line. A team can "win" for being the first team done passing. A team can "win" for scoring the most baskets.

■ Punt and Catch

Skills: Punting, receiving

Supplies: One football per game, field markings

Formation: Divide the class into teams of eight or nine players each. Set up the fields so there are two halves and a neutral zone.

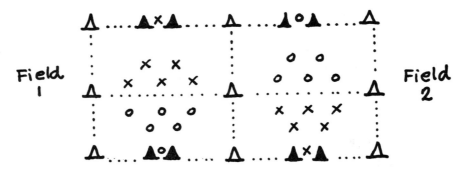

Description: This game involves punting and receiving. One team is in possession of the ball and punts the ball over the neutral zone into the opponent's area. The opponent who is closest to the ball tries to catch it. Whoever catches the ball punts it back. If the punt is missed, the kicking team receives a point. If the ball enters the neutral zone, a member of the opposite team enters the zone to retrieve it.

■ Kickoff Football

Skills: Running, punting, receiving, lateral passing, dodging, deflagging

Supplies: One football per game, flags, field markings

Formation: Divide the class into teams of six to eight players each. Have one team on one side of the field and the other team on the other side.

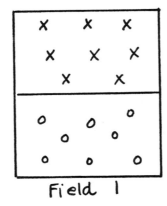

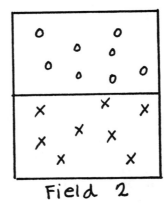

Description: This game provides practice in a variety of football skills. One team kicks off. The object is for the receiver to run with the football as far as s/he can without being deflagged. To avoid being deflagged, the player may use a lateral pass to a teammate. Team members can block for the ball carrier. When the ball carrier is deflagged, the ball is dead, and the other team kicks off.

■ Football Softball

Skills: Passing, receiving, punting, running

Supplies: A football, four bases

Formation: Divide the class in half to make two teams. One team is out in the field, and one team is up to "bat."

Description: This game is adapted from softball. Everything is the same except you use punting and passing instead of batting. One team is out in the field and sets up as in softball (first, second, and third basemen, shortstop, outfielders). The other team lines up to "bat." The first player to "bat" either punts or throws the ball out in the field and runs to first base. The fielders must use a pass to get the ball to the baseman to get a runner out. If the punted or thrown ball is caught in the air, the "batter" is out. "Batters" may not throw the ball to the ground. All players "bat" and then trade with the fielders.

■ Three-Person Football

Skills: Passing, punting, receiving, ball carrying, deflagging

Supplies: One football per game, field markers, flags

Formation: Divide the class into groups of three players each. Each group, two teams (six players) have a ball and a field. All players line up at their goal line.

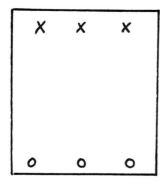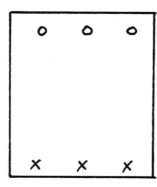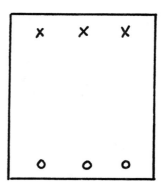

Description: This game is great for focusing on punting, receiving, and ball carrying. It is a favorite because it enables maximum participation. The three players kicking off are the defensive team. One is the punter and the other two are the chasers. Each takes a turn at punting before they become the offensive (receiving) team. When the ball is punted, the punter stays out of the game while the two chasers attempt to deflag the ball carrier.

The offensive team receives the punt and attempts to run to score a touchdown. One is the ball carrier and the other two block the chasers. Each takes a turn at receiving before they become the punting team. The chasers may not run until the receiver picks up the ball. When the ball carrier is deflagged or a touchdown is scored, the ball goes back to the punting team. This continues until all have punted; then the offensive (receiving) team becomes the punting team and the punting team becomes the offensive (receiving) team.

■ Four vs. Four Football

Skills: Passing, receiving, punting, ball carrying, centering

Formation: Divide the class into teams with four players on each team: two linemen, a center, and a quarterback.

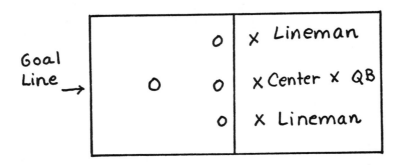

Description: This game is fantastic for modifying flag football down to four players on a team. This provides an opportunity for more participation. The game begins with one team kicking off. The receiver attempts to run past the goal line and score a touchdown. The ball is dead and play stops when:

1. The ball carrier is deflagged.
2. The ball is thrown, kicked, or carried out-of-bounds.
3. There is an incomplete pass.
4. The ball is fumbled.

Wherever the ball is dead is where play begins again, with centering the ball. The offensive team has four plays (downs) to score a touchdown. After four downs, the offensive team kicks off to the defensive team.

■ One-Down Football

Skills: Passing, receiving, centering, dodging

Supplies: A football for each game, field markings, flags

Formation: Divide the class into teams of five to nine players each.

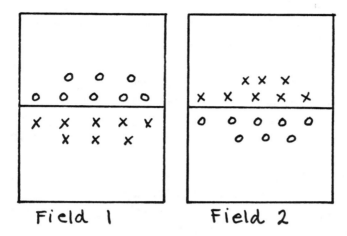

Field 1   Field 2

Description: The purpose of this game is to give teams several opportunities to be the offensive team, because each team has only one play to try to score a touchdown. Play begins at the midfield line with the offensive team centering the ball. After centering the ball, the team may run or pass. The defensive team attempts to deflag the player with the ball. If the defensive team deflags the ball carrier, play begins with his/her team at that spot. After a touchdown is scored, the opposing team starts with the ball at the midfield line.

TEACHING HINTS
FOR GYMNASTICS

1. Review animal walks in relay formation (see chapter 4).
2. Review stunts either in a scattered formation or relay formation (see chapter 4).
3. Set up a single mat for each group of six students and go through the tumbling skills one at a time.

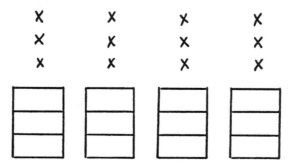

4. Combine tumbling (down the mat) and animal walks (coming back to the line, walking on the floor next to the mat).

5. Teach students how to spot skills in tumbling.

6. If students can do a number of tumbling skills, have them put the skills together in a sequence to create a routine.

7. Rhythmic gymnastics can be used along with, or in place of, another area of gymnastics. Have students make up routines to music and perform them for the class.

8. Divide students up and have some work on tumbling and some on the different areas of rhythmic gymnastics.

9. Have an in-class gymnastics meet where students can perform routines if they choose. Hand out participation awards.

SUGGESTED GYMNASTICS SKILLS SEQUENCE

TUMBLING

ROLLS	BACKBENDS
Log Roll	Bridge
Side Roll	Backbend
Forward Roll	Front Limber
Pike Forward Roll	Front Walkover
Forward Straddle Roll	Back Walkover
Dive Forward Roll	Valdez
Forward Roll to Handstand	
Back Roller	CARTWHEELS
Backward Roll	Cartwheel
Backward Roll to Knee Scale	One-handed Cartwheel
Backward Straddle Roll	Dive Cartwheel
Backward Pike Roll	Round-off
Back Extension	Forward Tinsica
INVERTED BALANCES	SPRINGS
Tripod	Knip-up
Tip-up	Headspring
Headstand	Front Handspring
Handstand	Back Handspring

TASK ANALYSIS OF GYMNASTICS SKILLS

LOG ROLL

1. Lie on back at one end of the mat.
2. Have legs straight and together.
3. Place arms straight overhead.
4. Roll sideways in a straight, smooth, continuous manner to the end of the mat.

Spotting the log roll

1. Spotter may need to help student get in starting position.
2. Spotter may need to give student a push.

SIDE ROLL

1. Lie on back and pull knees to chest.
2. Clasp hands around knees.
3. Lower head to knees.
4. Roll sideways to the end of the mat.

Spotting the side roll

1. Spotter may need to give student a push to get started.

FORWARD ROLL

1. Squat with arms outside of legs.
2. Place hands flat on the mat in front of feet and about shoulder width apart.
3. Tuck head to chest.
4. Lift hips, shifting weight from feet to arms.
5. Push with feet and land on back of neck then shoulders.
6. End in squat position and then stand.

Spotting the forward roll

1. Have student get in position.
2. Place one hand on the back of the student's head to help tuck his/her chin to chest.
3. Place the other hand on the student's bottom to help give a push.
4. As the student begins the roll, help tuck the head and give a push for momentum.

PIKE FORWARD ROLL

1. Assume piked push-up position (hands on mat, chin to chest, legs straight, seat in the air).

2. Lower head to mat and push off with feet.
3. Keep legs straight throughout the roll.
4. Roll to a V-sit position then flex knees and lower feet to the mat.
5. Stand.

Spotting the pike forward roll

1. Kneel to the side of the student's shoulders.
2. Place one hand on the back of the head close to the neck.
3. Place the other hand on the back of the mid-thigh area.
4. Have the student tuck the chin to the chest, bend elbows, and lower self to the mat.
5. As the head contacts the mat, assist in pulling the hips over the head (hand that's on thigh).

FORWARD STRADDLE ROLL

1. Stand in straddle position.
2. Place hands on the mat between the legs.
3. Lean forward and push downward.
4. Lower back of head to mat and push off with feet.
5. Remain straddled and reach for the mat between the legs.
6. Push self to straddle stand.

Spotting the forward straddle roll

1. The student should be able to do a forward roll and do a forward roll starting in a straddle position—the hard part is coming to a stand in a straddle position.
2. Spotter should kneel where the student will come out of the roll.
3. When the student comes out of the roll and places the hands between the legs on the mat, the spotter should grab the close arm with one hand (to stabilize student).
4. The spotter places the other hand on the thigh and lifts forward and upward.

DIVE FORWARD ROLL

1. Stand with feet together.
2. Jump up (reaching upward, lifting hips upward).
3. Reach for the mat (pike body, heels lift backward and upward).
4. Tuck head to chest.
5. End in squat position and then stand.

NOTE:
May want to place a rolled up mat for an obstacle to dive over and then contact the mat with the hands.

FORWARD ROLL TO HANDSTAND

1. Stand in pike position.
2. Tuck head to chest.
3. Reach for the mat and push off with feet.
4. Roll, ending in squat position.
5. Continue reaching arms forward, placing hands on the mat in front of the body.
6. Lift hips upward keeping arms straight and extend legs up into handstand position.

Spotting the forward roll to handstand

1. Have the student execute a forward roll.
2. As the student ends the roll in a squat position and reaches for the mat to do a handstand, the spotter can assist by grabbing the student's legs to bring them together and straighten them.

BACK ROLLER

1. Squat with knees together hands on mat.
2. Roll backwards bringing knees to chest and clasping them with arms.
3. Roll back and forth.
4. Roll back on neck and head.
5. Roll forward to original position.

BACKWARD ROLL

1. Squat with knees together.
2. Tuck chin to chest.
3. Place hands alongside head.
4. Roll backwards placing hands on mat.
5. Push hands on mat as hips move over the head.
6. Land on feet and come to a stand.

Spotting the backward roll

1. Spotter kneels next to the student and places one hand on the near shoulder and one hand under the near thigh.
2. Help the student roll back by pushing downward and backward on the shoulder.
3. Help the student roll over by pushing backward on the thigh.
4. Another way to spot is to face the student's back and grab his/her hips as student rolls back, lifting the student over his/her head and to a stand.

BACKWARD ROLL TO KNEE SCALE

1. Squat with knees together, chin tucked to chest, hands placed alongside head.
2. Roll backwards pushing off the mat with hands.

3. Lower one leg downward toward the mat (kneeling position) and extend the other leg back and up at a 45-degree angle.
4. Bend extended leg and come to a stand.

BACKWARD STRADDLE ROLL

1. Stand in straddle position.
2. Bend at the waist and reach between legs with arms.
3. Sit backward reaching for the mat with hands (briefly supports body weight).
4. Keep chin tucked to chest and roll on back continuing with legs straddled.
5. Move hands to shoulder position as weight is transferred from hands to hips.
6. Lower feet to the mat, place weight on the feet, and come to a stand.

Spotting the backward straddle roll

1. Spotter should stand at student's side and place one hand on the back and the other hand on the thigh.
2. Help keep the student in a pike position with a lifting action on the thigh, slowly lowering the hips to the mat.
3. As the student rolls, the spotter moves to face the student's back and grasps the hips to lift them over the head then the feet.

BACKWARD PIKE ROLL

1. Stand in pike position (legs straight and together, bend at waist).
2. Hold arms at either side of the legs.
3. Lower the chest toward the knees.
4. Extend the hips backward while reaching for the mat with the hands (weight supported by hands as hips are lowered to mat).
5. Move hands to shoulder position as weight is transferred to hips.
6. Continue rolling, maintaining pike position, place feet on the mat, return to stand.

NOTE:
Spot the same as for a backward straddle roll.

BACK EXTENSION

1. Stand and begin roll from standing position (gives momentum).
2. Extend legs to a low pike position while rolling backward onto shoulders.
3. Thrust legs straight upward as arms extend and head lifts (handstand position).
4. Lower one leg to the mat, placing the weight on that foot.
5. Come to a stand.

Spotting the back extension

1. Spotter should stand at the student's side and place one hand on the back and the other hand on the thigh.
2. As the student rolls and begins the leg thrust, grab the inside leg and lift to a handstand position.

TRIPOD

1. Squat and place the head and hands on the mat to form a triangle (hands shoulder width apart, head placed ahead of hands).
2. Position elbows directly above hands.
3. Place the inside of the right knee on the outside of the right elbow and the inside of the left knee on the outside of the left elbow (one at a time).
4. Balance in this position.
5. Return to squat position.

Spotting the tripod

1. Kneel to the right side of the student.
2. As the right knee is placed on the elbow, support the ankle by putting the left hand underneath it.
3. Place your right hand on the student's spine in the mid-area.
4. Keep the student balanced as s/he places the left knee on the left elbow.

TIP-UP

1. Assume tripod position.
2. Shift the hips toward the hands.
3. Kneel heavily on the elbows.
4. Press down with hands and slowly lift head while continuing to push downward with arms.
5. Balance in this position.
6. Return to squat position.

Spotting the tip-up

1. Begin spotting as in the tripod.
2. Grasp the student's thigh and shift the hips toward the hands.
3. Direct the student to push with the hands as the head is lifted.

HEADSTAND

1. Form a triangle on the mat with head and hands (as in tripod).
2. Extend legs directly above the head (either go from a tripod or kick legs up).
3. Arch back slightly.
4. Hold this position.
5. Bring feet back down to the mat or tuck head and roll out of the headstand.

Spotting the headstand

1. Stand facing the student's side.
2. As the legs are kicked up, grasp them.
3. Legs are held together.
4. Balance is maintained by the triangle formed with hands and head and slightly arched back.

HANDSTAND

1. Stand in forward stride position.
2. Stretch arms forward keeping palms down.
3. Place hands on the mat directly below the shoulders with arms straight.
4. Kick forward leg upward and follow immediately with the other leg.
5. Bring legs together, toes pointed, head up, back arched.
6. Hold this position.
7. Bring feet back down to the mat or tuck head and roll out of the handstand.

Spotting the handstand

1. Stand facing the student's side.
2. As the forward leg is kicked up, grasp the thigh or ankle.
3. Direct the student to kick up the other leg and place legs together.
4. Line up the hips over the shoulders and the shoulders over the hands.

BRIDGE

1. Lie on back, knees bent with heels close to seat.
2. Place hands under shoulders (hands turned backward, fingers pointing toward feet) with elbows pointing to the ceiling.
3. Push up straightening arms and legs lifting hips upward and toward the feet.
4. Drop the head between the arms and look toward the feet.
5. Lower self to the mat.

Spotting the bridge

1. Have the student lie on back and get in position. Spotter may have to place student's hands in correct position.
2. Spotter should either face the student in a forward stride position grasping the hips or by the side of the student grasping the hips, and help lift the student into a bridge position.
3. Direct student to drop head back and look for the mat.
4. Direct student to push with hands, shoulders, feet, and legs so that arms and legs are straight.

BACKBEND

1. Stand with feet shoulder width apart and arms extended overhead.
2. Arch the back and look for the mat while reaching for it (hips positioned over feet).
3. Lower self backwards.
4. Place hands on mat close to the feet, palms down, fingers toward heels.
5. Push off with hands, moving hips forward, and come to a stand.

Spotting the backbend

1. The spotter stands facing the student in a forward stride position and grasps the hips.
2. Direct student to arch back and look for mat while reaching for it.
3. Spotter positions hips of student over student's feet (helps arch instead of lean).
4. Spotter may help lower student if needed.
5. When student is in position spotter lets go so the student can balance.

FRONT LIMBER

1. Stand with weight supported on one leg and extend dominant leg forward, toes touching the mat.
2. Lift the front leg and step into a handstand (legs together, back straight, ankles extended).
3. Slowly lower feet to mat to a backbend or bridge position (ankles extend and toes reach for the mat).
4. Keep feet close together.
5. Move hips forward and upward as arms, hands, and fingers press off the mat and reach overhead.
6. Come to a stand.

Spotting the front limber

1. Stand facing the student's side.
2. As the forward leg is kicked up, grasp the leg.
3. Direct the student to kick up the other leg and place legs together.
4. As the student begins to arch over, place both arms under the student's back.
5. Readjust your hands, placing one hand on the small of the back, and one hand on the student's upper arm.
6. As student moves weight over the feet, press hips forward and upward and lift the upper arm.
7. Direct the student to thrust off the mat and stand.

FRONT WALKOVER

1. Stand on one leg with dominant leg forward, ankle extended, and toes touching the mat.
2. Lift forward leg and step into the skill.
3. Perform a momentary split handstand (legs straight, back arched).
4. Lower the lead leg toward the mat.
5. Thrust off the mat with the arms, reaching the hands and fingers upward so arms come to an overhead position.
6. Lower extended leg to the mat.
7. Come to a stand.

212 Lead-Up Games For Super Sports

Spotting the front walkover

1. Spotter stands to the side of the forward leg and in the direction of where the handstand position will take place.
2. As the student gets in the split handstand position, place one arm around the small of the student's back and the other arm under the extended leg.
3. As the student begins to stand, press the hips forward and upward with the arm around the back.
4. Also extend the free leg forward and upward with the arm that is under that leg.

BACK WALKOVER

1. Stand in forward stride position, weight on the rear leg, arms extended overhead.
2. Arch backward and look for the mat.
3. Lift the forward leg upward and push off the mat with the rear leg as the hands contact the mat.
4. Lower the forward leg to the mat following with the rear leg.
5. Push off the mat with the hands and come to a stand with arms extended overhead.

Spotting the back walkover

1. Stand on the side of the forward kicking leg, facing the shoulder area.
2. Place one hand around the small of the student's back and one hand under the thigh of the kicking leg.
3. The student begins by arching backward, looking for the mat and arms are overhead.
4. Direct the student to push away from the mat with the shoulders and lift the forward leg.
5. Remove hand from leg and grasp the other leg to keep the student in split position as s/he steps down with the forward leg.
6. Student continues to push away from the mat and comes to a stand.

VALDEZ

1. Sit with the dominant leg extended on the mat and the other leg bent at the knee (foot near the thigh area).
2. Extend the dominant arm forward and upward.
3. Extend the other arm behind the hips placing the hand on the mat.
4. Throw the dominant arm overhead as the dominant leg kicks upward.
5. Extend the other leg pushing off the mat upward to a handstand balance.
6. Split legs and step downward one leg at a time.

Spotting the Valdez

1. Kneel facing the student's shoulder area on the dominant arm side.
2. Place one hand on the student's near hip, and one under the extended thigh.
3. Direct the student to throw the dominant arm backward and overhead.

4. Spotter will assist by lifting the hips and kicking leg.
5. The student should be in a split position.
6. The student finishes the skill as in the back walkover.

CARTWHEEL

1. Progression: Stand in a forward stride lunge position with hands on mat, directly under shoulders, arms straight, head up. Kick rear leg up and then the forward leg. Rear leg steps down first and then the forward leg.
2. Actual Cartwheel: Stand in a forward stride lunge position with dominant leg forward.
3. Pike the upper body downward and place the dominant hand just ahead of the dominant foot.
4. Reach farther forward with the other hand, keeping it in line with the legs and dominant hand.
5. Push with the arms and shoulders as the rear leg kicks and lands next to the forward hand.
6. Lift dominant leg upward to follow the other leg.
7. Come to a stand.

Spotting the cartwheel

1. Spotter stands facing the back of the student.
2. Spotter grasps student's waist.
3. Spotter guides the sideward motion.
4. Spotter assists by giving a lift.

ONE-HANDED CARTWHEEL

1. Stand in a forward stride lunge position.
2. Lift both arms straight overhead.
3. Place the near hand on the mat as the cartwheel begins and extend the other arm to the ceiling.
4. Place the opposite foot on the mat first, close to the hand (supporting one) after beginning the cartwheel.
5. Then place the other foot on the mat.
6. Come to a stand.

NOTE:
Spotting is the same as for the cartwheel.

DIVING CARTWHEEL

1. Step forward on one leg and hop on it while the other leg is stretched backward.
2. Lift arms above head during the hop.
3. Swing leg forward to go into the cartwheel and circle arms backward by the ears and toward the hips.

4. Reach forward and upward while jumping off leg which thrusts the body in the air (dive).
5. Reach to the mat with hands and complete the cartwheel action.
6. Come to a stand.

NOTE:
Spotting is the same as in the cartwheel *or* place one hand at the "near waist" area to help give a lift.

ROUND-OFF

1. Execute a slow cartwheel to a handstand position.
2. Snap legs together and pike them down to the mat.
3. Extend arms overhead.
4. Perform a rebounding jump at the end.

Spotting the round-off

1. Spotter stands facing the back side of student in the spot where his hands will be placed.
2. As the student places one hand on the mat, place your hand under the opposite shoulder.
3. The spotter will lift as the student pushes off the mat with his hands.

FORWARD TINSICA

1. Begin as if starting a cartwheel.
2. Hold shoulders at an oblique angle in the direction of the movement of the skill.
3. Hold hips in the oblique angle as one leg, followed by the other, contacts the mat (hands and feet are in a straight line).
4. Come to a stand.

NOTE:
As the student begins to bring down one leg, the spotter can place a hand under the small of the back to help lift the student to a stand.

KNIP-UP

1. Lie on back and extend the legs at a 45-degree angle overhead bringing the hips above the mat.
2. Place the hands under the shoulders with elbows pointing toward the ceiling (weight is supported on shoulders, head, hands).
3. Extend legs and hips forward and upward pushing the head off the mat.
4. Swing arms up and overhead then forward.
5. Finish in a standing position.

Spotting the Knip-up

1. Kneel on the right side of the student facing the shoulder area.
2. Place the left hand on the student's right bicep.
3. Place the right arm under the upper back to help lift the student.

HEADSPRING

1. Place forehead (at hairline) on the mat, with hands placed near the face and hips held high.
2. Perform a small jump extending the legs and forcing the hips overhead.
3. Thrust legs upward and forward.
4. Extend the body and thrust the hands off the mat.
5. Return feet to mat and swing arms up overhead then forward.

Spotting the headspring (two spotters)

1. Two spotters kneel on each side of the student's shoulder area.
2. Place the near arm around the small of the student's back.
3. Place the far hand on the back of the near thigh.
4. As the hips pass overhead, spotters move their hands from the thigh to the biceps.
5. The spotters then assist in lifting the upper body as the student executes a leg thrust.

FRONT HANDSPRING

1. Take steps to the mat and execute a handstand.
2. Thrust the shoulders, arms, and hands off the mat as soon as the hands contact the mat.
3. Keep legs together and arch back on the thrust.
4. Land on feet and come to a stand.

Spotting the front handspring (two spotters)

1. Two spotters kneel facing each other in the spot where the student will place his/her hands.
2. As the student's hands are placed on the mat, spotters grasp the upper arm with one hand, and place the other arm around the student's upper back near the shoulder area.
3. As the student pushes off the mat, the spotters lift the arms and upper back to help student get in a semi-squat position.
4. The spotters will continue to grasp the upper arm to help absorb the momentum.

BACK HANDSPRING

1. Stand with feet together and arms extended overhead.

2. Bend knees slightly to initiate the jump.
3. Jump, lean back, and look for the mat reaching for it with the hands.
4. Contact the mat with the hands and then push off with the shoulders, arms, and hands.
5. Suspend the body momentarily in the air as the arms lead the head and chest upward to an extended position with legs together.
6. Jump off the mat into a high rebounding jump before landing from the snap-down.
7. Whip arms overhead (past ears) during the rebound jump.

Spotting the back handspring (two spotters)

1. Two spotters kneel facing each other and on either side of the student.
2. Place one hand on the small of the student's back.
3. Place the other hand on the back of the student's thigh.
4. As the student bends knees and jumps, the spotters lift at the back and thighs.

SAMPLE TUMBLING ROUTINES
It is fun to have an in-class "Gymnastics Meet" using these or other routines. Allow the students a choice on whether to participate, since the routine is performed in front of the whole class. Consider giving gymnastics awards for those who choose to participate.

TUMBLING ROUTINE 1

1. Dive Roll
2. Forward Straddle Role
3. Forward Roll
4. Forward Straddle Roll
5. Forward Roll
6. Stand

ROUTINE 2

1. Cartwheel
2. Round-off
3. Backward Roll
4. Back Straddle Roll
5. Backward Roll
6. Back Extension
7. Stand

ROUTINE 3

1. Cartwheel
2. Roundoff
3. Rebound and Half-Turn
4. Cartwheel
5. Backward Roll
6. Back Extension
7. Stand

GYMNASTICS GAMES

Skills: Tumbling stunts, balance

Supplies: Mats

Formation: Varies according to the game

Description: These games are a great way to practice learned tumbling skills. Use these after going through basic tumbling stunts. Each game is described under its heading.

ROLL ALONG

1. This is a musical game. You will need a long row of mats and one leader.
2. All players stand in a circle around the mats, three yards away, facing counter-clockwise.
3. As the music starts, the leader skips around the inside of the circle and grasps a player's hand.
4. They skip to the mat, unclasp hands and perform a stunt (for example, forward roll).
5. Clasp hands again, skip around the circle, then the second player chooses another player and continues as above.

ADD ONE

1. The first person in a single-file line does a stunt.
2. The next person does that stunt and another one.
3. The third person does what the first person did, what the second person did, then another one.
4. This continues for all the members of the squad.

RELAY RACE

1. Divide the class into squads and have each squad line up single file behind a mat.
2. The first person does one stunt down the mat and one back (can be the same stunt or two different stunts).
3. The first person touches the second person who does the same.
4. Continue until everyone on the squad has had a turn.

NOTE:
This could also be done on beams.

RUSH

1. Divide the class into two teams and number off each team consecutively.
2. You need two identical pieces of apparatus (mats).
3. Each team stands in front of its apparatus, about fifteen feet away.
4. A number and the name of a stunt is called.
5. The player from each team runs to the apparatus, performs the stunt, and runs back to the line.

CHALLENGE

1. Divide the class into two teams.
2. A player from Team A performs a stunt, and challenges a specific player from Team B to do the same.
3. Then the player from Team B does a stunt and challenges a player from Team A to do the same.
4. No one can be called more than once in a game.

STUNT GOLF

1. Designate a certain number of "holes" around the gym.
2. At each hole have the name, picture, or description of a stunt on a card.
3. Divide the class according to the number of holes.
4. Each group goes around the course attempting the stunts at each hole.
5. Those who succeed on the first try, get one point; second attempt, two points; third attempt, three points; with a spotter, four points; not at all, five points.
6. The person with the lowest score wins.

RHYTHMIC GYMNASTICS

■ Gymnastics with a Ball

Skills: Rhythm, swinging, rolling, bouncing, tossing

Supplies: One ball (5½ inches to 7½ inches in diameter) for each student

Formation: Each student in a personal space

Description: With a limited amount of gymnastics equipment available, this is a great way to introduce a different type of gymnastics. Students may be more excited to participate in this type of activity rather than traditional gymnastics. This would also be great for a P.E. performance for parents.

SWINGING MOVEMENTS

1. *Forward Swing*
   a. Hold the ball in the right hand (wrist grasp) at your side.
   b. Swing right arm forward to shoulder height.
   c. Change the ball to the left hand.
   d. Swing the left arm back.
   e. Continue swinging the arms forward and backward.

2. *Swing Across the Body*
   a. Hold the ball in the right hand with a wrist grasp, arm extended to the side.
   b. Swing the right arm across the body to the left.
   c. Change the ball to the left hand and swing it across to the right side.
   d. Sway the body from side to side with the swing of the arms.

3. *Forward Circling*
   a. Hold ball in the right hand with a wrist grasp and at your side.
   b. Circle the ball forward, upward, backward, and forward again.
   c. Change the ball to the left hand in front of the body and repeat.

4. *Circling Around the Body*
   a. Hold the ball in the right hand with a wrist grasp, arm extended to the side.
   b. Swing the ball across the body (in front) to the left.
   c. Change ball to left hand.
   d. The left hand moves the ball around the back.
   e. Change the ball to the right hand.

5. *Trunk Bending*
   a. Hold the ball in the right hand with a wrist grasp, arm extended to the side.
   b. Bend forward at the trunk.
   c. Swing right arm to the left and back.
   d. Make a horizontal circle with the ball going to the left.
   e. Change hands and repeat movement in reverse direction.

6. *Body Wave*
   a. Hold ball in right hand with a wrist grasp, arm extended to the side.
   b. Bend backwards bringing arm backwards and overhead.
   c. As you come back up bring your right arm up and overhead and switch it to the left hand.

7. *Spiral*
   a. Stand in straddle position, hold ball in right hand with wrist grasp, arm extended to the side.
   b. Swing the right arm across the body to the left, shifting weight to the left foot.
   c. Bend the right elbow, circle the ball toward the body, under the elbow, turning the palm inward then outward.
   d. As the ball ends by the right side, shift weight to the right.

e. Carry the ball to the left overhead, shifting the weight to the left and bending to the left.

f. Continue moving the ball in a circle around the head while returning to the original position.

ROLLING MOVEMENTS

1. *Side Floor Roll*
   a. Stand in a straddle position.
   b. Hold the ball in the right hand with a wrist grasp, arm at the side.
   c. Bend at the waist and roll the ball on the floor to the left.
   d. Receive the ball into the left hand, shifting the weight to the left.
   e. Come to a stand but bend trunk to the left.

2. *V-Sit Roll*
   a. Sit with legs straight out in front.
   b. Hold the ball in the right hand with a wrist grasp, arm extended to the side.
   c. Lift straight legs upward to a V-sit (balance on seat).
   d. Roll the ball to the left side under the legs and back, then lower legs.
   e. Change the ball to the left hand and repeat.

3. *Roll Around Body*
   a. Sit with legs straight out in front.
   b. Hold the ball in the right hand with a wrist grasp, arm extended to the side.
   c. Bend the trunk forward.
   d. Roll the ball around the feet to the left.
   e. Change ball to left hand and roll the ball around the back.
   f. Change the ball to the right hand.

4. *Roll on Legs*
   a. Sit with legs straight out in front.
   b. Hold ball in both hands with a wrist grasp.
   c. Lift legs tilting the trunk backward and let the ball roll from feet to chest.
   d. Grasp the ball with both hands, reach overhead, bend forward, and place the ball on the feet again.

5. *Arm Rolling*
   a. Stand with arms stretched straight out in front of the body, arms together.
   b. Hold ball in the palms of both hands.
   c. Move arms slightly upward, turning palms downward, and let the ball roll down the arms toward the body.
   d. Catch the ball with both hands after it bounces on the floor (the ball drops between the arms by the chest at the end of the roll).

6. *Shoulder Roll*
   a. Stand with the ball in the right palm with arm extended sideward.
   b. Toss the ball slightly upward, quickly turn the palm downward, and let the ball roll down the right arm to the shoulder.

c. Bend body slightly to the left letting the ball go behind the body.

d. Twist to the left and catch the ball on the rebound with the left hand.

BOUNCING MOVEMENTS

1. *Bounce With Arm Swing*
   a. Hold ball in both hands with arms straight out in front.
   b. Bounce the ball in front of the body and swing arms horizontally to the side and back to the front.
   c. Catch the ball.
   d. Knees and body give with the bounce.

2. *Bounce With Knee Bend*
   a. Hold the ball in the right palm.
   b. Bounce the ball alternately with the left and right hands while gradually bending the knees.
   c. When you get to a deep knee bend position, gradually return to a standing position (keep ball bouncing using alternating hands).

3. *Bounce Across Body*
   a. Stand in straddle position, with weight on the right foot.
   b. Hold the ball in the right palm with arm at the side.
   c. Shift weight from right to left, bouncing the ball in front of the body, catching it with your left hand.

4. *Bounce and Turn*
   a. Hold ball straight out in front of the body with both hands.
   b. Bounce the ball with both hands, spin around, and catch the ball with both hands.

5. *Bounce Under Leg*
   a. Hold ball in right palm, arm extended to the side.
   b. Lift right leg and bounce ball diagonally under the leg. The leg swings over the ball.
   c. Catch the ball in the left hand.
   d. Reverse the action (under left leg).

6. *Bounce with Scissor Kick*
   a. Hold ball in right palm with both arms extended to the side.
   b. Bounce the ball under both legs diagonally as they scissor kick over the ball (lift right leg then left leg).
   c. Catch the ball with the left hand.
   d. Reverse the action (bounce with left hand).

7. *Bounce with the Grapevine Step*
   a. Stand in straddle position, weight on right foot, ball in right palm, arm extended sideward.
   b. Step to the left with left foot, cross the right foot over the left and bounce the ball with the right hand.

c. Catch the ball with the left hand and step to the left, reaching left with the ball.

d. Repeat in opposite direction.

TOSSING MOVEMENTS

1. *Two-Hand Toss*
   a. Stand with knees slightly bent and ball held with both hands, low and in front of the body.
   b. Toss the ball upward.
   c. Extend the body going up on toes.
   d. Catch the ball with the fingertips.
   e. Let the body bend as the hands carry the ball to starting position.

2. *One-Hand Toss*
   a. Stand in a stride position with right foot forward, weight on the left foot.
   b. Hold the ball in the right hand at the side.
   c. Toss the ball forward and transfer the weight forward.
   d. Reach and catch the ball with both hands.
   e. Transfer the ball to the right hand.
   f. Do the same thing with the left hand.

3. *Over-Head Toss*
   a. Stand in straddle position, ball in right hand, both arms extended to the side.
   b. Toss the ball overhead and catch it in the left hand. Weight is shifted from right to left foot.
   c. Repeat.

4. *Front-Swing Toss*
   a. Stand in straddle position, ball in right hand, both arms extended to the side.
   b. Toss the ball from right to left low across the front of the body.
   c. While throwing, bend the knees and thrust hips from right to left.
   d. Catch the ball with the left hand.
   e. Reverse the action.

5. *Flick Toss*
   a. Stand in a straddle position.
   b. Hold the ball in the right hand with a wrist grasp, arm extended to the side.
   c. Bend the elbow and wrist in an inward and downward arc.
   d. Flick the wrist, tossing the ball upward.
   e. Catch the ball with the right hand.

6. *Cross Catch*
   a. Hold ball with both hands, low and in front of the body.
   b. Toss the ball up with both hands.
   c. Reach up and cross hands, then catch the ball.
   d. Bring hands to chest level.

e. Make an outside turn, ball brought toward the body.

f. Toss the ball upward and catch it with both hands.

7. *Throw Behind Shoulder and Catch*

   a. Hold the ball in the right hand with a wrist grasp.

   b. Extend both arms to the side.

   c. Bend the trunk to the right swinging the ball downward and behind the body.

   d. Toss the ball straight upward behind the left shoulder.

   e. Catch the ball with the left hand.

   f. Reverse direction.

SAMPLE BALL ROUTINE

1. Swing Across the Body 4x

2. Over-Head Toss 4x

3. One-Hand Toss 4x

4. Bounce With Grapevine Step 4x

5. Front-Swing Toss 4x

6. Two-Hand Toss 4x

7. Arm Rolling 4x

8. Finish by reaching up overhead with the ball, then down to a squat.

NOTE:

Perform this routine to music. Have the students make up their own routines and bring their own music.

GYMNASTICS WITH A HOOP

Skills: Rhythm, swinging, jumping, circling, tossing

Supplies: One hoop for each student

Formation: Each student in a personal space

Description: This activity is suitable for those with limited gymnastics equipment.

SWINGING MOVEMENTS

Swinging movements are done with a straight arm, with the movement starting from the shoulder.

1. *Swing and Lean*

   a. Stand in straddle position.

   b. Hoop is in right hand with palm facing the rear, weight is on the right foot.

   c. Both arms are extended sideward.

   d. Swing the hoop down in front of the body to the left.

e. Grasp the hoop with the left hand, palm forward.

f. Transfer weight to left foot.

g. Swing hoop overhead to the right and then the left (both hands on hoop).

h. Return to original position.

2. *Swing Forward and Backward*

a. Stand with feet together, hoop in right hand at the side with palm facing in.

b. Swing hoop forward and backward bending knees.

c. Switch hands and repeat.

3. *Ballet Point*

a. Stand in stride position, left foot forward.

b. Hold hoop in right hand at the side with palm in.

c. Bend forward over left foot swinging the hoop to the rear.

d. Change the hoop to the left hand in the rear.

e. Swing the hoop forward transferring the weight to the left foot.

f. Reverse the movement.

4. *Back Arch*

a. Stand with left foot forward.

b. Hold hoop in right hand at the side with palm facing up.

c. Swing the hoop upward in front of the body (both hands swing forward).

d. Keep the left arm forward.

e. Bending the body backward, bring the hoop to the rear.

f. Swing hoop to original position.

5. *Body Wave*

a. Stand with feet together both arms extended forward.

b. Hold hoop in right hand palm facing upward.

c. Swing the hoop down, back, and up (do a body wave).

d. While swinging the hoop up, twist the hoop outward twice and finish in original position.

6. *Hoop Turn with Side Stretch*

a. Hold hoop horizontally to the right side, right palm forward, left palm backward.

b. Cross right arm horizontally over the left in front of the body, half turning the hoop.

c. Do a side stretch to the left transferring weight to the left foot.

d. Reverse movement.

e. Return to starting position.

7. *Horizontal Turns*

a. Hold the hoop with both hands in front of the body, arms horizontal, palms facing in.

b. Use a three finger grasp (thumb, index finger, middle finger).

c. Move the fingers, turn the hoop inward or outward.

JUMPING MOVEMENTS

1. *Forward Jump*
   a. Hold hoop in front of body, arms horizontal, palms downward.
   b. Swing the hoop down and jump through it as in jumping rope.
2. *Backward Jump*
   a. Hold hoop above the head, palms upward.
   b. Swing hoop downward in back of body and jump through it.
3. *Leap*
   a. Hold hoop diagonally upward, palms facing in.
   b. Run three steps forward, bring hoop down and leap through it with the right foot (left knee bent to rear).
4. *Waltz Turn*
   a. Hold hoop horizontal at right side, with right palm forward, left palm backward.
   b. Step on left foot to the left, swing hoop down in front and step through it with the right foot.
   c. Turn to the left and step left foot through the hoop to the right (end standing inside the hoop).
   d. Bring the hoop upward over the head, palms facing forward.
   e. Turn hoop down and return to original position.

CIRCLING MOVEMENTS

1. *Circling*
   a. Hold hoop in right hand, palm forward, both arms extended to the sides.
   b. Circle hoop starting inward.
2. *Circle in Front of the Body*
   a. Hold hoop in right hand, palm forward, both arms extended to the side.
   b. Circle the hoop inward, in front of body, change hoop to left hand.
   c. Stretch to the left.
   d. Reverse the movement.
3. *Alternate Hand Circling*
   a. Hold hoop in right hand, palm forward, both arms extended to the side.
   b. Circle the hoop inward with the right hand.
   c. Change to the left hand in front of the body.
   d. Continue circling outward on the left hand.
   e. Reverse directions.
4. *Change Hands Behind Body*
   a. Hold hoop in right hand, palm forward, both arms extended to the side.
   b. Swing hoop downward and in back of body, changing the hoop to the left hand.

    c. Swing hoop to the left side.

    d. Reverse direction.

5. *Circle Back and Swing Across Front*

    a. Hold hoop in right hand, palm forward, both arms extended to the side.

    b. Circle the hoop inward in back of the body and grasp the hoop, palm backward.

    c. Swing the hoop in front of the body and change to the left hand.

    d. Reverse directions.

6. *Circle Front, Back and Change*

    a. Hold hoop in right hand, palm forward, both arms extended to the side.

    b. Circle the hoop inward, turn palm to face backward, circle inward in back of the body.

    c. Swing the hoop in back of the body to the left and catch it with the left hand.

    d. Reverse the movement.

7. *Horizontal Circle in Front of Body and Front of Head*

    a. Hold hoop in right hand, palm down, both arms extended to the side, hoop is horizontal.

    b. Circle the hoop horizontally in front of the body, gradually raising the arm overhead as you continue to circle the hoop.

    c. Change to the left hand and gradually bring the hoop down and in front of the body.

TOSSING MOVEMENTS

1. *Stand and Toss*

    a. Hold hoop in right hand, palm inward, arms at sides.

    b. Toss the hoop up in front of the body and catch with the left hand.

    c. Alternate sides.

2. *Run, Toss, and Leap*

    a. Hold hoop in right hand, palm inward, arms at sides.

    b. Run, as you leap (right leg in front), toss the hoop up.

    c. Catch the hoop with the left hand.

    d. Stand on right foot, left leg extended backward and upward (scale).

    e. Swing hoop to rear toward extended leg.

    f. Bring left leg and arm forward and end in starting position.

3. *Change Feet*

    a. Hold hoop in right hand, palm inward, arms at side.

    b. As you jump into the air and change feet, toss the hoop up and then catch it with the left hand.

    c. Repeat.

4. *Toss Over Head*

    a. Stand with weight on right foot, hoop in right hand, palm facing forward, both arms extended to the side.

    b. Toss the hoop over the head, transfer weight to left foot, and catch with left hand.

5. *Toss in Front of Body*

    a. Stand with weight on right foot, hoop in right hand, palm backward, both arms extended to the side.

    b. Toss the hoop downward in front of the body to the left side.

    c. Catch hoop with left hand (palm forward).

    d. Turn palm to the rear and toss the hoop to the right.

6. *Outward Circle and Toss Over Head*

    a. Hold hoop in right hand, palm forward, both arms extended to the side.

    b. Circle the hoop outward, then toss it above the head and catch the hoop with the left hand.

    c. Repeat.

7. *Front, Back, Toss Behind*

    a. Hold hoop in right hand, palm forward, arm extended to the side.

    b. Circle hoop inward in front of the body, circle outward to the side, circle inward in back of body, and toss the hoop in back of the body.

    c. Catch the hoop with the left hand.

SAMPLE HOOP ROUTINE

1. Swing And Lean 4x
2. Waltz Turn 4x
3. Hoop Turn To Side Stretch 4x
4. Run, Toss, Leap 4x
5. Toss Over Head 4x
6. Body Wave 4x
7. Circle in Front of Body 4x
8. Outward Circle and Toss Over Head 4x
9. Ballet Point

NOTE:

Perform routine to music. Have students make up their own routines and bring their own music.

TEACHING HINTS
FOR SOCCER

1. Recommended grade levels for soccer are 3–6 in the fall and 1–2 in the spring. Since there are plenty of activities for grades 1–2 to develop their motor skills, soccer is not necessary.

2. Put the students into groups of six players each (three boys, three girls). Decide on what skills you plan to teach. Teach how to execute a skill by explaining and modeling.

3. Decide on the drills you would like to use and have each group of students practice the same drill, or set up stations of various drills working on various skills. You can teach the skills for each station, check for understanding, and assign stations; or write out task cards for each station which give a diagram and directions for the drill.

4. Other ways to teach skills:
   a. Teach several drills involving one skill, then do lead-up games involving that skill.
   b. Teach a few different skills, then do a lead-up game involving those skills.
   c. Teach all the skills, then do lead-up games.

5. For lead-up games, you can set up a few areas of the same game, or set up and explain a few different games.

6. Teach students the rules so that they can call their own rule infractions so they can learn to be independent of constant teacher intervention. This allows for more than one game to go on at a time, which then provides for maximum student involvement. This also teaches students to be honest about their "mistakes."

GLOSSARY OF SOCCER TERMS

Corner kick: a direct free kick taken by the attacking team taken from the corner of the field after the ball goes over the goal line having last been touched by a defending player.

Direct free kick: a kick awarded on a personal foul which can score directly from the kicker's foot.

Dribble: repeated short taps with the inside or outside of the feet, used to cover ground while retaining control of the ball.

Goal: the act of causing the ball to pass between the goal posts.

Goal kick: an indirect free kick taken by the defensive team after the ball goes out of bounds over the goal line having last been touched by an attacking player.

Heading: to change the direction of the flight of the ball by making an impact with the forehead.

Indirect free kick: a free kick which cannot score a goal unless touched by one other player besides the one taking the kick.

Kickoff: method of putting the ball into play from the middle of the field at the beginning of each period and after a goal has been scored.

Penalty kick: a free kick awarded the attacking team after a defending player commits a personal foul within the penalty area. The kick is taken in front of the goal and no player except the kicker and the goalkeeper, who must be stationary with both feet on the goal line, may be within the penalty area until the kick is taken.

Passing: skill used in moving the ball to a teammate.

Heel: used for a short pass to a teammate behind the player.

Inside-of-foot: generally used for accurate passing, but can be used for volleying and shooting.

Instep: the basic soccer kick.

Outside-of-foot: almost exclusively used for short, chop-like passes and for maneuvering the ball.

Punt: used only by the goalkeeper.

Position Responsibilities

Forwards: primary task is to score goals.

Midfielders: their role is to link the team's defense and attack. They defend their own goal as well as attacking the goal of the opposition.

Defenders: their role is to prevent the other team from scoring goals.

Goalie: the primary task of the goalie is to act as the team's last line of defense; must prevent opposing players from scoring at the goal.

Shooting: applying passing techniques to get the ball past the opposing goalie and into the goal.

Tackling: technique used to dispossess opponents of the ball in order to gain possession.

Throw-in: means by which the ball is put into play after it has gone out of bounds.

Trapping: means by which the ball is stopped and controlled with a part of the body.

Chest trap: used when the ball is descending from a high volley or when a player wants to prevent a high-rising ball from getting past.

Foot trap: used for stopping a rolling ball by putting the sole of the foot on it.

Leg trap: used when the ball is approaching from a high volley or low bounce.

Shin trap: used with a rolling ball.

Side-of-foot trap: the motion of the ball is stopped by the inside of the foot.

Volley: the change of the direction of a ball on the fly.

Suggested Soccer Skills Sequence

GRADE 1	GRADE 2	GRADE 3
DRIBBLING Inside of feet *Drills* Line Dribble Freeze	DRIBBLING Inside of feet *Drills* Same as grade 1, plus: Follow The Leader	DRIBBLING Inside of feet *Drills* Same as grades 1 and 2, plus: Cone Dribble, Partner Keepaway
PASSING Inside of foot *Drills* Passing Passing and Trapping Circle Pass	PASSING Inside of foot *Drills* Same as grade 1	PASSING Inside of foot *Drills* Same as grades 1 and 2
TRAPPING Foot Trap *Drills* Roll and Trap	TRAPPING Foot Trap *Drills* Same as grade 1	TRAPPING Foot Trap *Drills* Same as grades 1 and 2
SHOOTING *Drills* Shot Between Cones	SHOOTING *Drills* Same as grade 1	SHOOTING *Drills* Same as grades 1 and 2, plus: Shooting and Goaltending, Shoot in Stride
THROW-IN Two hands overhead	THROW-IN Two hands overhead	THROW-IN Two hands overhead
LEAD-UP GAMES Start with Dribble Call Ball. Pick and choose, but do not get any more difficult than Line Soccer.	LEAD-UP GAMES Do not get any more difficult than four vs. four Soccer.	LEAD-UP GAMES Do not get any more difficult than Cooperative Soccer.

Suggested Soccer Skills Sequence (Cont.)

GRADE 4	GRADE 5	GRADE 6
DRIBBLING Inside of feet Outside of feet	DRIBBLING Inside of feet Outside of feet	DRIBBLING Inside of feet Outside of feet Toes
Drills Cone Dribble Freeze Partner Keepaway Shuttle Dribble and Tackle	*Drills* Same as grade 4, plus: Ball Control Protect Your Ball	*Drills* Same as grade 5
PASSING Inside of foot Outside of foot Instep Punt	PASSING Inside of foot Outside of foot Instep Heel Punt	PASSING Inside of foot Outside of foot Instep Heel Punt Volley
Drills Pass Left and Right Soccer Bowling Dribble and Pass	*Drills* Same as grade 4	*Drills* Stationary Pass Pass and Move Quick Reaction Dribble and Pass Dribble, Pass, Tackle Advanced Skills (Volley)
TRAPPING Foot trap Side-of-foot trap Shin trap	TRAPPING Foot trap Side-of-foot trap Shin trap Leg trap	TRAPPING Foot trap Side-of-foot trap Shin trap Leg trap Body trap
Drills Roll and Trap Bounce and Trap	*Drills* Same as grade 4	*Drills* Same as grade 5, plus: Throw and Trap
SHOOTING *Drills* Shoot in Stride Run, Shoot, and Defend	SHOOTING *Drills* Pass and Shoot Drop, Pass, and Shoot	SHOOTING *Drills* Same as grade 5, plus: Quick Shooting
	HEADING Stationary	HEADING *Drills* Advanced Skills (Heading)
THROW-IN Two hands overhead	THROW-IN Two hands overhead	THROW-IN Two hands overhead

LEAD-UP GAMES
Any you feel are
  appropriate, including
  Line Soccer, four vs.
  four, Sideline Soccer,
  Cooperative, six vs. six
	LEAD-UP GAMES
	Same as grade 4.
		LEAD-UP GAMES
		Same as grades 4 and
		  5

TASK ANALYSIS OF SOCCER SKILLS

DRIBBLING

1. Stand, feet apart, weight evenly distributed.
2. Step forward on left foot.
3. Tap ball with inside or outside of right foot.
4. Place right foot down.
5. Tap ball with inside or outside of left foot.
6. Continue this until the ball is passed.

INSIDE-OF-FOOT KICK

1. Stand, feet apart, weight evenly distributed.
2. Keep eyes on the ball.
3. Move toward the ball.
4. Flex knees and shift weight to nonkicking leg.
5. Swing kicking foot toward the ball.
6. Contact the ball with the inside of the foot.

OUTSIDE-OF-FOOT KICK

1. Keep eyes on ball.
2. Place nonkicking foot near the ball.
3. Put weight on nonkicking foot with knee slightly bent.
4. Extend arms for balance.
5. Point toe of kicking foot inward and contact ball with outside of foot.
6. Follow through with kicking leg.

INSTEP KICK

1. Approach ball from slight angle, keeping eyes on ball.
2. Plant nonkicking foot next to ball.
3. Transfer weight to nonkicking foot as kicking foot is brought back, bent at knee, arms are extended for balance.
4. Bend upper body slightly forward as kicking foot is brought back.
5. Swing kicking foot downward, toe pointed slightly out and down.
6. Contact ball with inside of instep and follow through.

HEEL KICK

1. Place nonkicking foot beside ball, keeping knee bent.
2. Pass kicking foot over ball.
3. Bring kicking foot back to contact with heel.
4. Follow through.

VOLLEY

1. Keep eyes on ball and face ball.
2. Put weight on nonkicking leg and bring kicking foot back.
3. Extend arms for balance.
4. Contact ball with instep of foot making contact in front of body as ball is about knee height.
5. Follow through, bending upper body slightly forward for balance.

PUNT

1. Hold ball in front of body.
2. Stride forward with nonkicking foot, shifting weight onto that foot while bringing kicking foot back.
3. Drop ball and keep eyes on ball.
4. Bring foot through making contact with ball on instep.
5. Follow through.

FOOT TRAP

1. Keep eyes on ball.
2. Move toward ball.
3. Shift weight to nontrapping leg.
4. Point toe up, heel down, of trapping foot.
5. Trap ball between foot and ground.

TRAPPING WITH INSIDE OF FOOT

1. Face ball.
2. Keep eyes on ball.
3. Bend knee and point toe outward.
4. Contact ball in front of body, trapping it between ground and inside of foot.
5. Withdraw foot slightly on contact to avoid rebound.

TRAPPING WITH OUTSIDE OF FOOT

1. Keep eyes on ball.
2. Bend knee closer to ball and point toe inward.
3. Meet ball away from body with outside of foot.
4. Withdraw foot slightly on contact to avoid rebound.

SHIN TRAP

1. Keep eyes on ball.
2. Flex both knees as ball approaches.
3. Bend trunk slightly forward and extend arms to side.
4. Extend legs slightly and shift weight to nonkicking foot at moment of contact.

LEG TRAP

1. Face ball.
2. Keep eyes on ball.
3. Lift leg so that thigh is horizontal to ground.
4. Contact ball at midpoint of thigh.
5. Recoil thigh on contact.

CHEST TRAP

1. Face ball.
2. Keep eyes on ball.
3. Extend arms for balance.
4. Put one foot in front of the other and arch trunk back.
5. Contact ball at top of chest.
6. Recoil on contact to take speed off ball.

TACKLING

1. Place nontackling foot next to ball and shift weight to that leg.
2. Bend knees slightly and lean upper body slightly forward, shoulder on tackling side toward opponent.
3. Contact ball with inside of foot.
4. Push ball between opponent's legs or lift it over his/her foot after stopping the ball.

HEADING

1. Keep eyes on ball at all times.
2. Bend knees slightly as ball approaches, and place one foot behind the other, rocking back, transfering weight onto back leg.

3. Keep arms out for balance.
4. Arch upper body back, then snap upper body, neck, and head forward as ball is contacted on forehead.
5. Transfer weight to front leg on contact.
6. Drive head "through" ball and follow through.

JUMP HEADING

1. Keep eyes on ball.
2. Jump as ball approaches, arching upper body back.
3. Extend arms for balance.
4. Drive upper body, neck, and head forward to contact ball with forehead at apex of jump.

THROW-IN

1. Hold the ball with both hands over head.
2. Flex knees and shift weight forward while throwing the ball.
3. Swing arms forward when releasing the ball.
4. Stay balanced with weight on two feet behind the line until ball is released.

SOCCER DRILLS

■ Dribbling Drills

Skills: Dribbling

Supplies: Soccer balls, cones

Formation: Varies according to the drill

Description: Each drill is described under its heading.

LINE DRIBBLE

1. Divide the class into groups of six students each. Have each group get in a single file line. Give each group a ball.
2. Have each player in each line dribble to a designated line and back, give the ball to the next player in line, and go to the end of the line.
3. Continue until all players have had a turn to dribble.

CONE DRIBBLE

1. Divide the class into groups of six students each. Have each group get in a single file line. Give each group a ball.
2. Place a line of cones (three to six) in front of each line with space between them.

3. The first player in each line dribbles around the cones and back, then gives the ball to the next player.
4. This continues until all players have had a turn.

BALL EXCHANGE

1. Divide the class into groups of six students each. Have each group get in a single file line, divide in half with distance between them. Give each half a ball.
2. The first players in each half of the line dribble toward each other. When they meet in the middle, they exchange balls, and proceed to the line on the other side.
3. The next two players do the same. This continues until all players have had a turn.

FREEZE

1. Each player has a ball and finds a personal space in the designated area.
2. At the signal, the players begin dribbling the ball in the area without touching another person or ball.
3. When the teacher says "freeze," the players trap the ball and freeze in place.
4. Players who bump into another person or ball must freeze until directed to rejoin the game.

FOLLOW THE LEADER

1. Have the students get a partner, a ball, and a personal space.
2. One of the partners is the leader, and the other student follows the leader's dribbling and trapping patterns.
3. Leader and follower switch roles.

PARTNER KEEPAWAY

1. Have each student get a partner and a ball.
2. One player starts with the ball and tries to keep it from the partner by dribbling, dodging, trapping, and pivoting.
3. As soon as the partner touches the ball, the players exchange roles.

DIRECTION DRIBBLE

1. Each student has a ball and finds a personal space.
2. The students begin dribbling, and on command (right, left, forward), switch directions.

BALL CONTROL

1. Set up designated areas with six to twelve players assigned to each area, one ball for each player.
2. At the signal, all players begin to dribble within their area.
3. While dribbling, each player attempts to kick the other players' balls out of the area while preventing players from doing the same thing to his/her ball.
4. When a player loses the ball, s/he is out of the game.
5. The drill continues until only one player is left in the area, in possession of the ball.

SHUTTLE DRIBBLE AND TACKLE

1. Divide the class into groups of six students each. Have each group line up single file, then divide in half and get in shuttle formation.
2. One side of each line is the offense and the other side is the defense.
3. The first player of the offense starts dribbling the ball toward the defensive line.
4. The first player of the defense moves out to tackle the offensive player.
5. The offensive player attempts to dribble around the opponent, while the defensive player attempts to gain possession of the ball.
6. The players go to the end of each other's lines, and the next two players go. This continues until all players have played both offense and defense.

PROTECT YOUR BALL

1. Set up designated areas with six to twelve players in each area, and all but one player has a ball.
2. The player without the ball attempts to take a ball away from any of the players who are dribbling within the area.
3. The dribblers, without making contact with other players, try to evade the tackler.
4. Once a dribbler has lost possession of the ball, s/he must try to take a ball from any dribbler other than the one who tackled him/her.

■ Passing Drills

Skills: Passing, dribbling, trapping, tackling

Supplies: Soccer balls, cones, bowling pins (or plastic liter pop bottles)

Formation: Varies according to the drill

Description: Each drill is described under its heading.

WALL PASSING

1. Arrange the students in a side-by-side line formation facing a wall.
2. Each student stands about 6 feet away from the wall and has a ball.
3. Each student passes the ball to the wall and retrieves it by trapping it.

PASSING

1. Put the students in groups of six and have them line up single file. Each line has a ball.
2. Have the first person in each line take the ball and move a distance away from the line.
3. This player rolls the ball to the first player in line, who then passes it back to the tosser.
4. The tosser goes to the end of the line, and the passer becomes the tosser.
5. Continue this, practicing the different types of passes you plan to teach.

PASSING AND TRAPPING

1. Divide a line of six players in half (shuttle formation), with one ball for the group.
2. Have the halves stand 10 feet to 15 feet apart.
3. One player starts by passing the ball to the opposite player who traps the ball.
4. The player who trapped the ball returns it by passing it.
5. Both players go to the end of their lines, and the next two in line do the same thing.
6. Have the students use various passes and traps.

CIRCLE PASSING

1. Have each group of [6] players form a circle with one player in the middle.
2. The center player has the ball.
3. The center player passes the ball to a player in the circle, who traps it and passes it back to the center player.
4. This continues until the center player has passed to all the players in the circle.
5. The center player then changes with one of the players in the circle, and the procedure is repeated until everyone has had a turn in the middle.

PASS LEFT AND RIGHT

1. Divide each line of 6 players in half and have them face each other (shuttle formation).
2. Player 1 passes the ball to the right or left of player 2, who traps the ball.
3. Player 2 then passes the ball back to player 1 to the right or left, and player 1 traps it.
4. Both players go to the end of their lines, and it is the next two players' turns.

STATIONARY PASS

1. Divide the class into groups of five students each.
2. Have one student stand in the middle with one student to his/her left, one to the right, one in front of him/her, and one behind.
3. The player in the center has the ball and passes to the player on the right, then to the player on the left, to the player in front, and finally to the player behind. NOTE: Different passes and/or feet will be used for the various directions.
4. Change the player in the middle and continue until each player has had a turn to be in the middle.

SOCCER BOWLING

1. Set up ten bowling pins for each group.
2. Set up two cones about 4 feet apart, a distance away from the pins, for the players to pass from.
3. Have the students line up in a single file line behind the cones.
4. The first student in line passes at the pins, goes and resets them, and then goes to the end of the line.

PASS AND MOVE

1. Divide each line in half and have them stand side by side in single file lines with one ball.
2. Have the partners move down the field while using only passing and trapping. Stress control.
3. They pass and trap back and the next set of partners go. This continues until all partners have gone.

DRIBBLE AND PASS

1. Divide each line in half and have them stand side-by-side in single file lines with one ball.
2. One player begins to dribble while his/her partner moves along with him/her.
3. After a few dribbles, the player with the ball passes it to the partner, who dribbles the ball then passes it back.
4. This pattern continues to a designated line and back.
5. Then the next set of partners go. Continue until all partners have gone.

QUICK REACTION DRIBBLE AND PASS

1. Divide the class into groups of six students each, and have each group get in a single file line. Give each group a ball.
2. The first player in each line goes out a distance away to direct the pass.
3. The next player in line dribbles out toward the first player who points to the left or right.

4. The dribbler passes the ball in the direction given.

5. The dribbler stays there to direct the pass while the first player dribbles the ball back to his line, passes it to the next person, and goes to the end of his line.

6. Continue until all players have had a chance to pass and direct.

DRIBBLE, PASS, TACKLE

1. Two offensive lines are set up facing one defensive line as shown in the diagram.

2. The first players in the offensive line move forward dribbling and passing.

3. The first defensive player moves out and attempts to take the ball away.

4. ROTATION: Those in line A rotate to the end of line B. Line B goes to the end of line C. Line C goes to the end of line A.

Line B x x x ⟶

⟵ o o o Line A

Line C x x x ⟶

■ Trapping Drills

Skills: Trapping, dribbling, throwing, rolling, bouncing

Supplies: Soccer balls

Formation: Varies according to the drill

Description: Each drill is described under its heading.

ROLL AND TRAP

1. Divide the class into groups of six students each, and have each group line up single file.

2. Have the first player in each line take the ball, go out a ways, and face the line.

3. The player with the ball rolls it to the first player in line and calls out the type of trap to use.

4. The player traps the ball as called, and then goes out to be the tosser, and the tosser goes to the end of the line.

5. Continue until all players have had a turn rolling and trapping.

BOUNCE AND TRAP

1. Divide the class into groups of six students each, and have each group line up single file.

2. Have the first player in each line take the ball, move a distance away from his line, and face them.

3. The player with the ball bounces it to the first player in line who traps the ball, and then goes out to be the tosser. The tosser goes to the end of the line.
4. Continue until all players have had a turn tossing and trapping.

THROW AND TRAP

1. Divide the class into groups of six students each, and have each group line up single file.
2. Have the first player in each line take the ball, go out a ways, and face the line.
3. The player with the ball throws it (two hands overhead) to the first player in the line who traps it, then dribbles out to become the thrower. The thrower goes to the end of the line.
4. Continue until all players have had a turn throwing and trapping.

■ Shooting Drills

Skills: Dribbling, passing, trapping, shooting, goaltending

Supplies: Soccer balls, cones

Formation: Divide the class into squads of approximately six players each.

Description: Each drill is described under its heading.

SHOOT BETWEEN THE CONES

1. Put two groups of six players each together with one ball and two cones.
2. Set the cones about 5 feet apart, with the group with the ball lined up on one side of the cones about 10 feet to 15 feet away. Line up the other group on the other side of the cones.
3. The player with the ball kicks it between the cones to the player on the other (shuttle formation) side, who traps it and kicks it back.
4. Both players go to the end of their lines, and the next players take their turns.

SHOOTING AND GOAL TENDING

1. The formation is the same as for the above drill.
2. The group without the ball are the goaltenders.
3. The first goaltender positions her/himself between the cones.
4. The first kicker attempts to kick a goal as the goalie attempts to block it.
5. These two players switch lines by going to the end of each others line, thus getting a chance to practice the other skill.
6. Continue until all players have had a turn as goaltender and kicker.

SHOOT IN STRIDE

1. A goal is set up and has a goalie.
2. The remaining players form two equal lines, each with a ball.

3. The two lines alternate turns.
4. The first player pushes the ball forward on the ground, sprints after it, and shoots as soon as s/he reaches the ball, without breaking stride, using whichever foot is appropriate.
5. The player retrieves the shot and goes to the end of the line.
6. The first player in the other line goes. This continues, alternating lines each time.
7. The player who shoots could take the goalie's place or the goalie could stay there for a designated number of players.

RUN, SHOOT, AND DEFEND

1. A goal is set up for each group, with a goalie.
2. There is a "feeder," a defensive line, and an offensive line.
3. The "feeder" rolls the ball forward, and the offensive and defensive player sprint to the ball.
4. The offensive player tries to get to the ball and shoot a goal, while the defender tries to help defend the goal.
5. The offensive player becomes the goalie; goalie goes to the end of the defensive line; defensive player becomes the "feeder"; and the "feeder" goes to the end of the offensive line.
6. Continue until all players have had a chance to play both offense and defense.

TURN AND SHOOT

1. A goal is set up with a goalie.
2. Players line up in a single file line.
3. The first player goes out and faces the "feeder."
4. The "feeder" lofts the ball over the player's head, who turns, moves to the ball, and shoots it on contact.
5. The shooter retrieves the ball, gives it to the "feeder" and goes to the end of the line or becomes the "feeder."
6. Continue until all players have had a turn to shoot.

PASS AND SHOOT

1. Set up a goal with a goalie.
2. Have two groups line up single file on each side of the goal, a distance back from the goal. The lines will be side by side with distance between them.
3. The first player of line A passes to the first player in line B.
4. Player 1 then runs toward the goal, player 2 passes to player 1 and player 1 attempts to score a goal.
5. Players 1 and 2 go to the end of the opposite line after their turn.
6. Continue this procedure. Change the goalie periodically.

DROP, PASS, AND SHOOT

1. Divide the class into groups of twelve students each, give each group a ball and a goal.
2. Set up two lines of offensive players with one line with the balls.
3. Set up a line of defensive players by the goal with one player as goalie.
4. The first player in line A dribbles about halfway.
5. A defensive player comes out to confront the dribbler, who drops a diagonal pass to the first player in line B who has moved up to receive the pass.
6. The player from line B receives the pass and takes a shot at the goal.
7. After the shot, the two offensive players go to the end of the opposite offensive lines, and the defensive player goes to the end of the defensive line.

QUICK SHOOTING

1. Divide the class into groups of twelve students each.
2. Give each group a ball and a goal.
3. A line of offensive players lines up alongside a "feeder."
4. A line of defensive players lines up at the side of the field ahead of the goal.
5. Two defensive players serve as retrievers and one as a goalie.
6. The "feeder" passes the ball forward for the offensive player to dribble and shoot.

7. When the offensive player is about halfway to the goal, the defensive player sprints out to confront the offensive player.

8. The object is for the offensive player to shoot at the goal before the defensive player attempts to take the ball away.

■ Drills for Advanced Skills

Skills: Volleying, heading

Supplies: Soccer balls, cones

Formation: Varies according to the drill

Description: Each drill is described under its heading.

VOLLEYING

1. Divide the class into groups of four, each with a designated space and ball.
2. Three players stand in a line while the tosser faces them.
3. The tosser tosses the ball to the first player who volleys the ball back to the tosser and then goes to the end of the line.
4. After the tosser has tossed to each player, s/he goes to the end of the line, and the next player becomes the tosser.

VOLLEYING THREESOMES

1. Divide the class into groups of three, each with a designated space and a ball.
2. The object is to keep the ball in the air by using the feet, thighs, head, and chest.
3. Each member can take a turn and see how long s/he can keep the ball in the air before it hits the ground, or the group of three can try to keep it in the air using teamwork.

TOSS AND HEAD

1. Have the groups line up single file.
2. The first player in each line takes the ball, moves out a distance from the line, and faces them.
3. The player tosses the ball high in the air and the first player in line heads it forward and downward.
4. The tosser goes to the end of the line, and the header becomes the tosser.

GOAL HEADING

1. Have each group line up single file facing a goal.
2. The first player in line takes the ball and moves inside the goal area facing the line.

3. This player tosses the ball high in the air to the first player in line who attempts to head it through the goal.

4. The tosser goes to the end of the line and the header becomes the tosser.

NOTE:

In teaching heading, you may want to start with foam balls, then change to playground balls, and finally to soccer balls.

SOCCER LEAD-UP GAMES

■ Soccer Dribble Call Ball

Skills: Controlled dribbling, trapping

Supplies: A soccer ball for each group

Formation: Divide the class into groups of six to ten students each. Have each group form a circle with the ball in the center. Number each circle of players consecutively.

Description: This game is great for practicing controlled dribbling. To start the game, the teacher calls out a number. The player with that number runs to the center of his circle, dribbles the ball out of his space, around the outside of his circle, back to the center, and traps it. When every team is finished, another number is called. This continues until all players have had a turn. NOTE: This game can be used as a drill for dribbling skills.

■ Soccer Croquet

Skills: Kicking with accuracy

Supplies: A soccer ball (or another type of ball) for each student

Formation: A grassy area is needed. Groups of three or four students line up single file. The groups should be scattered around the area.

Description: This game is great for practicing controlled and accurate kicks. The object of the game is for one ball to hit the other, with each hit scoring a point. The first player in each group kicks the ball straight out from the line. The second player kicks his/her ball, trying to hit the first player's ball. The third player kicks his/her ball, trying to hit either of the other balls. This continues with the players taking their turns in sequence. When a player hits a ball, s/he gets one point and another turn. The game continues until a specified number of points is reached (recommended: five to ten points).

■ Soccer Golf

Skills: Kicking with accuracy and control

Supplies: A soccer ball for each team and a large box or wastebasket for each team

Formation: Divide the class into groups of six students each. Have each team line up single file behind the restraining line. A cardboard box is placed on its side about 40 yards in front of each team.

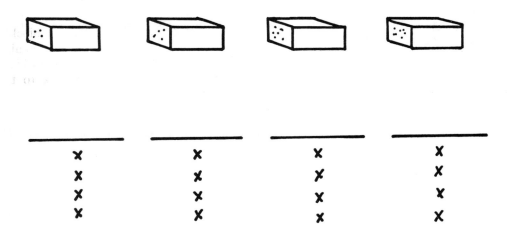

Description: This activity adds a challenge to kicking with accuracy and control. At the signal, the first player on each team kicks the ball until it rolls into the box. The player with the least number of kicks wins a point for his team. Continue this until all players have had a turn.

VARIATION: Set up "holes" scattered around the field with numbers on each box, and have the students move from hole to hole, keeping score.

■ Soccer Line Kick

Skills: Kicking, blocking, trapping, passing, tackling, teamwork

Supplies: A soccer ball, four cones

Formation: Divide the class into groups of eight to ten players each. Number each team consecutively.

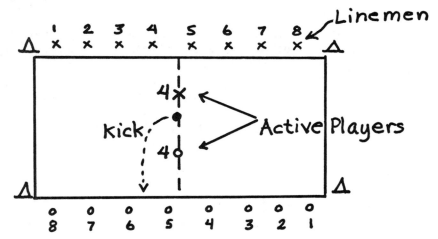

Description: This is a great game for practicing a variety of soccer skills with a focus on teamwork. The game starts with the ball in the center. The teacher calls a number and the player from each team with that number runs to the center and tries to gain possession of the ball in order to return it to his/her team. The player attempts to return it to one of the linemen and the lineman attempts to kick it through the other team's line. The active players try to steal the ball from the other team and block a kick going toward their team line. The linemen attempt to block the kick coming toward their line. Only the linemen can score. A point is scored when a lineman kicks the ball through the other team's line. After each score, the ball goes back to the center and another number is called. This continues until all players have had a turn to be the active player. Then call two numbers at a time, and so on.

■ Line Soccer

Skills: Dribbling, passing, trapping, shooting, tackling, defending

Supplies: Ten cones, one ball

Formation: Divide the class in half, lining up one half along one sideline and the other half along the other sideline.

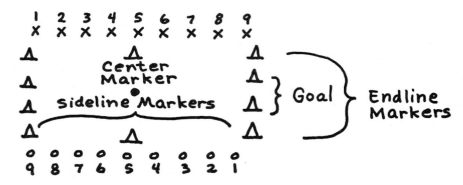

Description: This game is great for practicing and developing skills in a game situation, since the number of players on the field increases one player at a time. The teacher starts the game by calling a number. Those players run in, and each attempts to gain control of the ball, dribble toward the goal, and shoot. When a goal is scored the ball goes back to the center and the players go back to their places. Calling one number at a time continues until all players have had a turn.

Then two numbers are called. Players must use dribbling and passing with their teammate before they attempt to score a goal. This continues until all players have had a turn.

When three or more numbers are called at a time, the last number called is the goalie.

■ Four vs. Four Soccer

Skills: Dribbling, passing, trapping, shooting, tackling

Supplies: Cones, soccer balls, jump ropes for boundary lines

Formation: Divide the class into teams of four players each. There are three forwards and one goalie on each side. If you have the equipment, set up enough fields so all students can play.

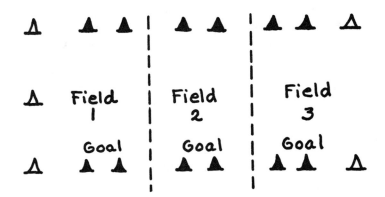

Description: This game is a favorite because it gives students an opportunity to be active and involved since there are only four players on a team.

The game is started by one team kicking off (center forward passes to one of the side forwards—defensive team 5 yards back), or by the two center forwards going for the ball at the same time. The object of the game is for the forwards to use dribbling and passing to move the ball down the field and score a goal. When a goal is scored, the ball goes back to the center and the team that did not score kicks off, or both center forwards go for the ball.

The rules include:

1. When the ball goes out of bounds, the ball is thrown in by the team that did not kick it out.
2. When "hands" are used (hand to armpit) it is a free kick for the other team at the spot where "hands" were used.
3. If the ball goes out at the endline, it is the goalie's ball to throw or kick in.

■ Soccer Kickball

Skills: Dribbling, passing, trapping, shooting, kicking

Supplies: One soccer ball, a goal, a base, and a restraining line

Formation: Divide the class in half. One team is the fielding team and one team is the kicking team. Set up the goal where home base would be and the base where first base would be. Fielders scatter behind the restraining line. The kicking team has one kicker and another "on deck" retrieving and waiting his/her turn.

Description: This game is wonderful for practicing controlled dribbling and passing and for accurate shooting skills. The first kicker kicks the ball, runs to the base, around it, and back to the goal line. The fielders get the ball, and using dribbling and passing, move the ball down the field and kick it through the goal. If the kicker makes it to

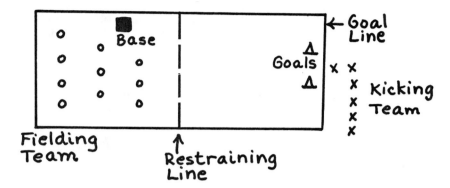

the goal line before the fielders kick a goal, the kicking team receives a point. If the ball goes through the goal before the kicker gets there, it is an "out." Fielding and kicking teams change places after all have kicked or after a designated number of "outs."

■ Soccer Softball

Skills: Dribbling, passing, trapping, kicking, teamwork

Supplies: Two soccer balls, four cones

Formation: Divide the class in half. One team is the fielding team, and one team is the kicking team. The cones are used as bases and set up as for softball. One soccer ball is put by home base, and the other ball is put between home and first base.

Description: This game uses soccer skills in a softball field setup. It focuses on controlled dribbling and passing as well as on teamwork. The first player kicks the ball at home plate out into the field. The kicker then runs to the ball placed between home and first and dribbles it around all the bases. The object is for the kicker to get back home before the fielding team gets the kicked ball home.

The fielding team must get the ball, kick it to the first baseman, who traps it and hits the first cone. Passes are then made to second, third, and home.

The rules are:

1. It is an out if the catcher hits home before the kicker.
2. It is an out if the kicker touches the ball with the hands.
3. The kicking team scores a run if the fielding team touches the ball with their hands.
4. A run is scored if the kicker hits home before the catcher.
5. The teams change places after two outs.

■ Sideline Soccer

Skills: Dribbling, passing, trapping, shooting, tackling

Supplies: Soccer ball, cones

Formation: Divide the class into teams of ten to fifteen players each. Five players from each team line up inside the playing area; remaining players line up outside the area.

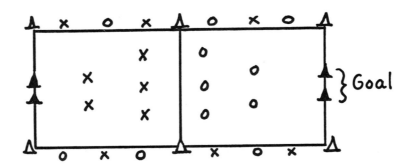

Description: This game is great for keeping all students involved whether they are a field player or a sideline player.

The game begins with a kickoff by the center players. Once the game has started, the field players can move anywhere on the field. Sideline players must stay behind the sidelines, but may shift sideward to the next player. Sideline players are allowed to trap and pass to the field players, but only the field players can score goals.

If the ball goes over the sidelines or end lines, the ball is given to the nearest sideline opponent of the team that touched the ball last. If a player touches the ball with the hands, or a sideline player enters the playing area, the ball is given to the nearest sideline opponent of the team that caused the infraction. Rotate the sideline and field players every two minutes.

■ Cooperative Soccer

Skills: Dribbling, passing, trapping, shooting, tackling, defending, cooperation

Supplies: Ten cones for each field, one soccer ball for each field

Formation: Divide the class into teams of six players, each with three forwards, two backs, and a goalie. The forwards can go everywhere on the field, and they attempt to score goals. The backs can only go on their half of the field (to the center line), and they pass to the forwards and help protect the goal. The goalie attempts to keep the opponents from scoring.

Description: This is a fantastic lead-up game for developing the concept of teamwork. The game is started by the center forward of one team passing to one of his/her other forwards. The rule is that all forwards must contact the ball by dribbling and passing before a goal can be scored. If a goal is scored before all forwards on a team have contacted the ball, the score does not count and it becomes the goalie's ball. When a legal score is made, the ball goes back to the center and the team that did not score kicks off.

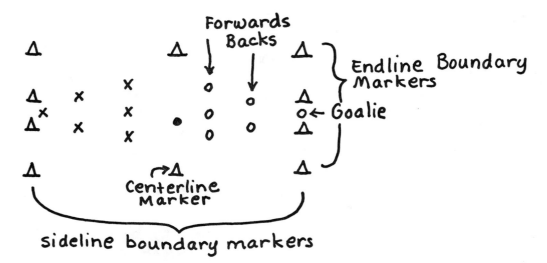

If the ball goes out of bounds on the sideline, it's a throw-in from that spot. If the ball goes out of bounds on the endline, it's the goalie's ball. The goalie can either throw or kick the ball in. If a player touches the ball with hands (from fingers to armpit), it's a free kick for the other team from that spot.

Periodically (for example, every 5 minutes) change positions (forwards to backs and goalie/backs and goalie to forwards) so all players get a chance to score goals.

A team wins once everyone on that team has scored a goal.

■ Six vs. Six Soccer

Skills: Dribbling, passing, trapping, tackling, defending, goaltending, teamwork

Supplies: A soccer ball and set of goals for each field

Formation: Divide the class into groups of six players each. Each team consists of six players (three forwards who go all over the field and attempt to score goals; two backs who can only go to the center line, passing the ball to forwards and helping the goalie protect the goal; one goalie who attempts to keep the opponents from scoring).

Description: This game provides a wonderful opportunity for students to be actively involved, since there are only a few players on each team. The game begins with a kickoff by one team's center forward. The object of the game is for the players to use their learned soccer skills along with teamwork to move the ball down the field and score goals.

The rules are:

1. If the ball goes out of bounds at the sideline, it is a throw-in.
2. If the ball goes out at the endline it is the goalie's ball to throw or kick in.
3. If hands are used it is a free kick at the spot where hands were used.
4. When a goal is scored, the ball goes back to the center, and the team that did not score kicks off.

TEACHING HINTS
FOR SOFTBALL

1. Softball is recommended for grades 3–6, but it can be adapted to grades 1 and 2.
2. After teaching the basic techniques of the various skills, have the students practice in stations. Here is a station example:

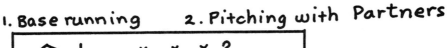

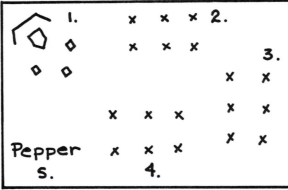

1. Base running   2. Pitching with Partners

3. Fly ball catching with partners

Pepper
5.   4.

4. Grounders with partners

3. You may need to have some third graders start out using a tee for batting, or pitching to them yourself. You may want to use a 6-inch playground ball to begin with.
4. To practice not throwing the bat, have the batter drop the bat in a bucket before running to first base (throwing the bat is a common error among students).
5. If you need to be in the gym, use a whiffle ball and plastic bat.
6. Consider not using strike outs. Have every batter bat until s/he gets a hit. Help out by pitching to them or helping them with batting.
7. Teach students the rules and have them call their own rule infractions so they can learn to be independent of constant teacher intervention. This allows for more than one game to go on at a time, which then provides for maximum student involvement. This also teaches students to be honest about their "mistakes."
8. Set up as many fields as possible so that all students can be active.

Suggested Softball Skills Sequence

GRADE 3	GRADE 4	GRADE 5	GRADE 6
THROWING & CATCHING (Use a rubber softball.) Underhand Overhand Grounders Fly Balls	THROWING & CATCHING (Use a regular softball.) Underhand Overhand Pitching Grounders Fly Balls Taking throws at first, second, third, catcher	THROWING & CATCHING Same as grade 4	THROWING & CATCHING Same as grades 4 and 5
Drills Throw and Catch Zig zag Throw Pitch and Catch	*Drills* Same as grade 3, plus: Softball Pop-Up	*Drills* Same as grade 4, plus: Pitching With a Target	*Drills* Same as grades 4 and 5, plus: Overtake Throw
BATTING *Drills* Batting With a Tee Informal Hitting	BATTING *Drills* Informal Hitting	BATTING *Drills* Five Hundred Pepper	BATTING *Drills* Pepper Home Run Babe Ruth Ball
BASE RUNNING *Drills* Around the Bases	BASE RUNNING *Drills* Around the Bases	BASE RUNNING *Drills* Overtake the Base	BASE RUNNING *Drills* Same as grade 5
	INFIELD *Drills* Infield Plays	INFIELD *Drills* Same as grade 4	INFIELD *Drills* Swing at Four
LEAD-UP GAMES Twenty-One Softball	LEAD-UP GAMES Hit Pin Softball Twenty-One Softball Three Team Softball	LEAD-UP GAMES Same as grade 4, plus: Two Pitch Softball Hurry Softball	LEAD-UP GAMES Same as grades 4 and 5

GLOSSARY OF SOFTBALL TERMS

Ball: a pitched ball that isn't in the strike zone and is not swung at by the batter.

Baseline: the line drawn from home to first, to second, to third, and back home.

Diamond: softball playing field.

Double: a hit ball that enables the batter to reach second base.

Double play: a play by the fielding team in which two base runners are put out.

Fair territory: area between first and third base lines which continue into the outfield.

Fly ball: any ball that is batted in the air.

Force out: to put out a base runner who has to leave a base because of an advancing runner.

Foul territory: the area outside the first and third base lines.

Home run: a hit that enables the batter to make it around all the bases and back home, scoring a run.

Pitching plate: where pitcher stands.

Pop-up: a fly ball that doesn't go beyond the baselines.

Single: a hit that enables the batter to get to first base.

Strike: a ball that passes over home plate between the batter's knees and shoulders and which batter does not swing at, or a ball that the batter swings at and misses.

Tag out: when a fielder who is in possession of the ball touches a base runner with the ball; also, touching the base with the foot while in possession of the ball.

Triple: a hit that enables the batter to reach third base.

Overthrow: a ball thrown toward a base which goes beyond the intended baseman.

TASK ANALYSIS OF SOFTBALL SKILLS

THROWING

Gripping the Ball

1. Grip the ball with four fingers spread on top.
2. Place the thumb to the side or underneath.
3. Have only the pads of the fingers touching the ball.

Overhand Throw

1. Raise throwing arm to shoulder height, with elbow bent and back, wrist cocked.
2. Stand with opposite side facing the direction of the throw and that arm extended forward.

3. Have weight on rear foot.
4. Simultaneously move the throwing arm upward and forward (elbow leading) with nonthrowing arm moving down and back as the weight shifts to the front foot.
5. Release the ball with a snap of the wrist at shoulder height.
6. Follow through with hand pointing toward the target, downward direction, ending with palm of throwing hand facing the ground.
7. Swing the back leg around into a balanced position.

Sidearm Throw (for shorter, quicker throws)

1. Extend the upper throwing arm diagonally out and down from the shoulder.
2. Extend the forearm of the throwing arm straight up from the elbow.
3. Swing arm forward, dropping the forearm down and swinging it parallel to the ground.
4. Lean the body slightly toward the throwing-arm side.
5. Release ball with a whiplike action with arm continuing across and around the body.

Underhand Toss

1. Bring throwing arm and hand back with palm facing forward, as the weight shifts to the back foot.
2. Bring arm forward and downward and shift weight to front foot.
3. Release the ball with a snap of the wrist.
4. Follow through with the upper arm and hand in the direction of the throw.

Pitching

1. Stand with both feet on the pitcher's rubber, facing the batter.
2. Hold the ball in front with both hands about waist high.
3. Hold the ball in pitching hand with palm facing upward.
4. Bring pitching arm down and back.
5. Take a step forward on nonthrowing foot as the pitching arm swings forward and close to the body, releasing the ball.
6. Follow through with the pitching arm.

CATCHING

Stance (Ready Position)

1. Infielder is in semi-crouch position with feet shoulder width apart, knees slightly bent, hands on or in front of knees. Weight is shifted to the balls of the feet as the ball is pitched.
2. Outfielder is also in a semi-crouch position but a little more erect.

Catching Balls

1. For a ball above the waist, the thumbs are together and fingers are pointed upward.

2. For a ball below the waist, the little fingers are together and the fingers are pointed downward.
3. Make the initial contact with the glove; the other hand secures the ball. As the ball hits the pocket of the glove, "give" with the hands toward the body.

Fielding Grounders

1. Infield
   a. Face the batter with feet spread, knees bent, weight forward, and eyes on the ball.
   b. Move to get in line with the ball.
   c. Keep body and glove low to the ground with throwing foot forward.
   d. Look the ball into the glove and secure it just inside of front foot and with throwing hand.
   e. Stand up and step in the direction of the throw.
2. Outfield
   a. Move in line with the ball.
   b. Turn body slightly, touching to the ground the knee that is closest to the ball (sets up a body block).
   c. Secure the ball in the glove.
   d. Assume the position for an overhand throw.

Fielding Fly Balls

1. Stand with feet spread, knees bent, weight forward, and eyes on the ball.
2. Move in line with the ball. (If you have to move back, run, turning to watch the ball over the shoulder.)
3. Catch the ball slightly above eye level.
4. Absorb the force of the ball with the glove.
5. Either run the ball to the infield (if infield pop-fly) or assume throwing position.

CATCHER

1. Assume a crouched position.
2. Place feet shoulder width apart with the catching foot slightly ahead.
3. Point fingers of the glove upward (provides a target for the pitcher).
4. Secure the ball with the throwing hand.
5. Step to a throwing position.

TAKING A THROW AT FIRST BASE

1. Move to the base when the ball is hit.
2. Assume a relaxed, ready position.
3. Extend one leg toward the ball while touching the base with the other foot (throw to left requires extending left leg; throw to right requires extending right leg).

TAKING A THROW AT SECOND OR THIRD BASE

1. From infield or right field: Straddle the base and turn upper body to face throw.
2. From left field: Face the throw, catch the ball, pivot on catching foot, face runner with glove in position to make the tag.
3. From center field: Face the thrower, catch the ball, pivot on throwing foot into a position to make the tag.

BATTING

Grip

1. Grip the bat with hands together, fingers and thumbs wrapped around the handle.
2. Place the lower hand (left for right-handed batters; right for left-handed batters) about one or two inches from the knob.

Stance

1. Stand with feet parallel to the plate, knees flexed.
2. Face the plate squarely with hips and shoulders.
3. Bend elbows and hold them away from the body (back elbow is raised to shoulder level and points backwards).
4. Hold the bat back of the head at about shoulder height.

Swing

1. Shift weight to the rear foot as the pitch is made and move front foot forward.
2. Rotate shoulders and project weight forward.
3. Pivot at the hips as the bat comes around with hands, leading the swing in front of the body.
4. Keep eyes on the ball.
5. Snap the wrists to contact the ball.
6. Roll hands and follow through.

SOFTBALL DRILLS

■ Throwing and Catching Drills

Skills: Throwing, catching

Supplies: Softballs, gloves, bases

Formation: Varies according to the drill

Description: Each drill is described under its heading.

THROW AND CATCH

1. Divide students into groups of two, each with a ball.
2. Practice the following:
   a. Throw back and forth, using various throws.
   b. Throw ground balls back and forth.
   c. One student is the first baseman, throws grounders to the others, and receives the putout throw.
   d. Throw fly balls back and forth.
   e. Establish four bases and throw from base to base.

OVERTAKE THROW

1. Divide the class into teams with six to eight players each.
2. Two teams form a circle with players of opposing teams alternating.

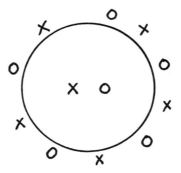

3. A player from each team is in the center and each has a ball.
4. The center players start their balls on opposite sides of the circles.
5. Both balls are passed clockwise, throwing only to their team members.
6. The object is for one team to throw and catch the ball so fast that it overtakes the other team's ball.
7. After each round, a new player goes in the center.
8. If you choose to score, a point is scored for a team if they are able to overtake the other team's ball.

ZIGZAG THROW

1. Divide the class into teams with eight to ten players each.
2. Give each team a ball.
3. Divide each team in half, forming two lines facing each other.

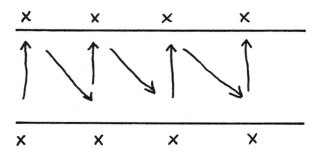

4. The object is for the teams to throw the ball through the zig-zag pattern in the shortest time.

SOFTBALL POP-UP

1. Divide the class into teams with six to eight players each.
2. One team forms a circle and has a ball.
3. Another team scatters in the center of the circle.
4. Each member of the throwing team has a number (outside circle).
5. Each member of the fielding team has a corresponding number (inside circle).
6. Each member of the throwing team (in turn) throws a fly ball and the person with the corresponding number attempts to catch it.
7. After each has had a turn, teams change roles.

■ Pitching Drills

Skills: Pitching (underhand), catching

Supplies: Softballs, gloves, bases

Formation: Varies according to the drill

Description: Each drill is described under its heading.

PITCH AND CATCH

1. Divide class up in pairs, each pair with a base.
2. One student pitches over the plate to his/her partner.
3. After several pitches, change places.

PITCHING WITH A TARGET

1. Divide the class into groups of four, each group with a base.
2. One student pitches, one catches, one is a stationary batter, one is an umpire.
3. After a certain number of pitches, rotate positions (pitcher becomes umpire, umpire becomes catcher, catcher becomes batter, batter becomes pitcher).

■ Batting Drills

Skills: Batting, catching, fielding, timing, pitching
Supplies: Bats, softballs, batting tees (a cone on top of a cardboard box), gloves
Formation: Varies according to the drill
Description: Each drill is described under its heading.

BATTING WITH A TEE

1. Set up a tee for each group.
2. Have three to five students for each tee.
3. One student bats, one is a catcher (gets incoming balls from field), others are fielders.
4. After a certain number of hits, rotate positions (batter to fielder, fielder to catcher, catcher to batter).

INFORMAL HITTING

1. Divide class into groups of five.
2. Have one batter, one pitcher, one catcher, and two fielders.
3. After a certain number of hits, rotate positions (batter to fielder, fielder to pitcher, pitcher to catcher, catcher to batter).

PEPPER

1. Divide the class into groups of five.
2. Give each group a bat and ball.
3. A line of four players faces the batter.
4. Each player tosses the ball to the batter, who attempts to hit it back to them.
5. After each player has tossed, rotate batter and players.

FIVE HUNDRED

1. Divide class into groups with five to twelve students in each.
2. One player bats, the other players are scattered in the field.
3. The fielders attempt to become the batter by getting a score of 500.
4. Point system:
   a. 200 points for catching a fly ball.
   b. 100 points for catching a ball on the first bounce.
   c. 50 points for fielding a grounder.
5. When a fielder becomes the new batter, the game starts over.

HOME RUN

1. Divide class into teams with at least four players in each.
2. There needs to be a batter, catcher, pitcher, and one fielder.
3. The batter hits a pitched ball and runs to first base and home before the ball is returned to the catcher.
4. The batter is out when:
    a. A fly ball is caught.
    b. The ball beats him back to home plate.
5. Rotate positions after each hit.

BABE RUTH BALL

1. Divide the class into groups of at least six players.
2. Divide the three outfield zones (left, right, center) with cones.

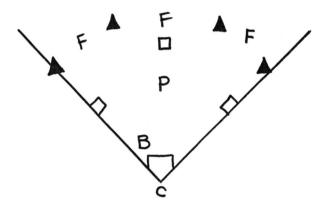

3. The batter calls out the field to which s/he intends to hit.
4. The pitcher pitches to the batter.
5. The batter stays as batter as long as s/he can hit to the designated field, but field choices must be rotated.
6. The batter gets one swing.
7. There is no base running.
8. Rotate players.

■ Infield Drills

Skills: Catching, throwing

Supplies: Softballs, gloves, bases

Formation: Varies according to the drill

Description: Each drill is described under its heading.

INFIELD PLAYS

1. Divide students into groups of six.
2. There is one catcher, one first baseman, one second baseman, one third baseman, one shortstop, and one "batter."
3. Start out by throwing the ball around the bases.
4. Have the "batter" throw the ball to the various players who throw to a certain base (batter calls out the play).
5. After a certain number of throws, rotate positions (batter to first, first to second, second to shortstop, shortstop to third, third to catcher, catcher to batter).

SWING AT FOUR

1. Divide the class into groups of ten to twelve players.
2. Arrange the group with a player in each infield position (first, second, third, shortstop, pitcher, catcher), and have the remaining players line up behind home plate.
3. The pitcher throws four balls to each batter who tries to hit the ball to the infield.
4. Infield players retrieve the ball and throw it to first base.
5. The first baseman throws the ball back to the pitcher.
6. After a player has had four hits, rotate all players (batter to third, third to shortstop, shortstop to second, second to first, first to pitcher, pitcher to catcher, catcher to "waiting" line).

■ Base-Running Drills

Skills: Running

Supplies: Bases, bats, softballs

Formation: Varies according to the drill

Description: Each drill is described under its heading.

AROUND THE BASES

1. Divide the class into two teams for each softball diamond.
2. Both teams line up on the inside of the diamond at diagonally opposite bases.
3. At the signal, the first player on each team runs around all four bases and then tags the next player in line.
4. The team finishing first wins.

OVERTAKE THE BASE

1. Divide the class into six groups (A, B, C, D, E, F).

2. Group A is at the pitcher's line, group B is at home plate, group C is on first base, group D is on second base, group E is on third base, group F is the one that runs bases.
3. When the whistle blows player A throws to player B, B to C, and so on. At the same time, player F runs to first base and so on.
4. Player F attempts to reach home before the ball does.
5. The players rotate after each run (A to B, B to C, C to D, D to E, E to F, F to A).

SOFTBALL LEAD-UP GAMES

■ Two-Pitch Softball

Skills: Catching, throwing, pitching, fielding, batting, base running

Supplies: A softball, bat, gloves, four bases

Formation: Divide the class into two teams, a batting team and a fielding team.

Description: This game is played like regulation softball with the following changes:

1. A member of the batting team is the pitcher.
2. The batter has two pitches in which to hit the ball.
3. The pitcher can't field the ball.
4. A member of the fielding team acts as the fielding pitcher.

After three outs or all have batted, the teams change roles.

■ Hit Pin Softball

Skills: Batting, catching, fielding, pitching, throwing

Supplies: A softball, bat, gloves, four bases, four Indian clubs (bowling pins, plastic liter pop bottles).

Formation: Divide the class into two teams, one batting team and one fielding team. Set the Indian clubs on the outside corner of each base.

Description: This game focuses on throwing with accuracy. A new twist is added to regular softball by having the Indian clubs at each base. The object of the game is to throw the batted ball to each base and knock down the pins before the batter gets home.

The first batter hits a pitched ball and runs the bases. The fielding team fields the ball and throws it to the first baseman, second, third, and home. When the baseman receives the ball, he knocks down the pin, and throws it to the next base. A batter is out by regulation softball rules and/or the four pins being knocked down before the batter gets home. After all the players have batted, change roles. Rotate field positions each inning.

■ Twenty-One Softball

Skills: Throwing, catching, pitching, fielding, batting

Supplies: A softball, bat, gloves, four bases

Formation: Divide the class into two teams, a batting team and a fielding team.

Description: This game is a great encouragement for those students who have difficulty getting good hits, because they score points for each base they are safe at.
This game uses regulation softball rules with the following exceptions:

1. A batter gets as many swings as needed to hit the ball.
2. When the batter hits the ball, s/he runs the bases until put out.
3. A runner safe at first gets one point, safe at second two points, safe at third three points, safe at home four points.
4. Teams exchange places after three outs.
5. The first team to score twenty-one points wins.

■ Three-Team Softball

Skills: Throwing, catching, pitching, batting, fielding

Supplies: A softball, bat, gloves, bases

Formation: Divide the class into groups of twelve players each. If possible, give each group a softball diamond to play on.

Description: This game is good for practicing softball skills in small groups. Each group of twelve players are divided into three teams: outfield team (four players), infield team (four players), and batting team (four players). Regulation softball rules are used with the following exceptions:

1. After three outs, the teams rotate—outfield to infield, infield to batting, and batting to outfield.
2. An inning is over when all three teams have batted.

■ Hurry Softball

Skills: Throwing, catching, batting, pitching, batting, base running

Supplies: A softball, bat, gloves, four bases

Formation: Divide the class into two teams, one batting team and one fielding team.

Description: This game adds a fun challenge to softball. The object is to make rapid changes from batting to fielding and fielding to batting. The differences in this game include:

1. The pitcher is from the batting team.
2. The team coming to bat does not wait for the fielding team to get set in their positions. Since it has its own pitcher, s/he gets the ball and pitches it to the batter as soon as possible.
3. The fielding team tries to run onto the field as soon as possible.

4. Only one pitch is allowed per batter.

5. The pitcher stands closer to the batter than normal.

6. There are three outs and then the teams change roles.

HINT: The team in the field should put their next batter as catcher, so on the third out s/he can take his/her place as the first batter immediately.

■ Beanbag Softball Toss

Skills: Tossing with accuracy, scoring

Supplies: Targets, beanbags

Formation: Divide the class into small groups according to the number of targets you have available.

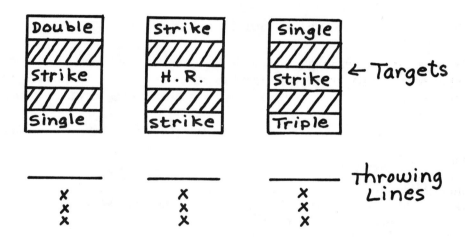

Description: This game is fun to use if inclement weather interrupts your softball unit or as a way of combining beanbag skills and softball terminology. The first player in each line stands behind the throwing line and tosses a beanbag at the target until s/he gets three strikes. The number of runs scored before getting an out is the score for the inning. Each player in line does the same thing.

VARIATIONS: Strike could be replaced with OUT to make the game go faster. Students could form teams and play a certain number of innings.

TEACHING HINTS
FOR VOLLEYBALL

1. Volleyball is recommended for grades 3–6. If you choose to do basic skills with younger students, use beach balls or foam balls with grades 1 and 2, and teach only the bump and set. Some third

graders are not able to manage volleyball either; use your judgment for deciding when to introduce this sport.

2. If you choose to do volleyball in grade 3, use nerf balls or playground balls and teach bump, set, and serve (serve from the front line position). Give students a choice later on whether they want to use the type of balls they have been using or volleyballs.

3. For grades 4–6 use volleyballs.

4. Begin by teaching the bump and the set using different drills. After teaching these skills, do games using just these two skills. Then add the serve. Some students will need to stand close to the net to serve and then move back a little at a time. Allow them to serve from whatever spot will make them successful in getting the ball over the net. There can be no game without a good serve.

5. The *overhand pass* and *set* are the same skill. The *forearm pass* and *bump* are the same skill.

6. When playing a game (grades 1–3) have more players on the court (nine to twelve). Later with third grade, you may be able to go to only six players on the court. With grades 4, 5, and 6, have six players on the court.

7. Lower the net according to the students' height. Take an average-size student and have him/her stand facing the net with arms stretched straight up. The top of the net should be even with the fingertips.

8. Teach students the rules and have them learn how to call their own rule infractions so they can learn to be independent of constant teacher intervention. This allows for more than one game to go on at a time, which then provides for maximum student involvement. This also teaches students to be honest about their "mistakes."

9. If possible, set up more than one court so that all students can be active.

GLOSSARY OF VOLLEYBALL TERMS

Block: defensive skill used in defending against an oncoming spiked ball.

Dig: a one handed hit used as an emergency return.

Forearm pass (bump): used when ball is below waist level; hands are connected and ball is rebounded off forearms.

Suggested Volleyball Skills Sequence

GRADE 3	GRADE 4	GRADE 5	GRADE 6

PASSING
  Bump
  Set
Drills
  Toss and Hit
  Circle Volley
	PASSING
	  Bump
	  Set
	Drills
	  Same as grade 3,
	    plus:
	    Toss-Set/Toss-
	    Bump
		PASSING
		  Bump
		  Set
		Drills
		  Same as grade
		    4, plus:
		    Net Set and
		    Bump
		    Zig zag Volley
			PASSING
			  Bump
			  Set
			Drills
			  Same as grade
			    5, plus:
			    Circle Volleyball
			    Pass Placement

SERVING
  Underhand
 	
Drills
  Serve 'em Up
	SERVING
	  Underhand
	
	Drills
	  Same as grade 3,
	    plus:
	    Regulation Serve
		SERVING
		  Underhand
		
		Drills
		  Same as grade 4
			SERVING
			  Underhand
			  Overhand
			Drills
			  Regulation Serve
			  Target Ball

	COMBINATION
	  Partner Serve and
	    Set
		COMBINATION
		  Same as grade
		    4, plus:
		    Circuit Volleyball
			COMBINATION
			  Same as grade
			    5, plus:
			    Wall Serve and
			    Set

		ADVANCED
		  Dig
			ADVANCED
			  Dig
			  Spike
			  Set, Spike, Block

LEAD-UP GAMES
  Clean Out Your
    Back Yard
  Newcomb
	LEAD-UP GAMES
	  No Serve
	    Volleyball
	  Mass Volleyball
	  Modified
	    Volleyball
	  Regulation
	    Volleyball
		LEAD-UP GAMES
		  Same as grade
		    4, plus:
		  Three-and-Over
		    Volleyball
		  Regulation
		    Volleyball
			LEAD-UP GAMES
			  Same as grade
			    5, plus:
			  Sideline
			    Volleyball
			  Regulation
			    Volleyball

Overhand pass (set): a hit where the ball is contacted with the fingertips and is used to set up the ball.

Serve: the means of scoring points. The ball must go over the net without touching the net.

Setup: pass which sets the ball up for a possible spike. The setup is usually the second pass in a series of three, and is the overhand pass (set). It is used to pass the ball about 15 inches above spiker and about 1 foot from the net.

Spike: offensive skill; a ball that is hit downward into the opponent's court.

TASK ANALYSIS OF VOLLEYBALL SKILLS

OVERHAND PASS (Set)

1. Stand with knees bent, feet in an easy, comfortable position.
2. Have elbows bent and out to the side.
3. Hold hands at forehead level with fingers spread apart, thumbs pointing toward each other (forms a "window").
4. Move underneath the ball and contact it with fingertips.
5. Extend body upward and forward, straightening legs and following through with arms and hands.

FOREARM PASS (Bump)

1. Stand with knees bent, feet shoulder width apart.
2. Clasp hands together so forearms are kept parallel.
   a. Method 1: The thumbs are kept together and parallel.
   b. Method 2: Place the back of one hand in the palm of the other, bend wrists downward which causes elbows to rotate in, forming a flat surface with forearms.
3. Move underneath the ball and contact it.
4. Allow the ball to rebound off arms with movement of shrugging the shoulders (not swinging arms upward).
5. Straighten legs on ball contact.
6. Follow through in the direction of the ball.

DIG

1. Reach sideways with one arm.
2. Stiffen arm.
3. Rebound the ball off of cupped fist, heel of hand, or inside of forearm.
4. Use this only as an emergency return when unable to return the ball with an overhand or forearm pass.

UNDERHAND SERVE

1. Stand with the nonhitting foot (left for right-handers, right for left-handers) slightly forward of the hitting foot.
2. Put weight on the rear foot and bend the body slightly forward.
3. Hold the ball with the nonhitting hand with the arm across the body.
4. Extend the hitting arm backward and upward.
5. Swing the hitting arm down and forward, and at the same time begin to shift weight to front foot.

6. Hit the ball with the heel of the hand or side of fist.
7. Follow through with the hitting arm and step forward with the hitting foot.

OVERHAND SERVE

1. Stand with nonhitting foot slightly forward.
2. Turn the nonhitting side slightly toward the net.
3. Hold the ball in the nonhitting hand.
4. Have hitting arm flexed and cocked, with hand back near the ear.
5. Toss the ball 2 feet to 3 feet above the head so it descends 1 foot in front of the shoulder of the hitting hand.
6. Shift weight to back foot on toss, and shift weight to front foot on descent.
7. Snap the hitting arm forward and contact ball 1 foot above head.
8. Contact the ball with the open hand.
9. Follow through in the direction of the ball.

SPIKE

1. Take running steps toward the net.
2. Jump up, bringing both arms upward and twisting trunk slightly.
3. Continue to extend nonhitting arm upward above head.
4. Cock hitting arm back.
5. Simultaneously draw nonhitting arm down, whipping hitting arm forward and downward, contacting the ball with an open hand.
6. Land facing the net.

BLOCK

1. Time jump according to spike.
2. Face net and jump up at the same time the spiker does.
3. Swing both arms upward with palms facing the opponent.
4. Keep hands stationary so as to rebound the ball back over the net.

VOLLEYBALL DRILLS

■ Passing Drills

Skills: Bump, set
Supplies: Volleyballs, net, standards
Formation: Varies according to the drill
Description: Each drill is described under its heading.

TOSS AND HIT (Do with overhand & forearm pass)

1. The first player in line has the ball and moves a distance away from the squad and faces them.
2. Player 1 tosses the ball to player 2 who uses the designated hit.
3. Player 2 goes to the end of the line, and player 1 tosses ball to player 3.
4. This continues until player 1 has tossed the ball to all in the squad. Then player 2 tosses it to all players.
5. This continues until all have had a chance to toss the ball to all players.

TOSS-SET/TOSS-BUMP

1. Player 1 tosses the ball to self and sets it continuously as many times as s/he can.
2. Player 2 does the same thing.
3. This continues until all have had a turn.
4. Do the same thing with the bump.

NOTE:
Activity works best when each student has a ball.

WALL SET

1. Player 1 (in a squad) faces a wall about 6 feet away.
2. Player 1 throws the ball against the wall and continuously sets the ball back to the wall.
3. Player 2 does the same thing.
4. This continues until all have had a turn.

NET SET AND BUMP

1. Arrange squads so half of the squad is on one side of the net and the other half of the squad is facing them on the other side of the net.

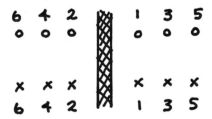

2. Player 1 tosses the ball over the net to player 2 who sets the ball back over the net to player 1. Player 1 catches the ball.
3. Player 1 rolls the ball under the net to player 2.

4. Player 2 tosses the ball to player 1 who sets the ball back over the net to player 2. Player 2 catches the ball.
5. Player 2 rolls the ball under the net.
6. Players 1 and 2 go to the end of their lines.
7. Players 3 and 4 do the same as players 1 and 2 did.
8. This continues until all have had a turn.
9. Repeat this process with the bump.
10. Repeat this process except have the two players attempt to pass the ball back and forth over the net with the set, bump, or both.

CIRCLE VOLLEYING

1. Have each squad of 6 players form a circle with a ball.
2. One player tosses the ball to another player who sets it.
3. Players attempt to keep the ball in the air using sets.
4. Players need to "call it" when going for the ball ("I got it.").
5. Do the same thing with the bump.
6. Then repeat using either hit.

ZIGZAG VOLLEY

1. Two teams of 6 players each stand facing each other and use first the set to go zigzag down the line, then the bump. The idea is to keep the ball going.

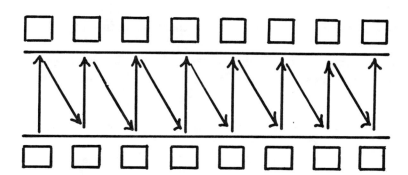

2. NOTE: You may need to use smaller groups to achieve success (varies according to ability).

PASS PLACEMENT

1. Divide the class up so there are about four players in each line.
2. Player 1 tosses to player 2 who passes it to player 3.
3. Player 3 passes it to player 4.

4. This continues down the line as long as the ball doesn't hit the floor.

5. If the ball hits the floor, team 1 goes to the back and team 2 moves up and repeats the process.

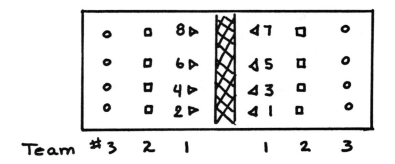

CIRCLE VOLLEYBALL

1. Class is divided into two teams of 6 players each.

2. Each team forms a circle. One team is offense, the other team is defense.

3. Offensive players attempt to pass the ball over the defensive players' heads to their center offensive players. The defensive players attempt to intercept the passes.

4. The center player catches the ball then tosses it to a teammate.

5. The game is started with an offensive player tossing the ball and passing it to a teammate. It can then be passed to a center player.

6. If the ball gets to the center player without being intercepted, the offensive team gets a point.

7. Have the center player change places with an offensive player.

8. Have the offensive and defensive teams trade places after a designated period of time.

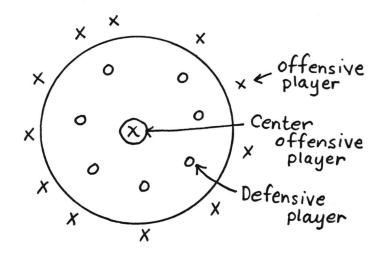

■ Serving Drills

Skills: Serving

Supplies: Volleyballs, net, standards

Formation: Varies according to the drill

Description: Each drill is described under its heading.

SERVE THEM UP

1. You will need a net, volleyball standards, and a volleyball.
2. Set the students up in a regular volleyball formation.

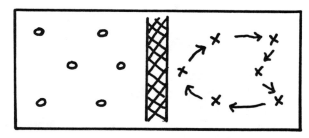

Rotation

3. One team serves the ball over the net to the other team which catches the ball.
4. The player who catches the ball serves the ball from that spot.
5. This procedure is repeated.
6. If the ball hits the floor, it is a point against the team whose court the ball landed in.
7. When the whistle blows, both teams rotate positions.
8. The team with the lowest score wins.

TARGET BALL

1. Divide the class into as many groups as you have wall target space for.
2. The object is to serve for placement.
3. Player 1 on each team serves the ball to the target.
4. If the server hits the number area, s/he gets the number of points shown in that area.
5. The team that scores the most number of points wins.

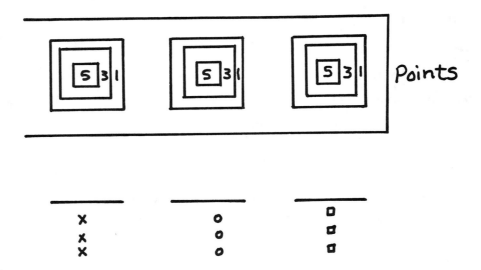

REGULATION SERVE

1. Divide the class into two teams.
2. Line up one team along the serving line on one side of the net and the other team on the other serving line.
3. Player 1 on team 1 serves the ball over the net (if students can't make it from the serving line, have them move close to the net and move back a little each time. Some students may not be able to serve from the serving line. Have them stand wherever they need to).
4. Player 1 on team 2 serves the ball over the net.
5. Both player 1s go to the end of their own lines.
6. Both player 2s of both teams serve the ball.
7. This is repeated until all have had a turn. Keep practicing.

■ Combination of Skills (Passing and Serving)

Skills: Bump, set, serve

Supplies: Volleyballs, net, standards

Formation: Varies according to the drill

Description: Each drill is described under its heading.

WALL SERVE AND SET

1. Have each squad line up single file and face a wall, about 10 feet from the wall.
2. Give each squad a ball.
3. The first player serves the ball to the wall and on the rebound, sets the ball back to the wall, then catches it.

4. The first player goes to the end of the line, and the second player repeats the skill.

PARTNER SERVE AND SET

1. Have two squads face each other in a single file line on either side of the net.
2. Player 1 on team 1 serves the ball over the net to player 1 on team 2.
3. Player 1 on team 2 sets or bumps the ball back over the net.
4. The two players go to the end of the opposite line.
5. This continues until all players have had a chance to serve and bump or set.

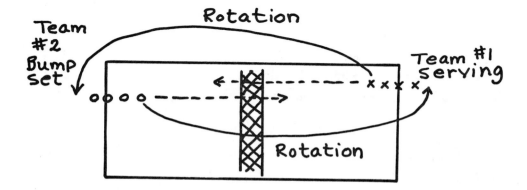

■ Circuit Volleyball

Skills: Bump, set, serve

Supplies: Eighteen volleyballs

Formation: Divide the class into groups according to the number of stations you set up.

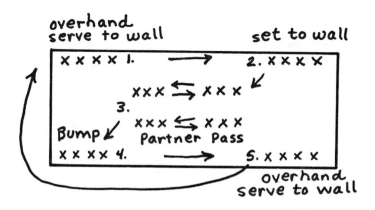

Description: This activity is great for practicing learned skills in a setting which permits the teacher to give individualized instruction. The students practice the designated skill until the whistle blows. The students then rotate to the next station. This continues until the students have been to all stations.

The stations include:

1. Underhand serve to the wall
2. Set to the wall
3. Partner pass (bump and set)
4. Bump
5. Overhand serve to the wall

■ Advanced Skills Drills

Skills: Dig, spike, block

Supplies: Volleyballs, net, standards

Formation: Varies according to the drill

Description: Each drill is described under its heading.

DIG

Divide the class into groups of six students each. Have each group line up single file. The first player in each line is the tosser.

1. The tosser tosses the ball low and to the right or left of the first player in line.
2. The player reaches to the side with his right arm (if on right side) or left arm (if on left side) and contacts the ball on the wrist or fist.
3. Then the tosser tosses to the other side.
4. The hitter becomes the tosser and the tosser goes to the end of the line.
5. This continues until all players have had a chance to toss and dig.

SPIKE

Divide the class in half with each half on a different side of the net. One side is the spikers, the other side the retrievers.

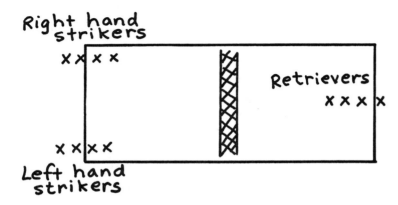

Rotation

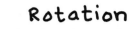
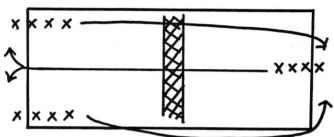

Strikers to end of retrieving line. Retrievers to end of striking line.

1. Level 1: The teacher stands on a chair holding the ball above the net. The first spiker runs and spikes the ball out of the teacher's hand. Rotate.
2. Level 2: The teacher tosses the ball high and near the net, and the spiker runs and spikes the ball. Rotate.
3. Level 3. The teacher sets the ball high and near the net, and the spiker runs and spikes the ball. Rotate.

SET, SPIKE, BLOCK

Divide the class in half with each half on a different side of the net.

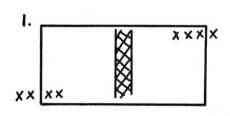

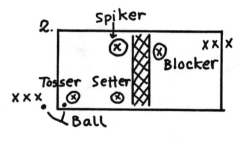

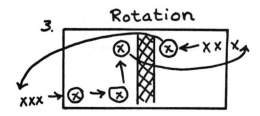

Tosser → Setter
Setter → Spiker
Spiker → End of blocking line
Blocker → End of tosser line

1. The first player in the tosser line tosses the ball high to the setter.
2. The setter uses an overhand pass (set) to set up the ball for the spiker.
3. The spiker attempts to spike the ball into the opposite court.
4. The blocker attempts to block the spiked ball.
5. Players rotate.
6. Repeat process.

VOLLEYBALL LEAD-UP GAMES

■ Clean Out Your Backyard (K–2)

Skills: Throwing over an obstacle

Supplies: Fleece balls, net, standards

Formation: Divide the class in half and have one half get in a personal space on one side of the net, and the other half on the other side of the net. Give each half an equal number of fleece balls.

Description: This game is a lot of fun and gives the students a good workout. The object of the game is to keep the balls going over the net so that your team ends up with the least number of balls on your side at the end of the designated time.

At the signal, the students begin to throw their fleece balls over the net. As the balls come over the net, the players on that side pick them up and throw them over the net. At the signal to stop, have one student on each side count how many balls are left on their side (Vary this period of time, for example, 30 seconds, 1 minute, 3 minutes). The side with the least number of balls scores a point.

■ Newcomb (3–4)

Skills: Throwing, catching, teamwork

Supplies: A volleyball, net, standards

Formation: Divide the class in half. Place nine to twelve players on a side, with the remaining players on the sideline to rotate in.

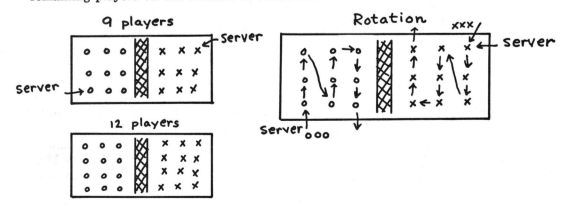

Description: This game is an introduction for rotation and teamwork for volleyball. It provides an opportunity for success for those students who are not quite ready to start volleyball.

The game starts with a serve (tossing the ball over the net) by the back right-hand corner player who may move as close to the net as is needed to get the ball over the net. The serving team scores a point if the receiving team fails to return the serve or if the receiving team throws the ball out of bounds. Only the serving team can score. The receiving team attempts to catch the ball and either throw it to a teammate or over the net (three throws are allowed with the third going over the net). The receiving team may not run with the ball or touch the net. The receiving team wins the serve if:

1. The server fails to get the ball over the net.
2. The serving team fails to return a volleyed ball by the receiving team.
3. The serving team throws the ball out of bounds.

Each time a team gets the ball back to serve, players rotate positions.

VARIATION: Give students the choice of using bumps, sets, and serves or throwing and catching, with both being acceptable in the game.

■ No-Serve Volleyball (4–6)

Skills: Bump, set

Supplies: Net, standards, volleyball

Formation: Divide the class into teams with six players on each team. Have two teams set up on either side of the net with the remaining teams along the sidelines. VARIATION: Divide the class in half and rotate in.

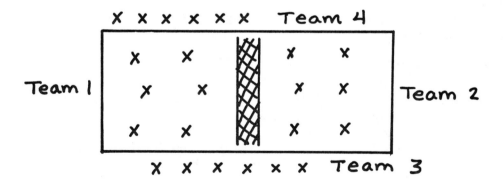

Description: The object of this game is to keep the ball going back and forth over the net using bumping and setting skills. It gives the students an opportunity to play a game using these skills without the pressure of having to serve.

The team that starts with the ball tosses it over the net to the receiving team. The receiving team attempts to return the ball by using bumps and sets. As many hits as needed can be used to keep the ball in play, or you may choose to go with the regulation number of three hits.

When the ball hits the floor or goes out of bounds, the player who retrieves the ball starts the game again by tossing it over the net.

Rotate positions periodically or whenever the ball is dead. Change teams after a designated period of time (for example, 5 minutes).

■ Mass Volleyball (4–6)

Skills: Bump, set, serve, teamwork

Supplies: A volleyball, net, standards

Formation: Divide the class in half. Set up nine to twelve players on a team with the same number of players in each row. The remaining players on each team line up at the sidelines and rotate in.

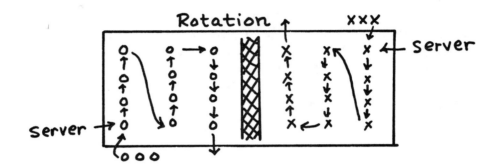

Description: This game provides encouragement to use bumping and setting skills as well as teamwork, because there is no limit to the number of hits on a side before the ball goes over the net.

The game starts with a serve by the back right-hand corner player. The serving team scores a point when:

1. The receiving team fails to return the serve.
2. The ball touches the floor.
3. The ball is hit out of bounds.
4. A player catches the ball.

Only the serving team can score.

The receiving team attempts to return the serve using an unlimited number of bumps and sets. The receiving team wins the serve when:

1. The server fails to serve the ball over the net.
2. The serving team fails to return the volleyed ball.
3. The serving team allows the volleyed ball to hit the floor.
4. The serving team hits the volleyed ball out of bounds.
5. A player catches the volleyed ball.

A game is 11 or 15 points.

■ Sideline Volleyball (4–6)

Skills: Bump, set, serve, teamwork

Supplies: A volleyball, net, standards

Formation: Divide the class in half with a team on each side of the net. Six players from each team are on the court. The other players stand around the sidelines and backline.

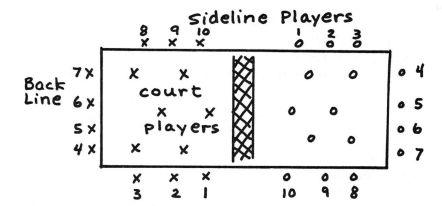

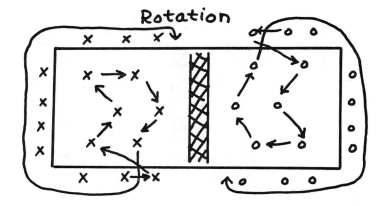

Description: This game is great for keeping everyone involved. There are six court players per team and the rest are sideline and backline players who help keep the ball in play, yet their hits do not count as one of their team's three hits.

The game starts with a serve by the back right-hand corner player who may move as close to the net as needed to get the serve over. The six players on the court are the team players. The sideline and backline players are active, but must stay in their positions. These players attempt to pass the ball to the court players before it hits the floor. The receiving team has as many hits as needed to get the ball over the net. Only the serving team can score. Points are awarded:

1. If the receiving team fails to return the ball.
2. If the ball hits the floor.
3. If the ball is hit out of bounds.

The serving team continues to serve until:

1. The served ball hits the net or does not go over the net.
2. The serving team fails to return a volleyed ball.
3. The volleyed ball hits the floor.
4. The serving team hits the volleyed ball out of bounds.

Teams rotate whenever they get the ball to serve. Rotate sideline and backline players in.

■ Modified Volleyball (4–6)

Skills: Bump, set, serve, teamwork

Supplies: A volleyball, net, standards

Formation: Divide the class in half. Place six players on the court on each side of the net with the rest of the players on each team lined up on the sidelines to rotate in.

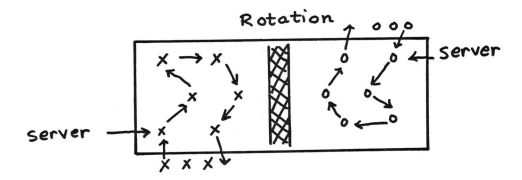

Description: The rules of this game are the same as for Mass Volleyball and Sideline Volleyball in regard to the serving team and receiving team. The differences are:

1. The server has two chances to serve.
2. Students attempt to use only three legal hits to get the ball over the net, but may use as many legal hits as necessary.
3. The same person cannot hit the ball twice in a row.

■ Three-and-Over Volleyball (5–6)

Skills: Bump, set, serve, teamwork

Supplies: A volleyball, net, standards

Formation: Divide the class into two teams. Place six players from each team on their half of the court. Have the remaining players line up along their sideline to rotate in.

Description: This game has the same rules as Modified Volleyball with the exception that students *must* use three legal hits to return the ball. This emphasizes teamwork. If fewer than three hits or more then three hits are used, the ball goes to the other team.

BIBLIOGRAPHY

American Heart Association *Jump For The Health Of It.* 1988.

BENTLEY, WILLIAM G. *Physical Education for Young Children.* Monterey Park, CA: Creative Teaching Press, 1975.

BIERI, ARTHUR PETER. *Action Games.* Belmont, CA: Fearon-Pitman Publishers, n.d.

BLAKE, O. WILLIAM, and ANNE M. VOLP. *Lead-Up Games to Team Sports.* Englewood Cliffs, NJ: Prentice-Hall, 1964.

BRALEY, WILLIAM T.; GERALD KNOCKI, and CATHERINE LEEDY. *Daily Sensorimotor Training Activities.* Freeport, NY: Educational Activities, 1968.

BRAMLISH, RICHARD. *Elementary Floor Exercise Routines.* Freeport, NY: K.B.H. Productions, 1971.

BRYANT, ROSALIE; and ELOISE MCLEAN OLIVER. *Complete Elementary Physical Education Guide.* West Nyack, NY: Parker Publishing, 1974.

CAPON, JACK J. Perceptual Motor Development Series: Book 1, *Basic Movement Activities;* Book 2, *Ball, Rope, Hoop Activities;* Book 3, *Balance Activities;* Book 4, *Beanbag, Rhythm Stick Activities;* Book 5, *Tire, Parachute Activities.* Belmont, CA: Fearon-Pitman Publishers, 1975.

Coaching Youth League Football. Chicago: The Athletic Institute, 1974.

Coaching Youth Soccer. Chicago: The Athletic Institute, 1974.

Coaching Youth Softball. Chicago: The Athletic Institute, 1974.

COMPLO, JUANITA MARIE. *Funtactics.* Belmont, CA: Fearon-Pitman Publishers, 1979.

COTLER, HAROLD I. *Galaxy of Games, Stunts, and Activities for Elementary Physical Education.* West Nyack, NY: Parker Publishing, 1980.

Course of Study in Physical Education. Rochester, Minnesota Public Schools, 1970.

DAUER, VICTOR P. *Fitness for Elementary School Children.* Minneapolis: Burgess Publishing Co., 1965.

DAUER, VICTOR P., and ROBERT P. PANGRAZI. *Dynamic Physical Education for Elementary School Children.* Minneapolis: Burgess Publishing Co., 1975.

DRURY, BLANCHE, and ANDREA BODO SCHMID. *Gymnastics for Women.* Palo Alto, CA: National Press Books, 1970.

Elementary Physical Education. Coeur d'Alene, Idaho Public Schools, n.d.

EWING, NEIL. *Games, Stunts, and Exercises.* Belmont, CA: Fearon-Pitman Publishers, 1964.

FLUEGELMAN, ANDREW. *More New Games.* Garden City, NY: Dolphin Books, Doubleday and Co., 1981.

GREGSON, BOB. *The Outrageous Outdoor Games Book.* Belmont, CA: Pitman Learning, 1984.

HOHENSTEIN, MARY. *Games.* Minneapolis: Bethany House Publishers, 1980.

KIRCHNER, GLENN. *Physical Education for Elementary School Children.* Dubuque, IA: Wm. C. Brown Co., 1981.

KOKASKA, SHAREN METZ. *Creative Movement for Special Education.* Belmont, CA: David S. Lake Publishers, 1974.

NAGWS Sports Guide. American Alliance for Health, Physical Education and Recreation, 1971.

New Games Foundation. *The New Games Book.* Garden City, NY: Dolphin Books, Doubleday and Co., 1976.

Nuts and Bolts and Climbing Ropes. State of Idaho Department of Education, 1984.

ORLICK, TERRY. *The Cooperative Sports and Games Book.* New York: Pantheon Books, 1978.

ORLICK, TERRY. *The Second Cooperative Sports and Games Book.* New York: Pantheon Books, 1982.

REDFIELD, JOY HOPE. *Dance/Movement Experiences.* Carson, CA: Educational Insights, 1974.

REEVES, JOHN A. *The Coach's Collection of Soccer Drills.* West Point, NY: Leisure Press, 1981.

SIEDENTOP, DARYL; JACQUELINE HERKOWITZ; and JUDY RINK. *Elementary Physical Education Methods.* Englewood Cliffs, NJ: Prentice-Hall, 1984.

SMITH, PAUL. *Rope Skipping.* Freeport, NY: Educational Activities, 1969.

SOBEL, JEFFREY. *Everybody Wins.* New York: Walker and Co., 1983.

EDITORS of *Sports Illustrated. Basketball.* Philadelphia and New York: J.B. Lippincott Co., 1971.

TILLMAN, KENNETH G., and PATRICIA RIZZO TONER. *What Are We Doing in Gym Today?* West Nyack, NY: Parker Publishing, 1983.

TILLMAN, KENNETH G., and PATRICIA RIZZO TONER. *You'll Never Guess What We Did in Gym Today!* West Nyack, NY: Parker Publishing, 1984.

TORBERT, MARIANNE. *Follow Me.* Englewood Cliffs, NJ: Prentice-Hall, 1980.

WILT, JOY, and TERRE WATSON. *Rhythm and Movement.* Waco, TX: Creative Resources, 1977.

WINKLEMAN, GRETCHEN, and PATRICIA ANN ZEZULA. *Lifetime Treasury of Elementary Physical Education Activities.* West Nyack, NY: Parker Publishing, 1980.